JASON AND THE ARGOBOTS™

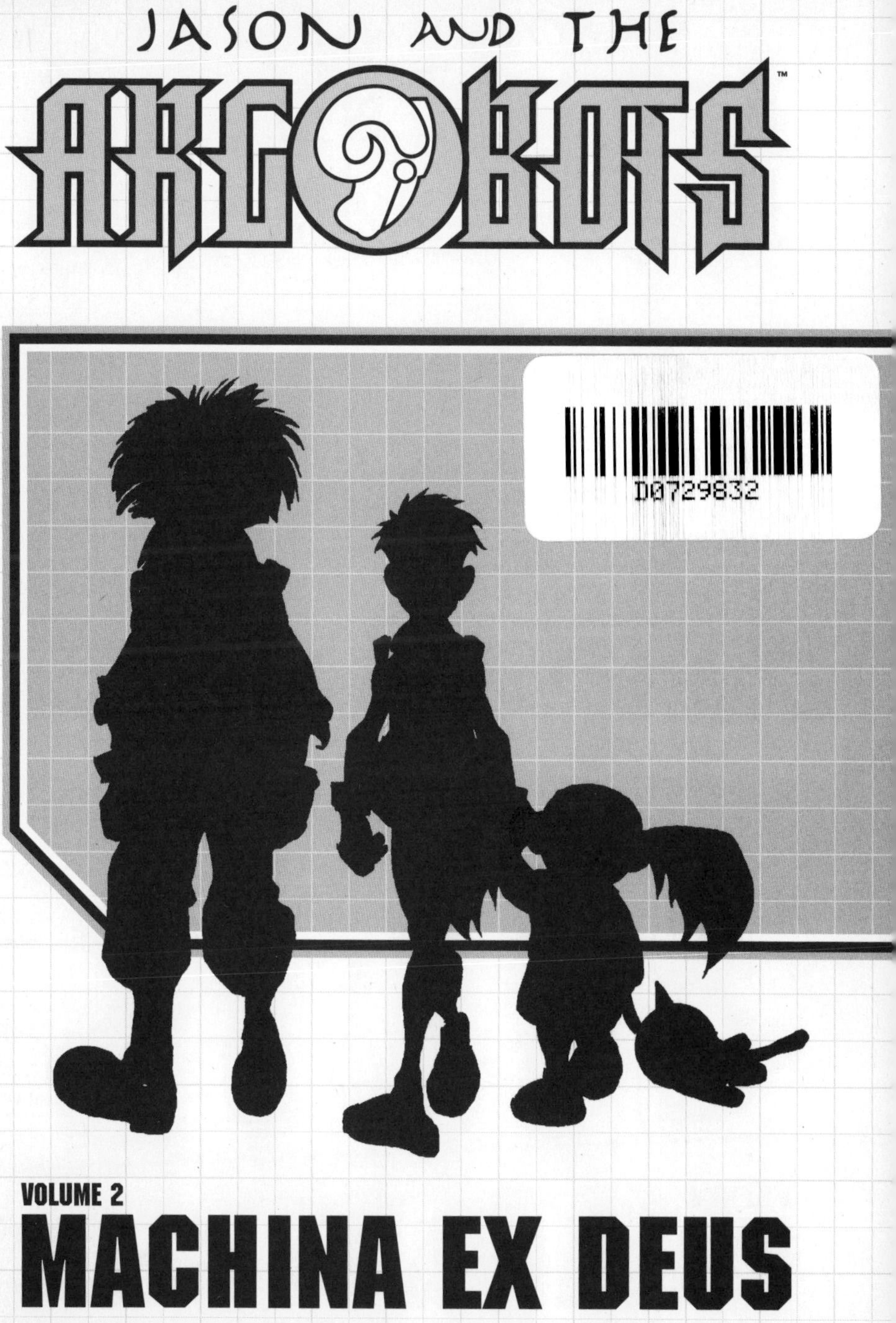

VOLUME 2

MACHINA EX DEUS

JASON AND THE ARGOBOTS™

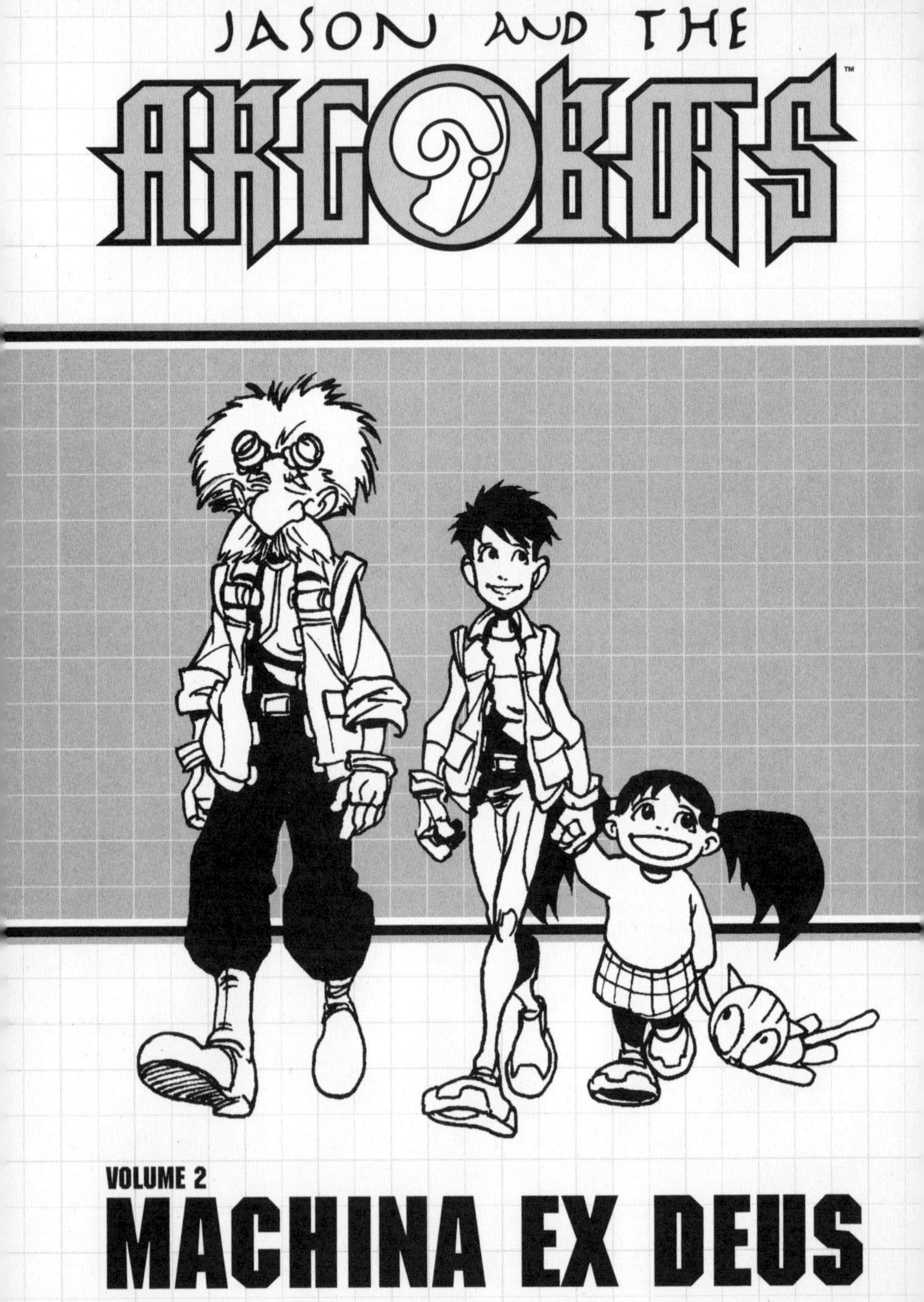

VOLUME 2

MACHINA EX DEUS

Written by
J. TORRES

Illustrated by
MIKE NORTON

Lettered by
NATE PIEKOS @ BLAMBOT

Cover by
MIKE NORTON with **CHRIS CRANK**

Cover colors and chapter break tones by
LONG VO @ STUDIO XD

Designed by
KEITH WOOD

Edited by
JAMES LUCAS JONES

Published by Oni Press, Inc.
JOE NOZEMACK, publisher
JAMIE S. RICH, editor in chief

ONI PRESS, INC.
6336 SE Milwaukie Avenue, PMB 30
Portland, OR 97202
USA

www.onipress.com
www.jtorresonline.com
www.ihatemike.com

First edition: September 2003
ISBN 1-929998-56-2

1 3 5 7 9 10 8 6 4 2
PRINTED IN CANADA.

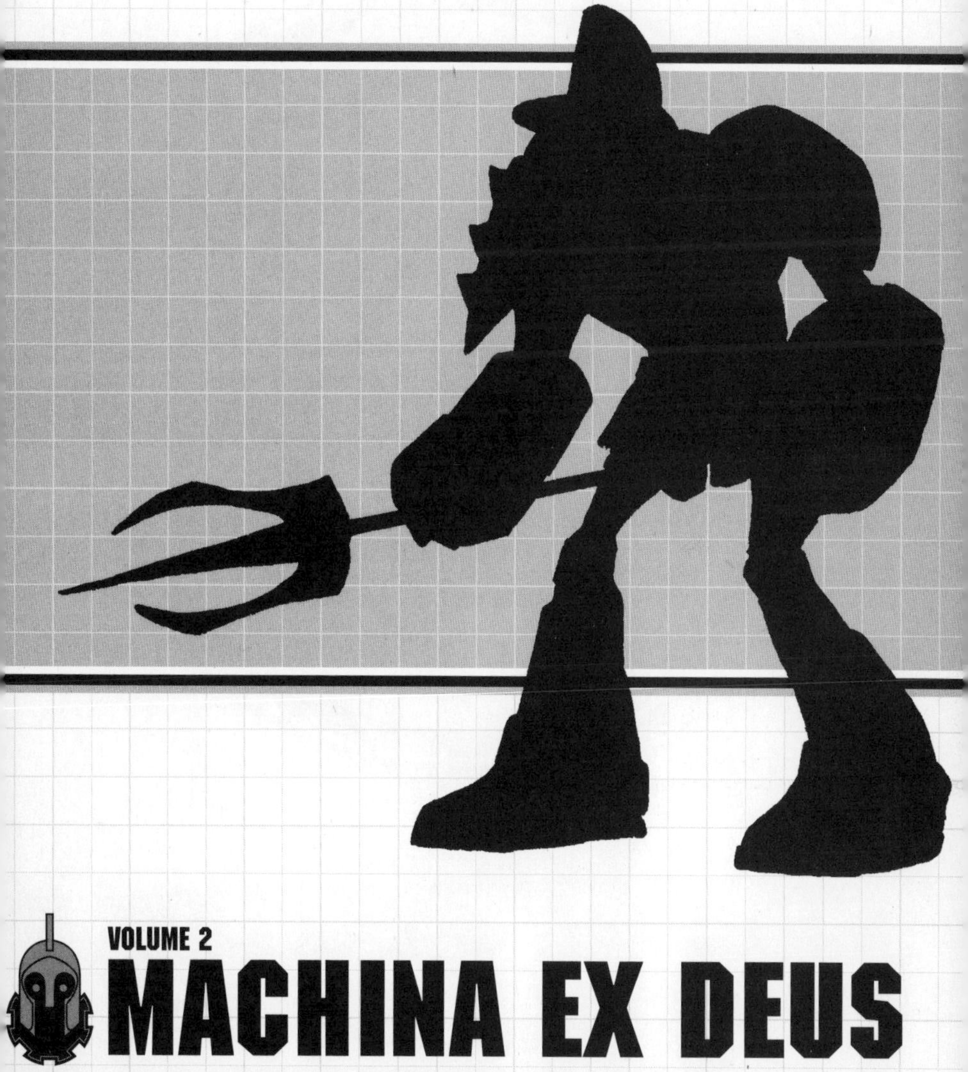

VOLUME 2

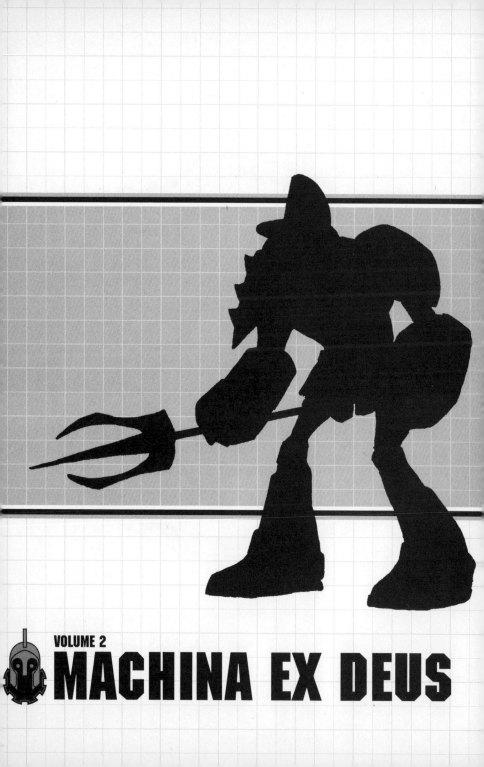

MACHINA EX DEUS

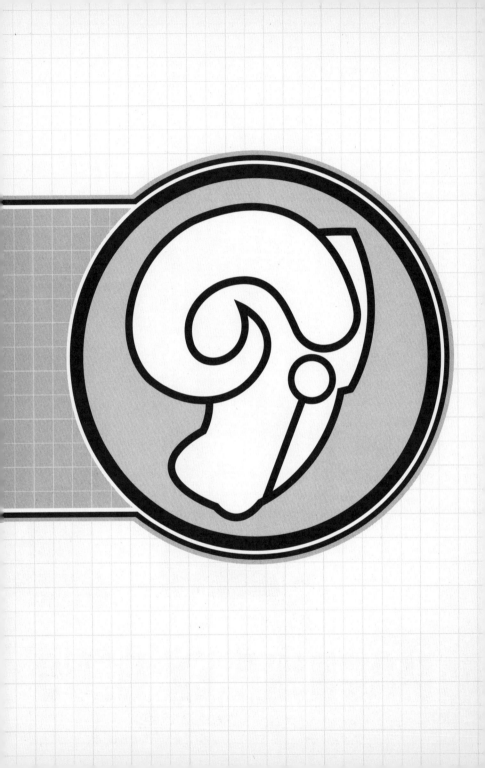

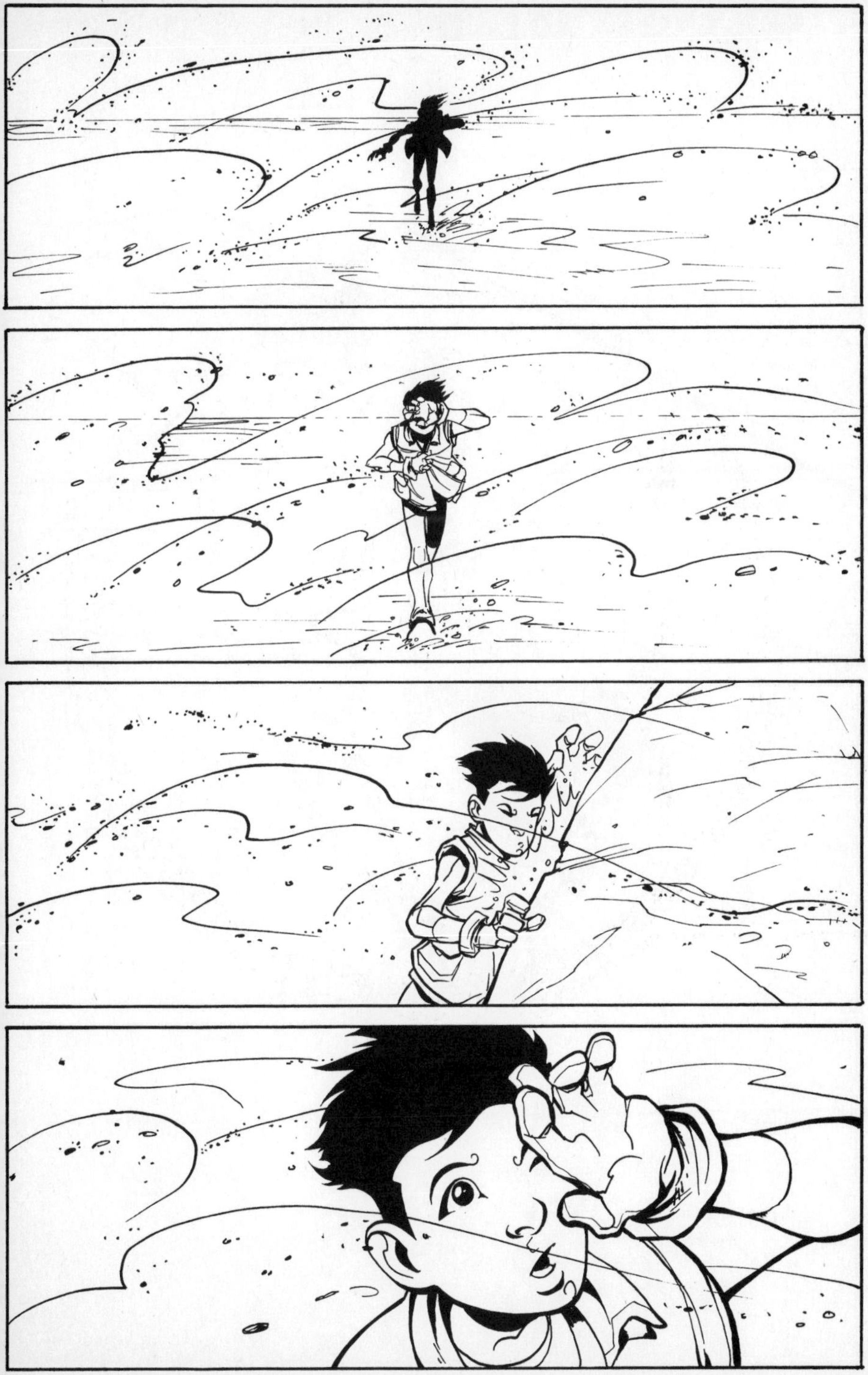

PART 1: GEARS

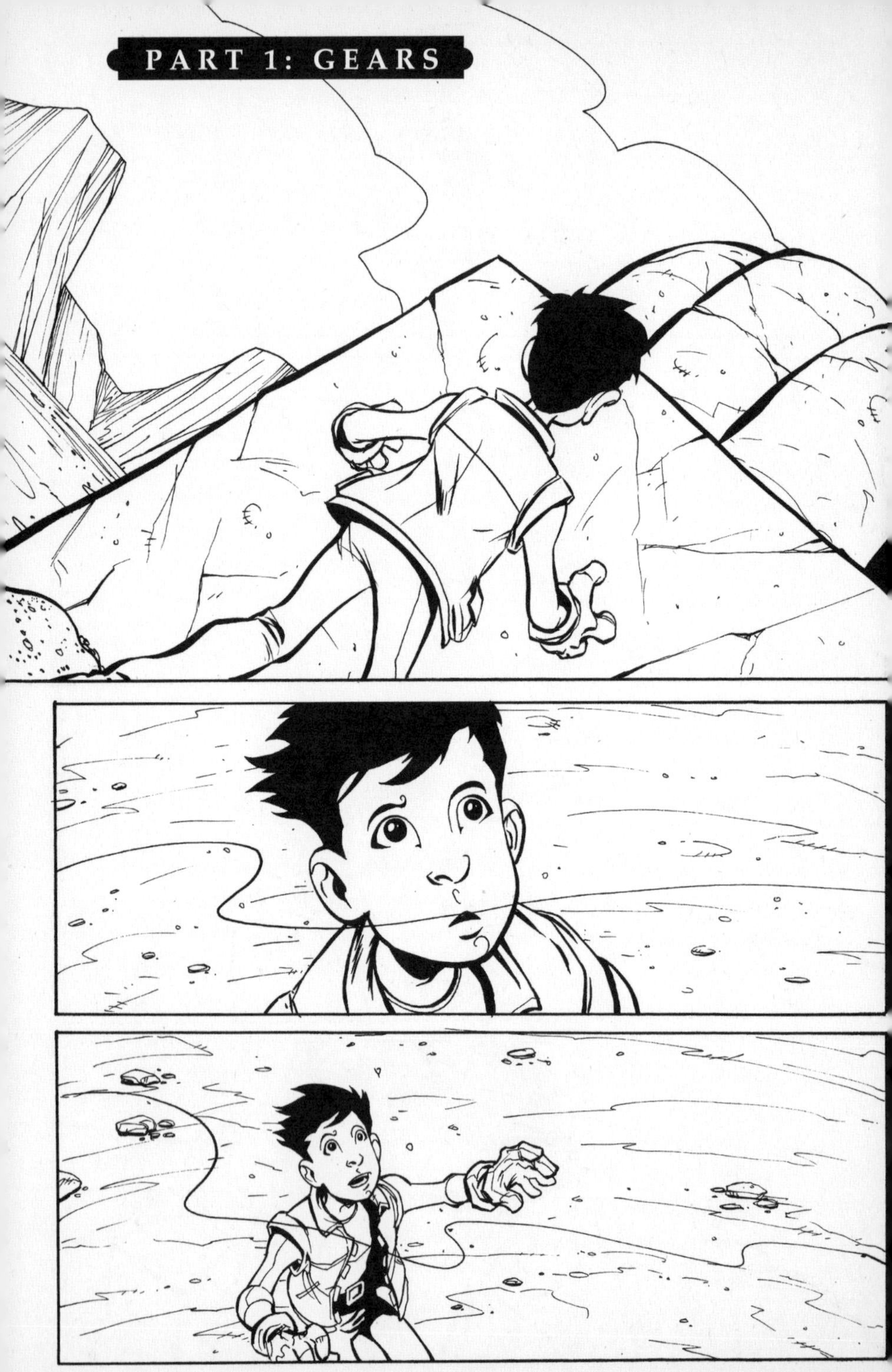

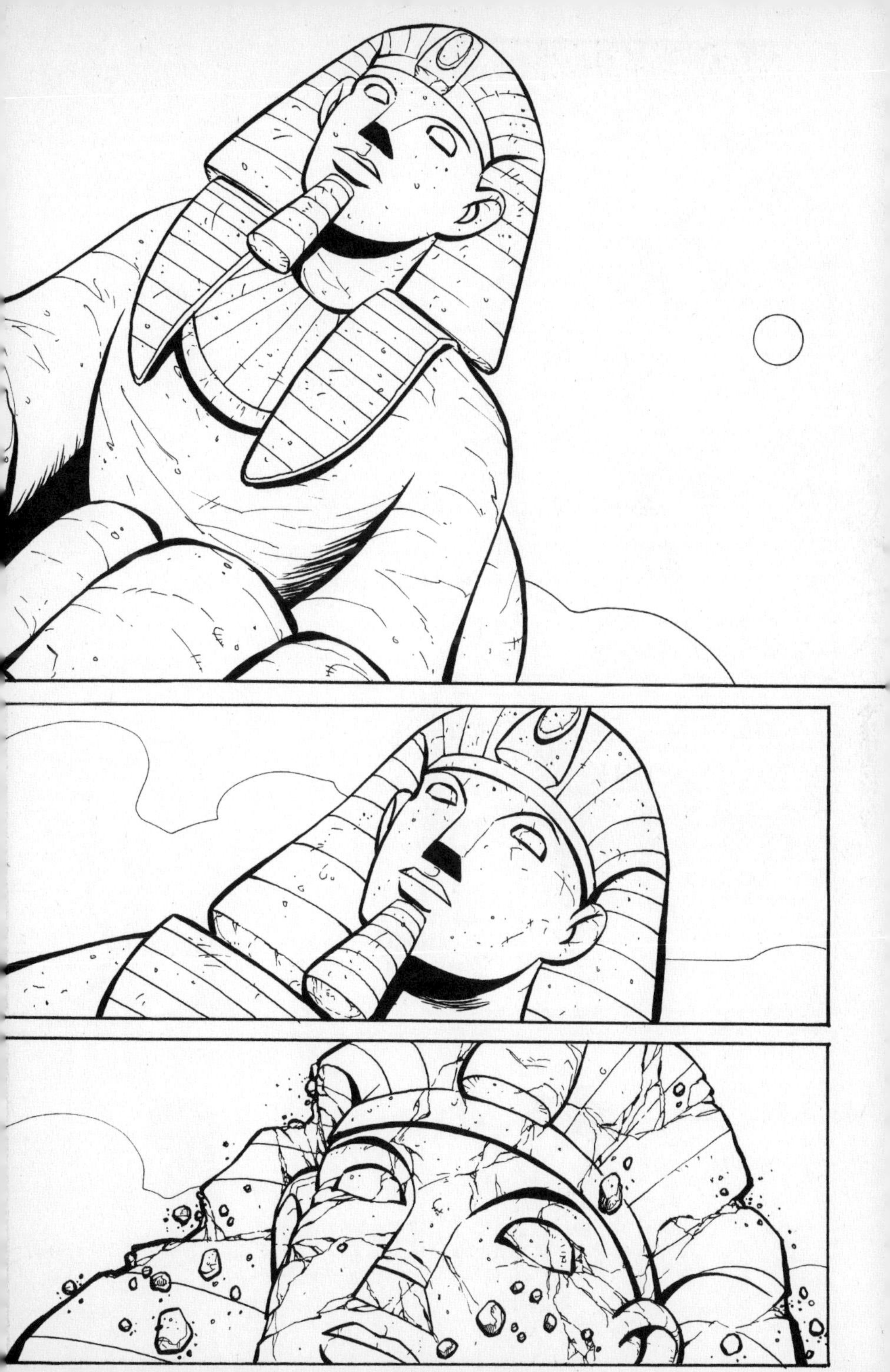

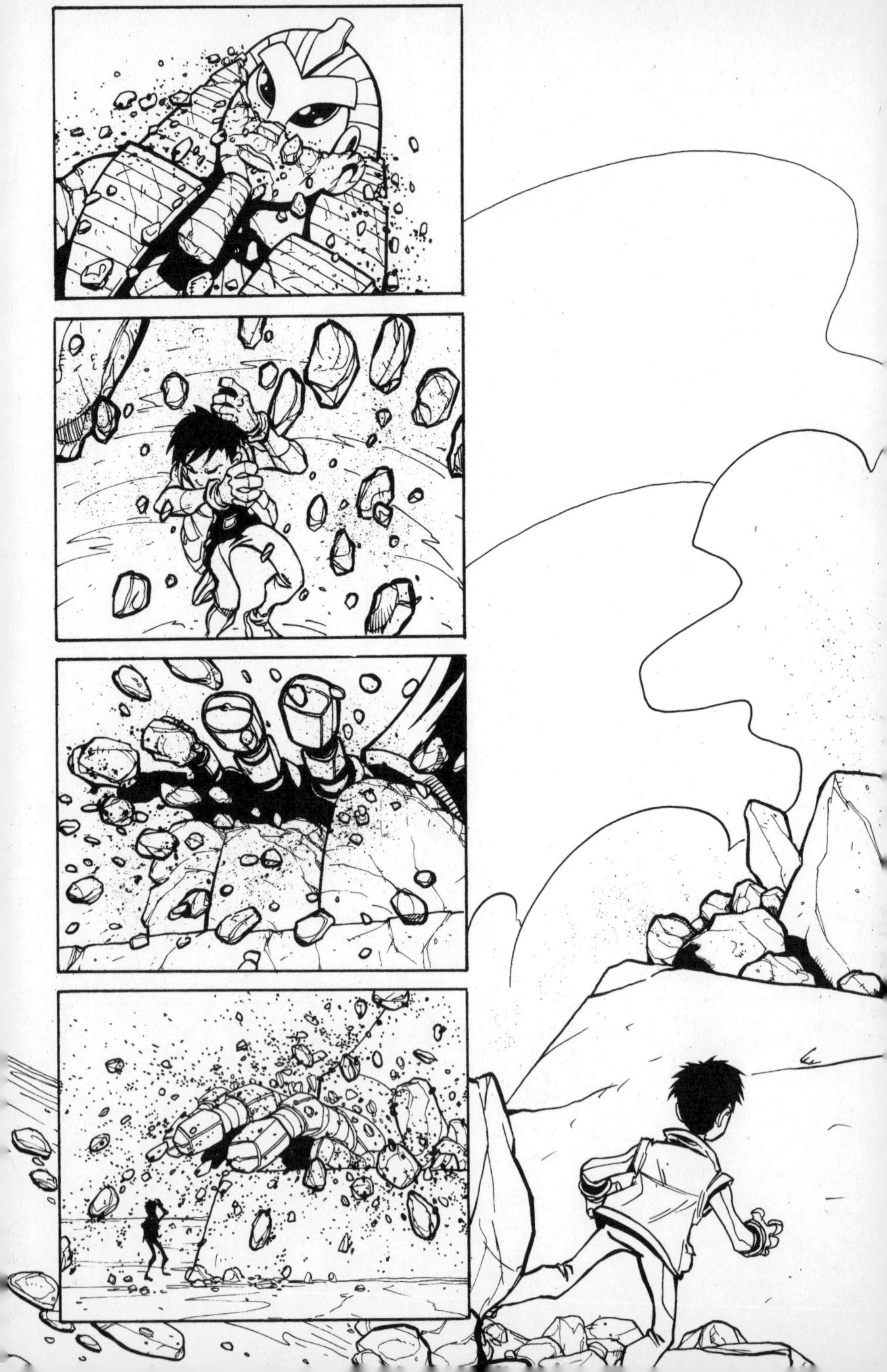

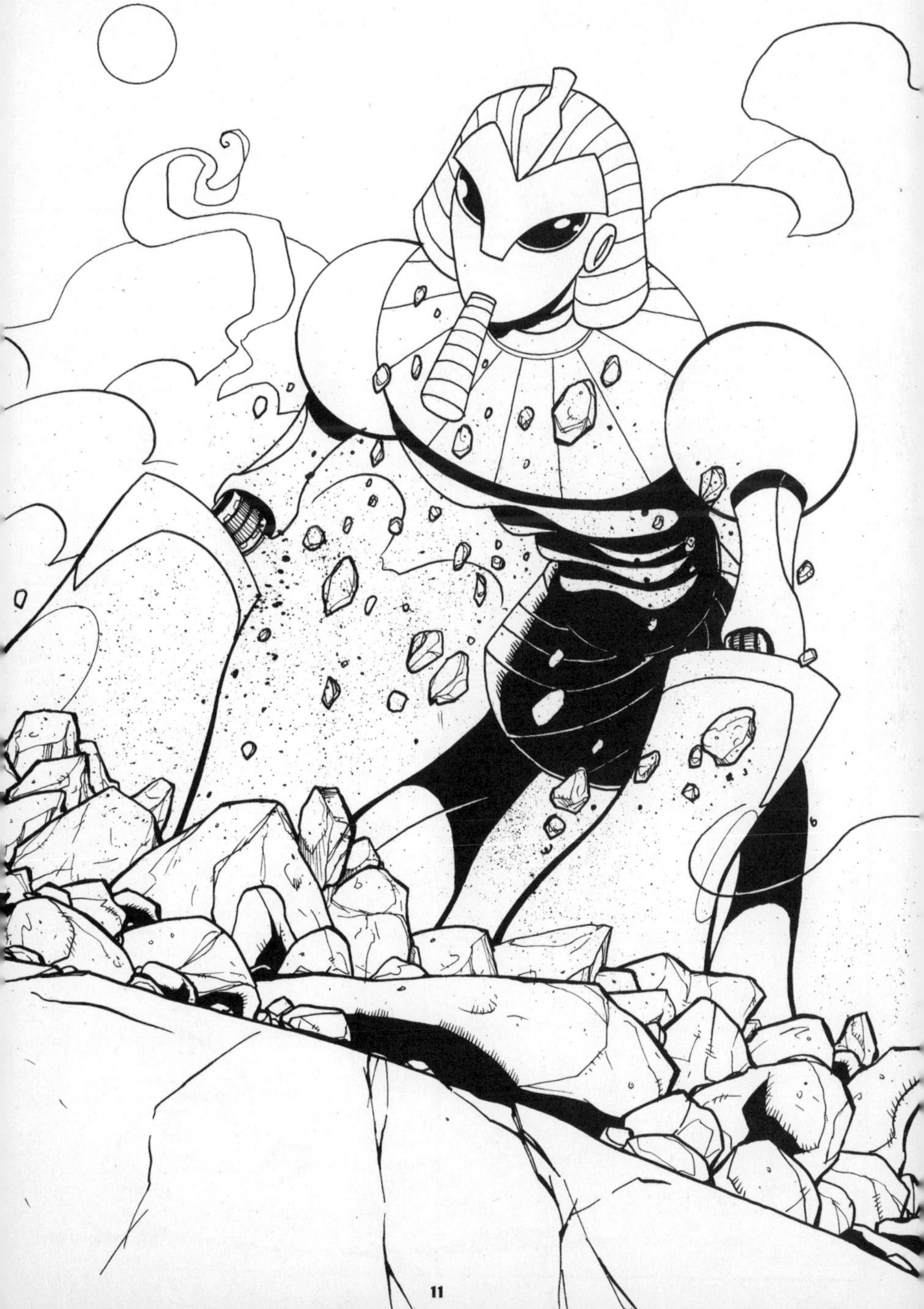

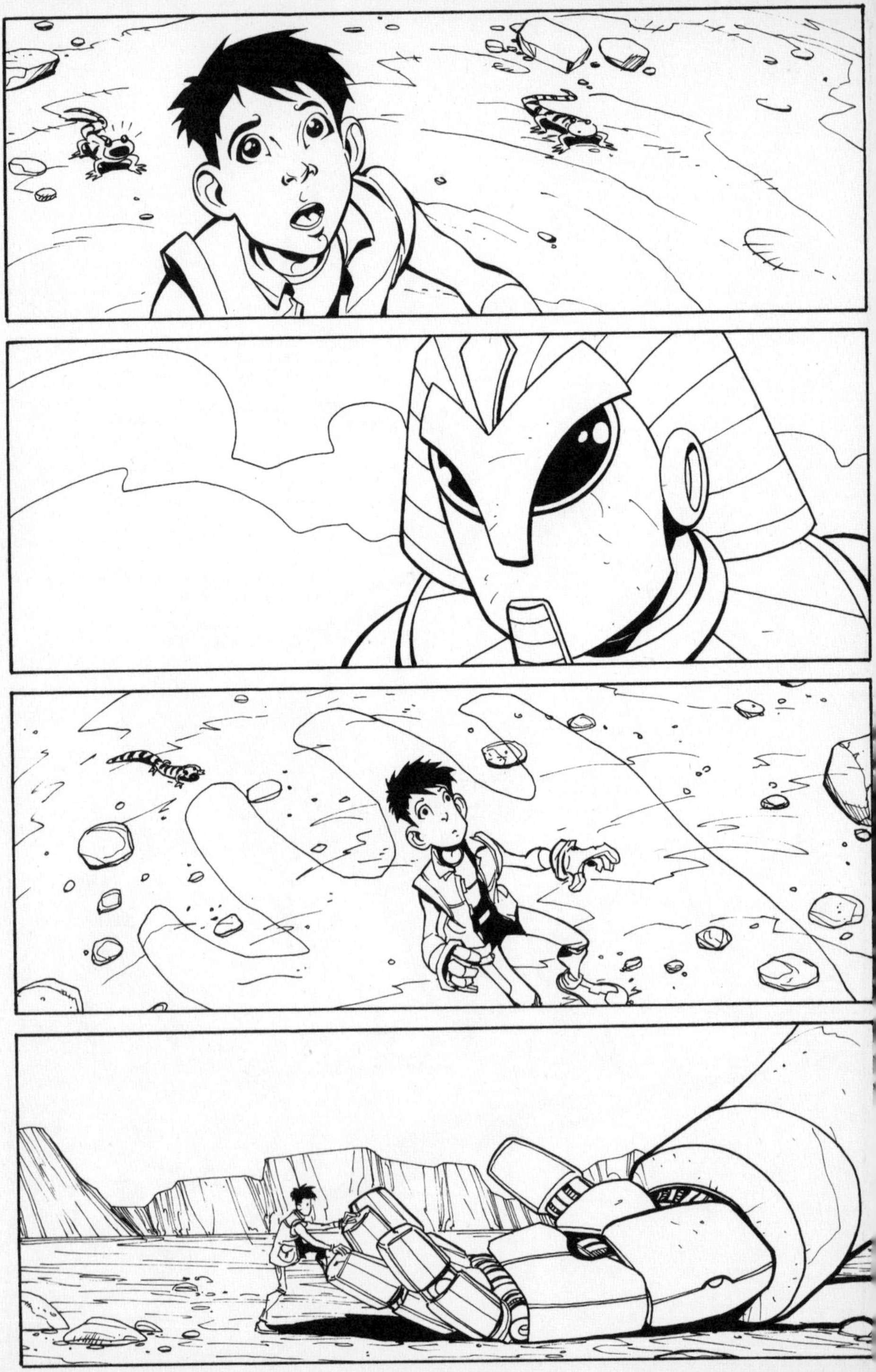

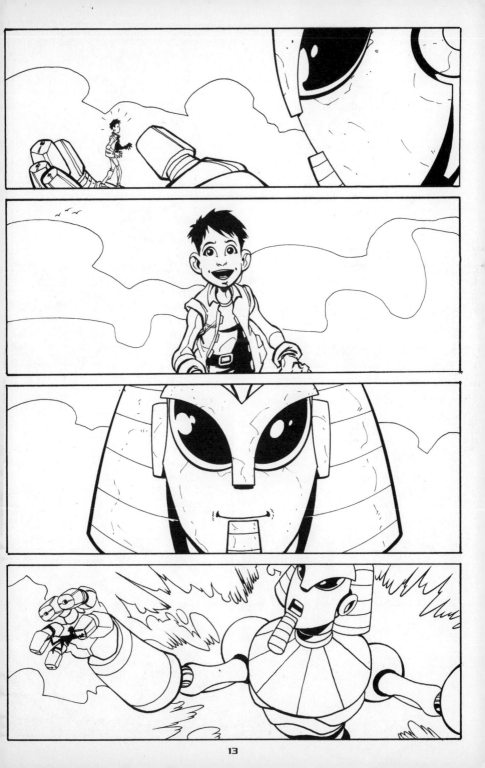

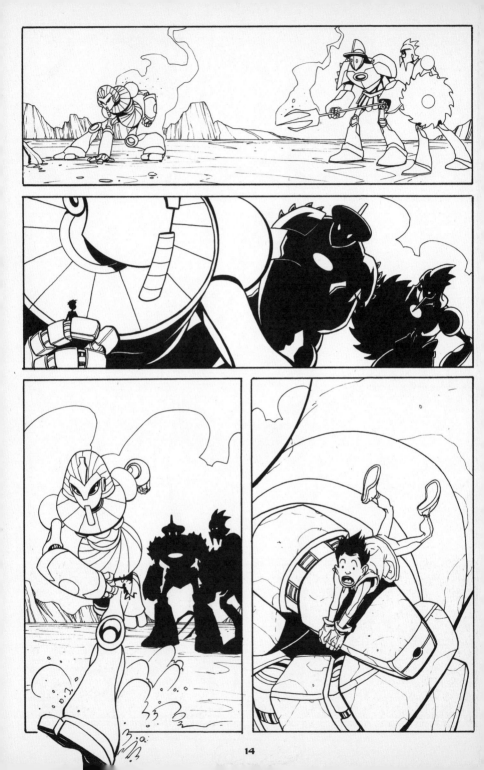

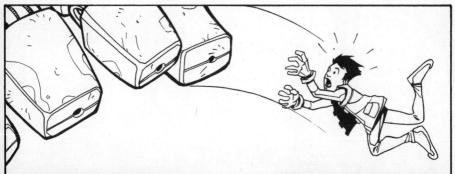

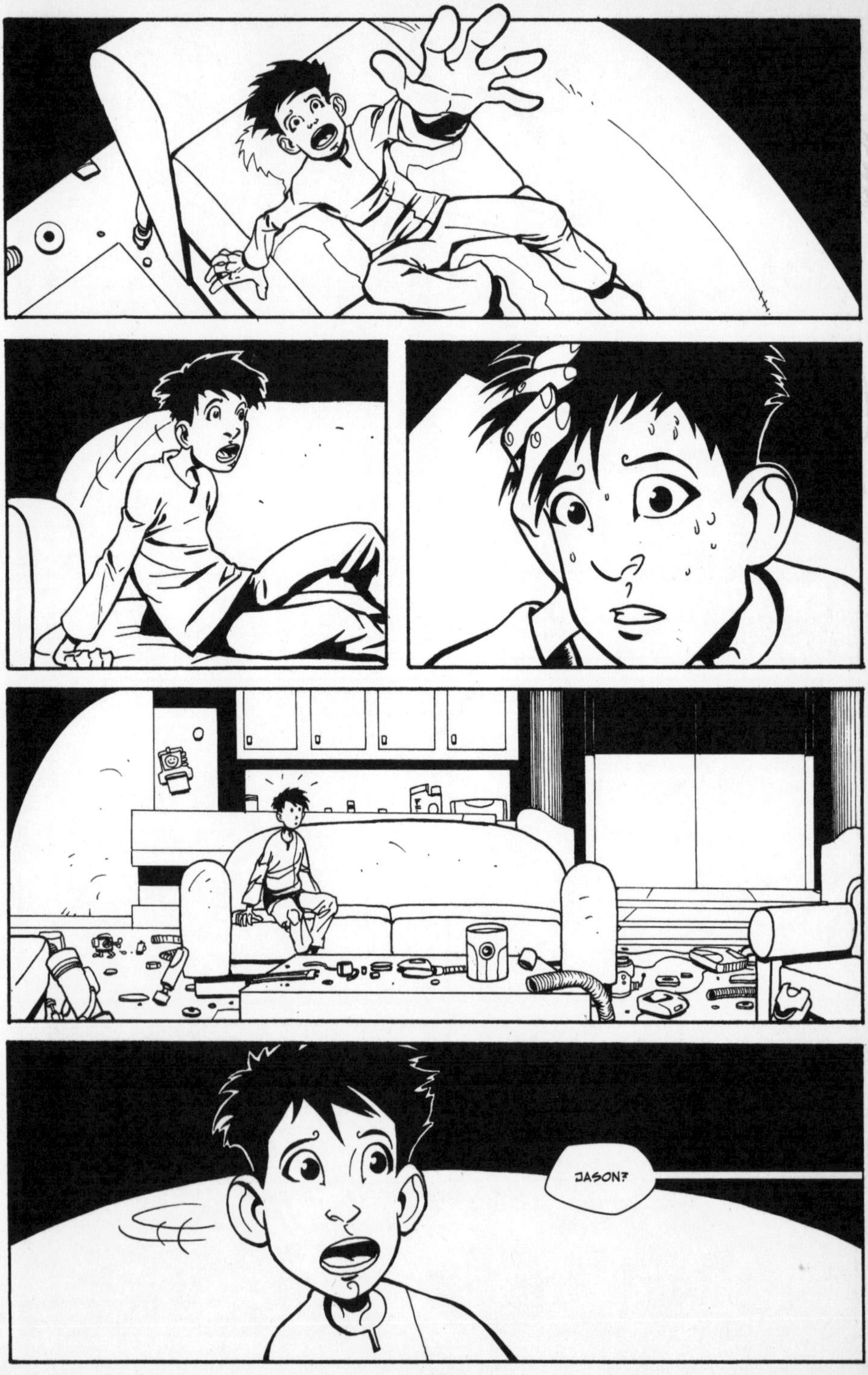
JASON?

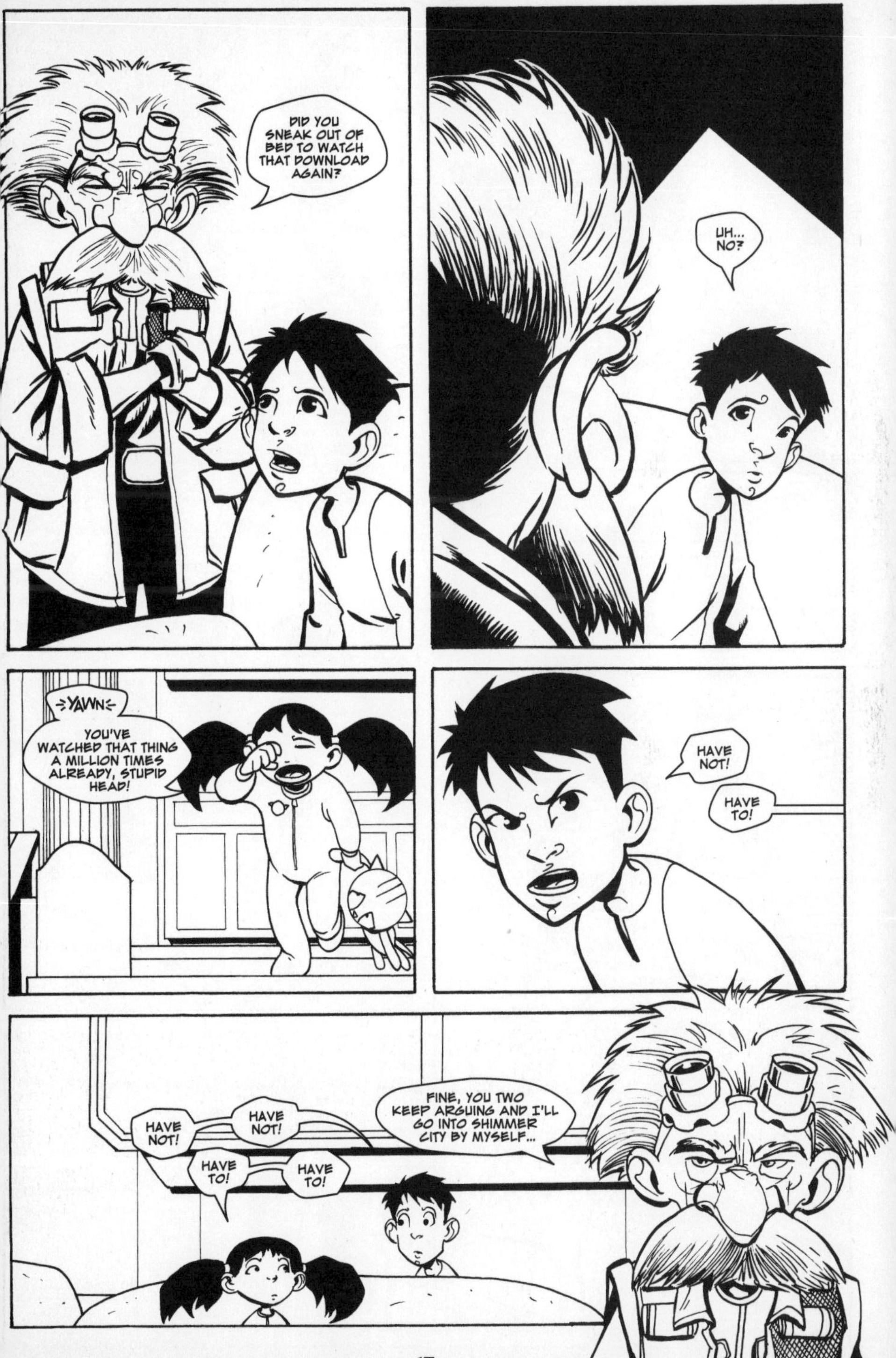
DID YOU SNEAK OUT OF BED TO WATCH THAT DOWNLOAD AGAIN?
UH... NO?
YAWN
YOU'VE WATCHED THAT THING A MILLION TIMES ALREADY, STUPID HEAD!
HAVE NOT!
HAVE TO!
HAVE NOT!
HAVE NOT!
HAVE TO!
HAVE TO!
FINE, YOU TWO KEEP ARGUING AND I'LL GO INTO SHIMMER CITY BY MYSELF...

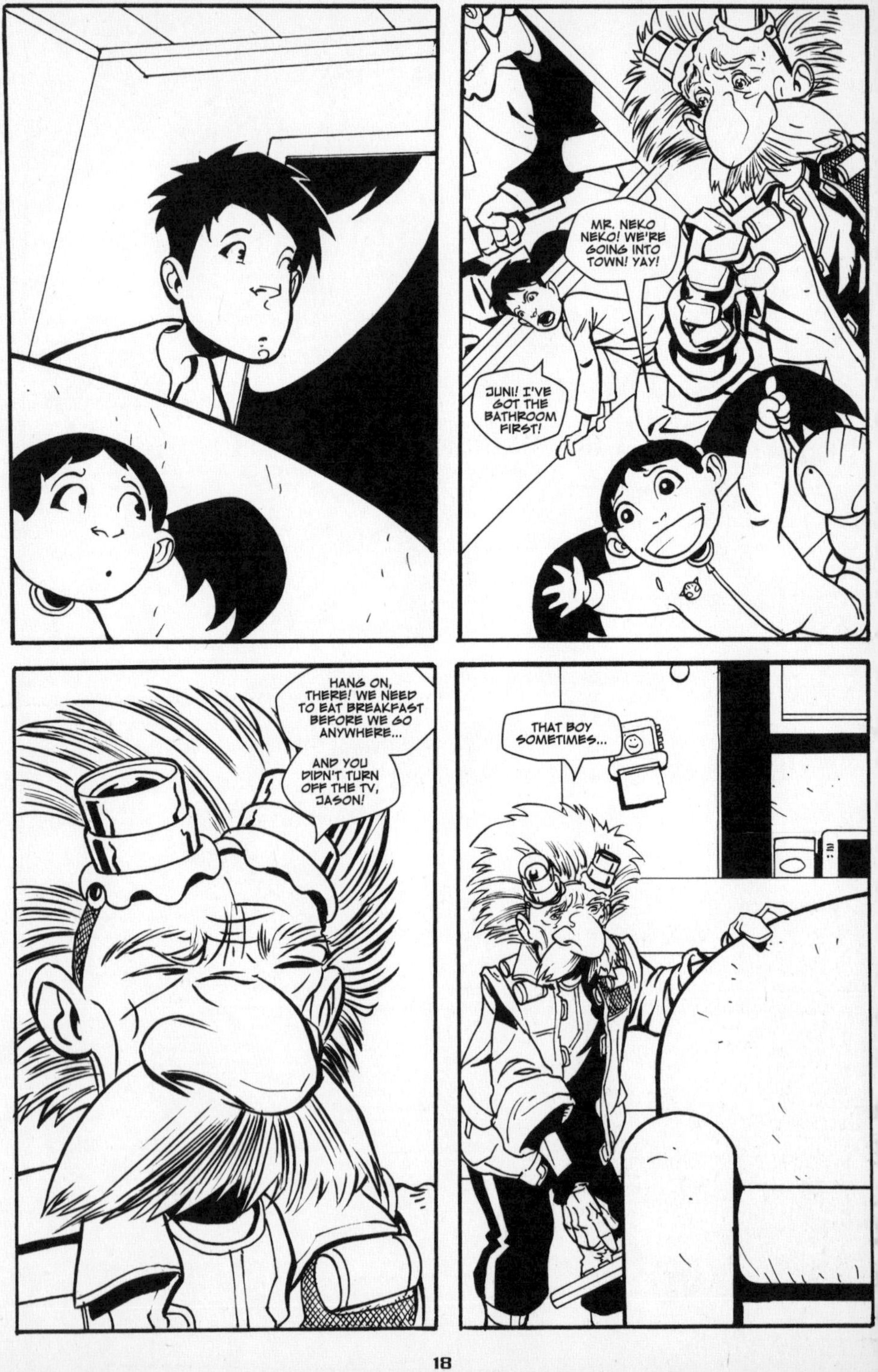
MR. NEKO NEKO! WE'RE GOING INTO TOWN! YAY!
JUNI! I'VE GOT THE BATHROOM FIRST!
HANG ON, THERE! WE NEED TO EAT BREAKFAST BEFORE WE GO ANYWHERE...
AND YOU DIDN'T TURN OFF THE TV, JASON!
THAT BOY SOMETIMES...

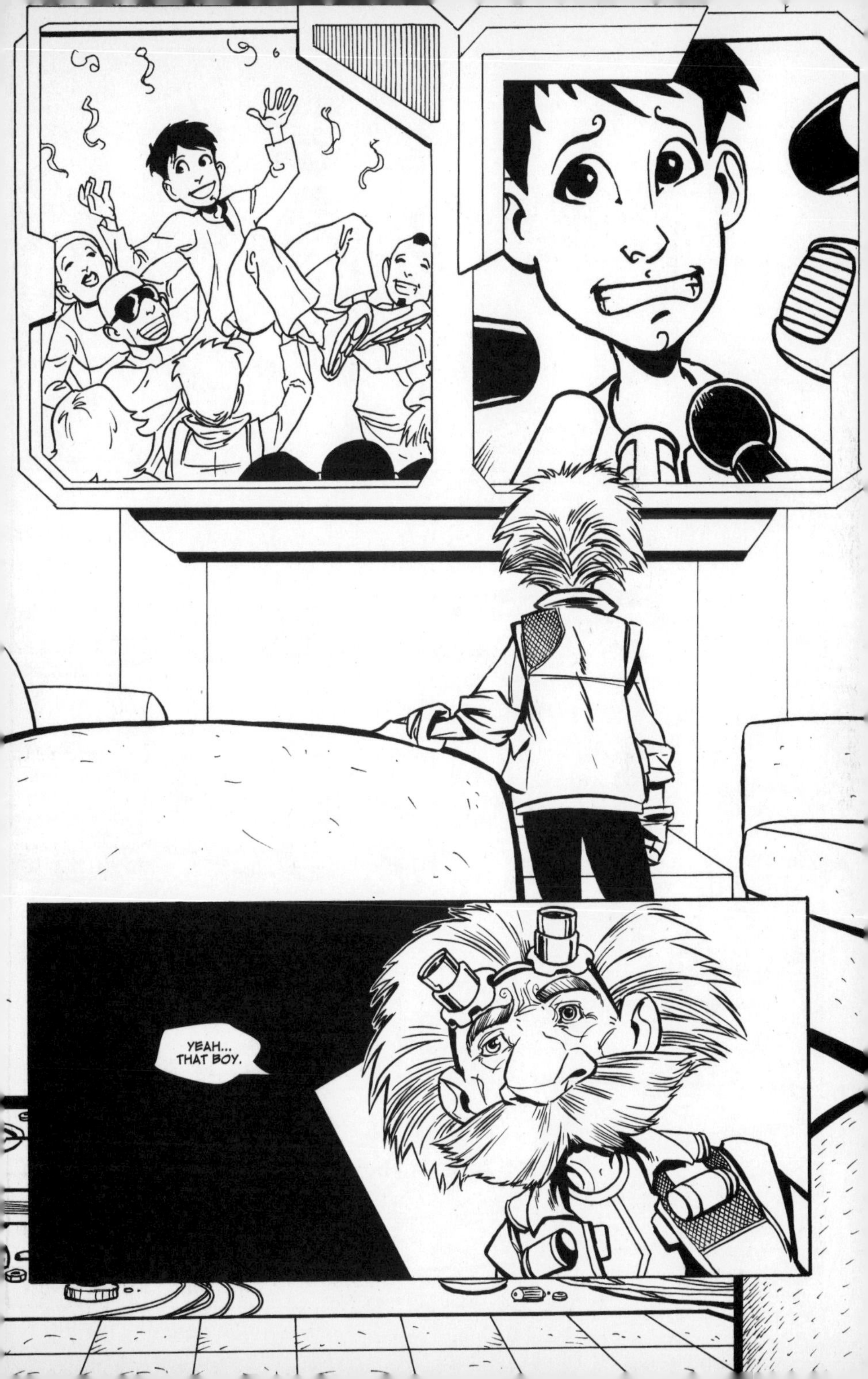
YEAH... THAT BOY.

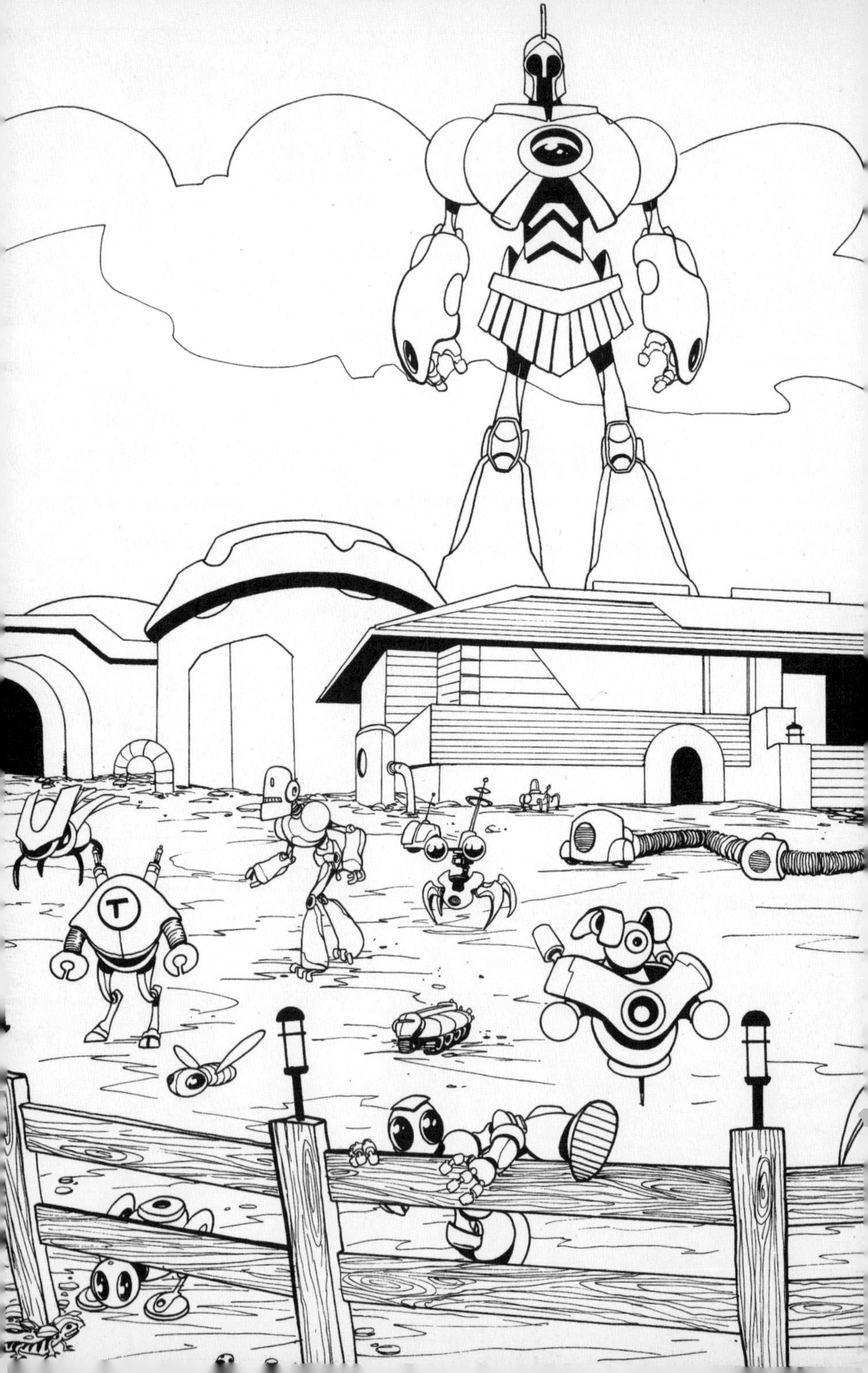
T

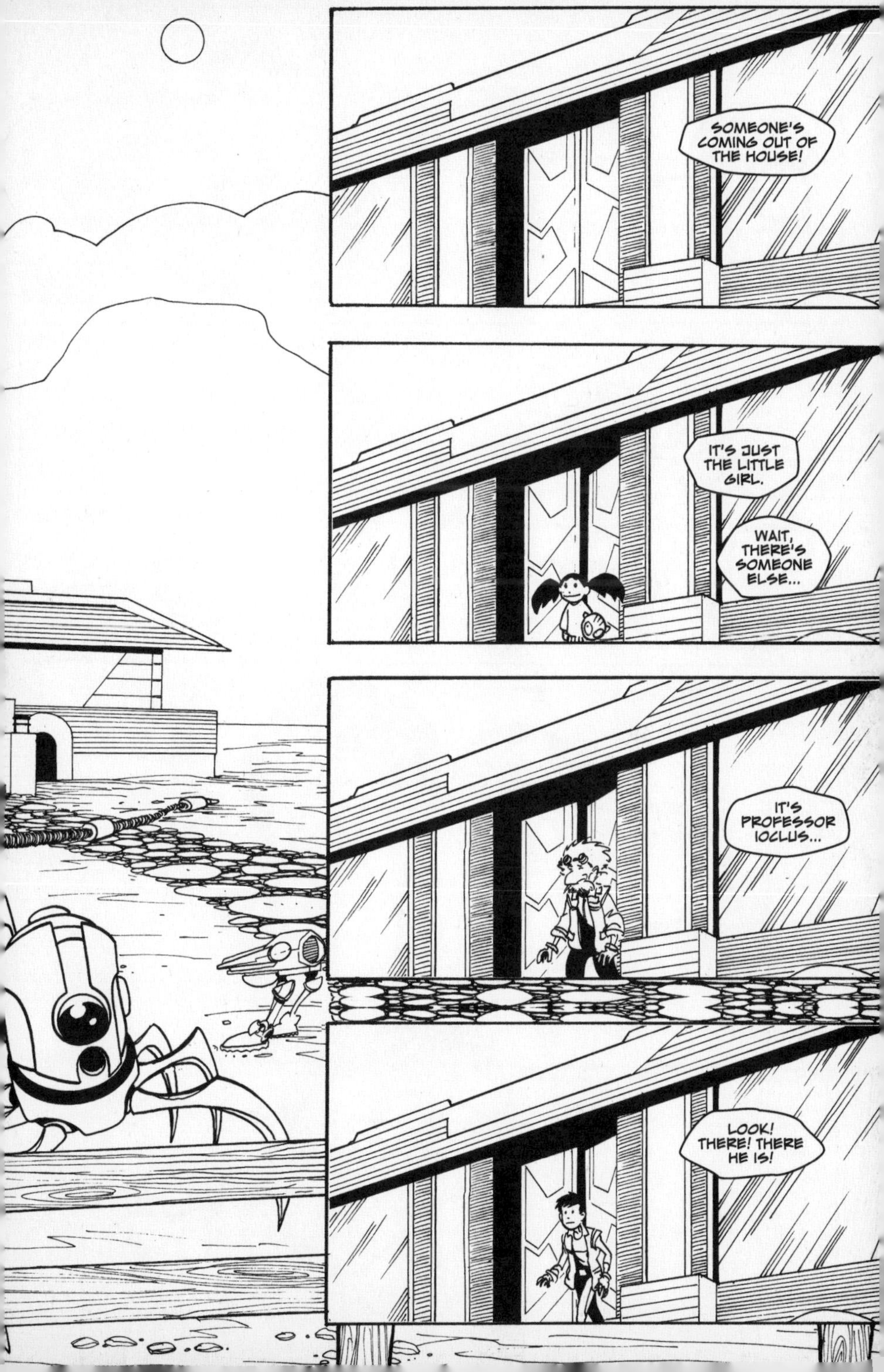
SOMEONE'S COMING OUT OF THE HOUSE!
IT'S JUST THE LITTLE GIRL.
WAIT, THERE'S SOMEONE ELSE...
IT'S PROFESSOR IOCLUS...
LOOK! THERE! THERE HE IS!

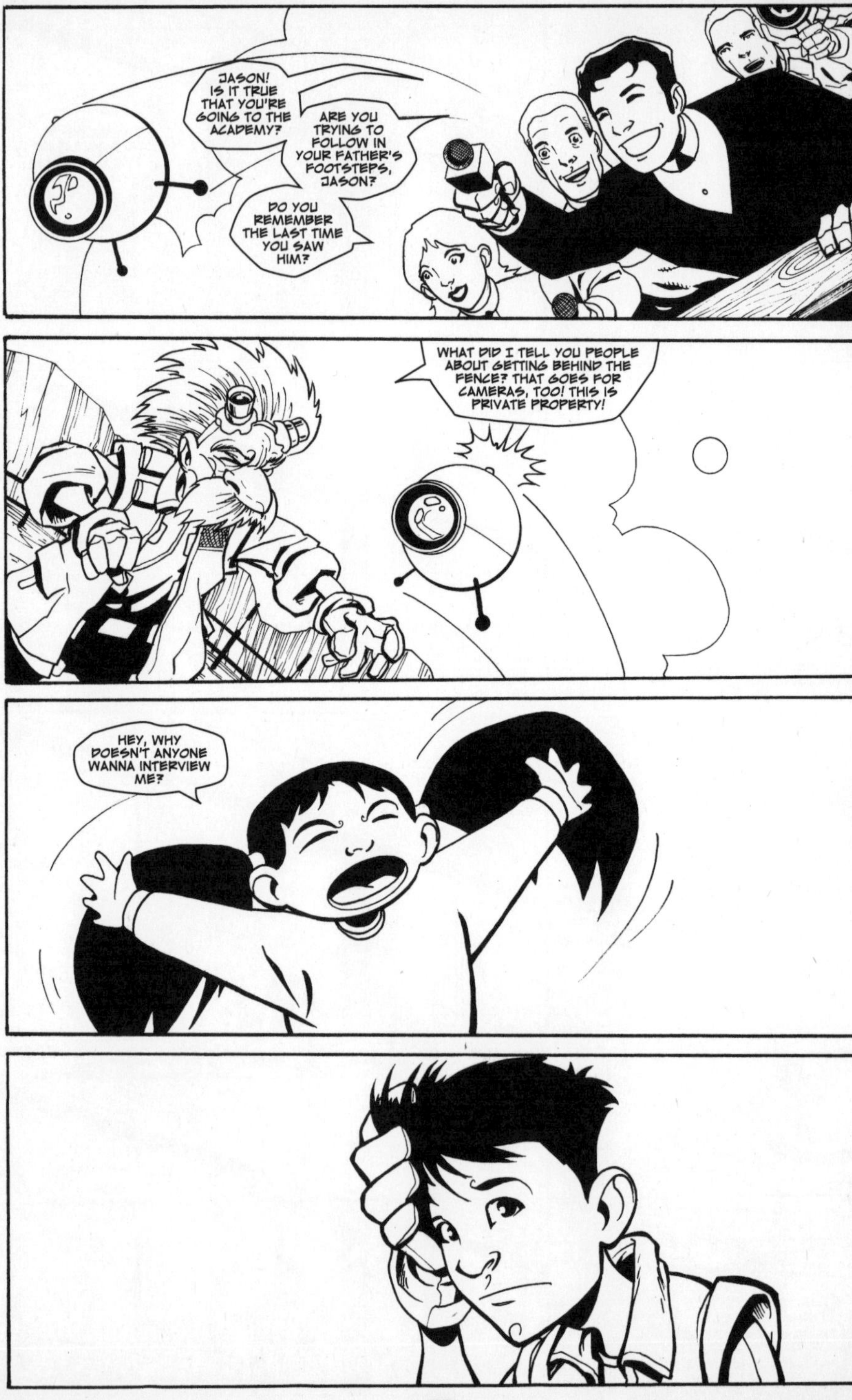
JASON! IS IT TRUE THAT YOU'RE GOING TO THE ACADEMY?
ARE YOU TRYING TO FOLLOW IN YOUR FATHER'S FOOTSTEPS, JASON?
DO YOU REMEMBER THE LAST TIME YOU SAW HIM?
WHAT DID I TELL YOU PEOPLE ABOUT GETTING BEHIND THE FENCE? THAT GOES FOR CAMERAS, TOO! THIS IS PRIVATE PROPERTY!
HEY, WHY DOESN'T ANYONE WANNA INTERVIEW ME?

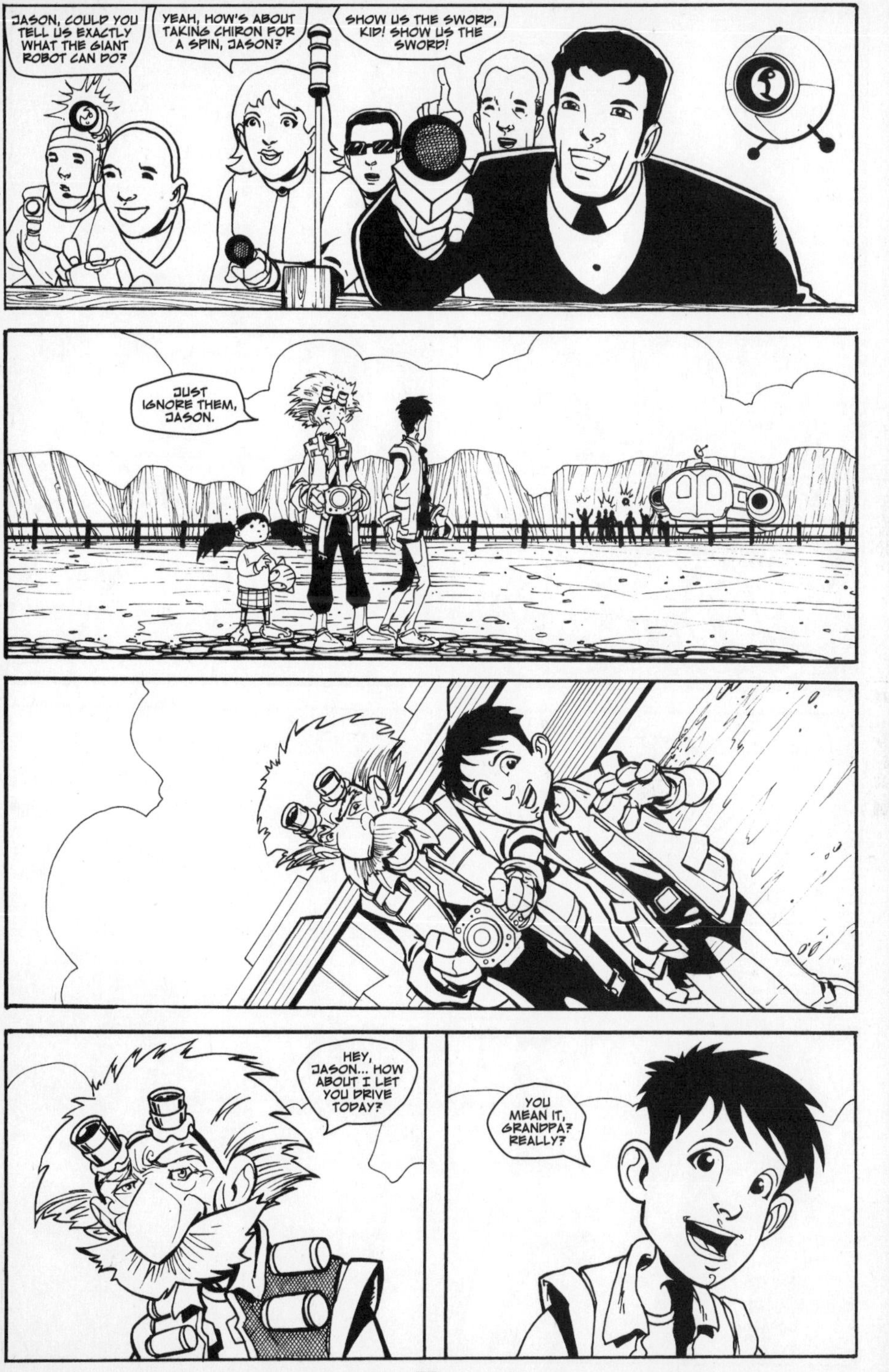
JASON, COULD YOU TELL US EXACTLY WHAT THE GIANT ROBOT CAN DO?
YEAH, HOW'S ABOUT TAKING CHIRON FOR A SPIN, JASON?
SHOW US THE SWORD, KID! SHOW US THE SWORD!
JUST IGNORE THEM, JASON.
HEY, JASON... HOW ABOUT I LET YOU DRIVE TODAY?
YOU MEAN IT, GRANDPA? REALLY?

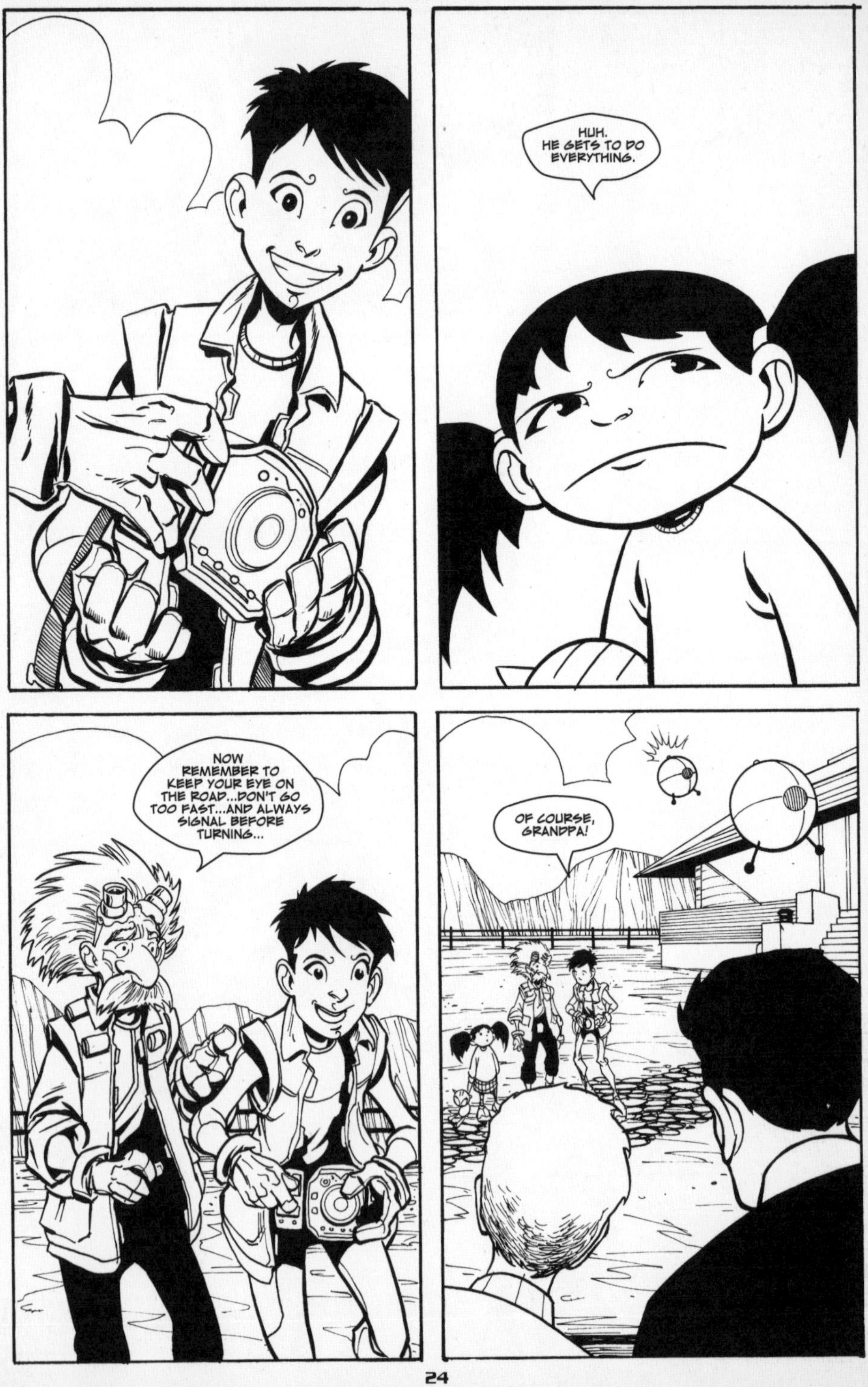
HUH.
HE GETS TO DO EVERYTHING.
NOW REMEMBER TO KEEP YOUR EYE ON THE ROAD...DON'T GO TOO FAST...AND ALWAYS SIGNAL BEFORE TURNING...
OF COURSE, GRANDPA!

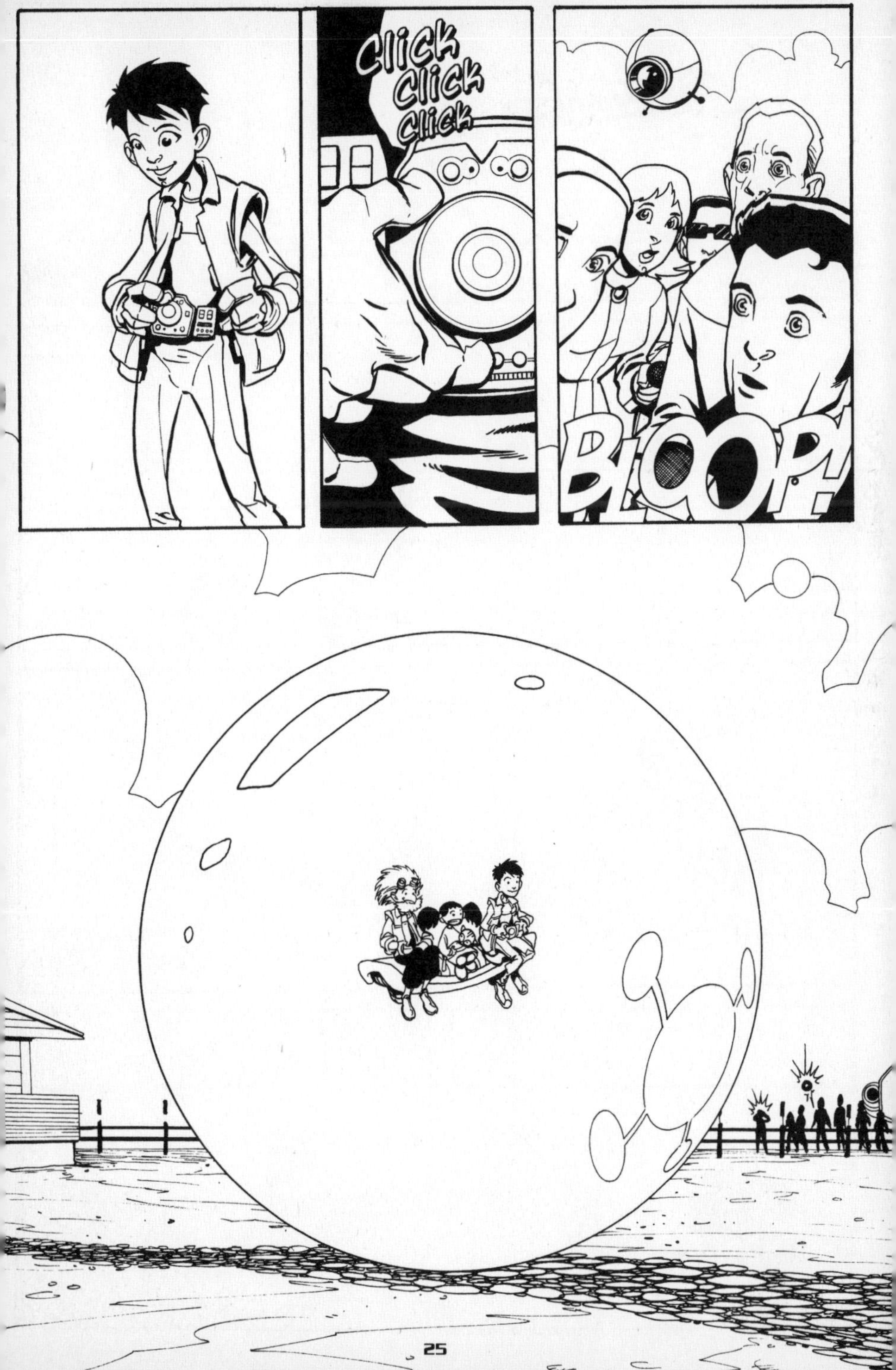
CLICK
CLICK
CLICK
BLOOP!

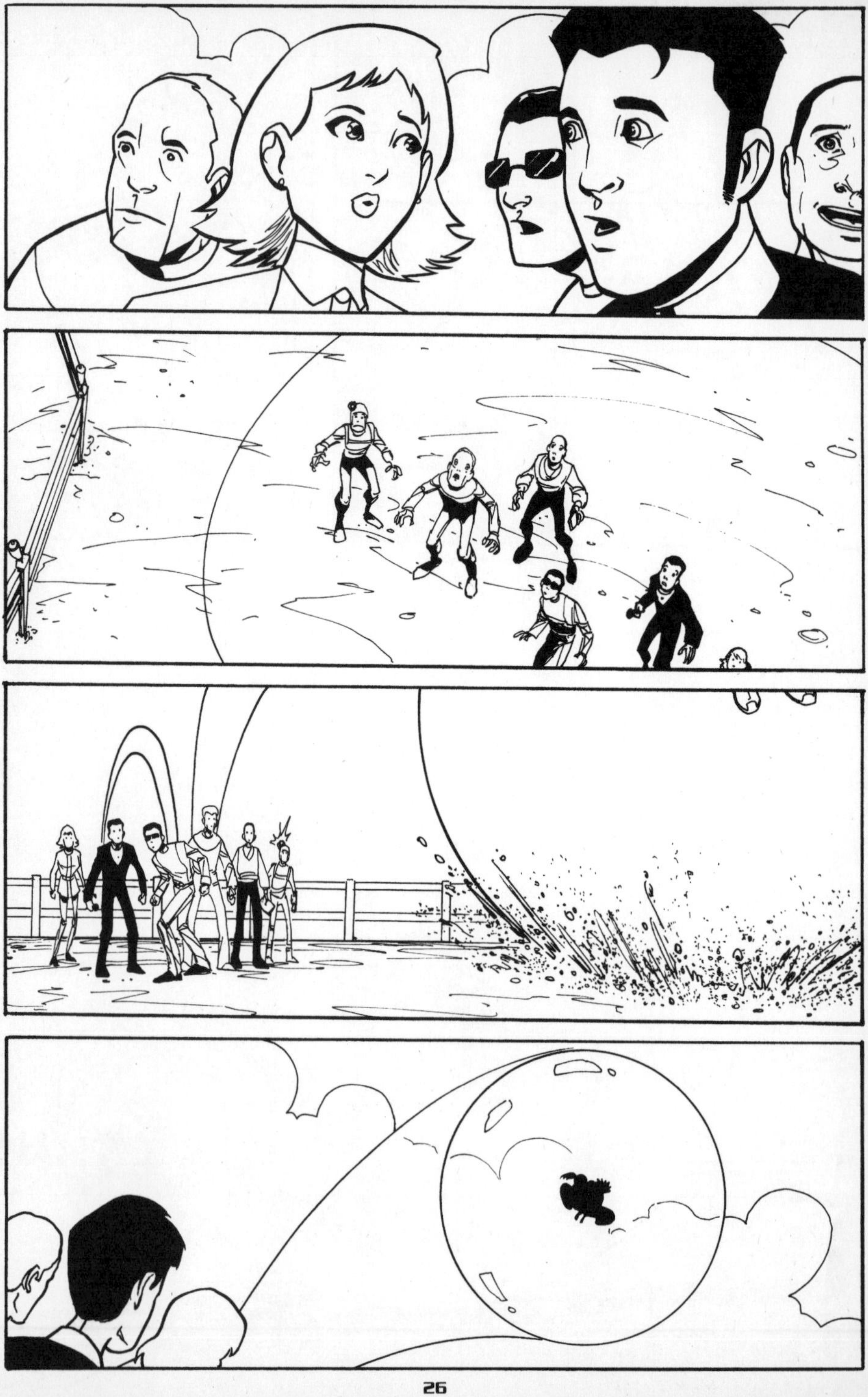

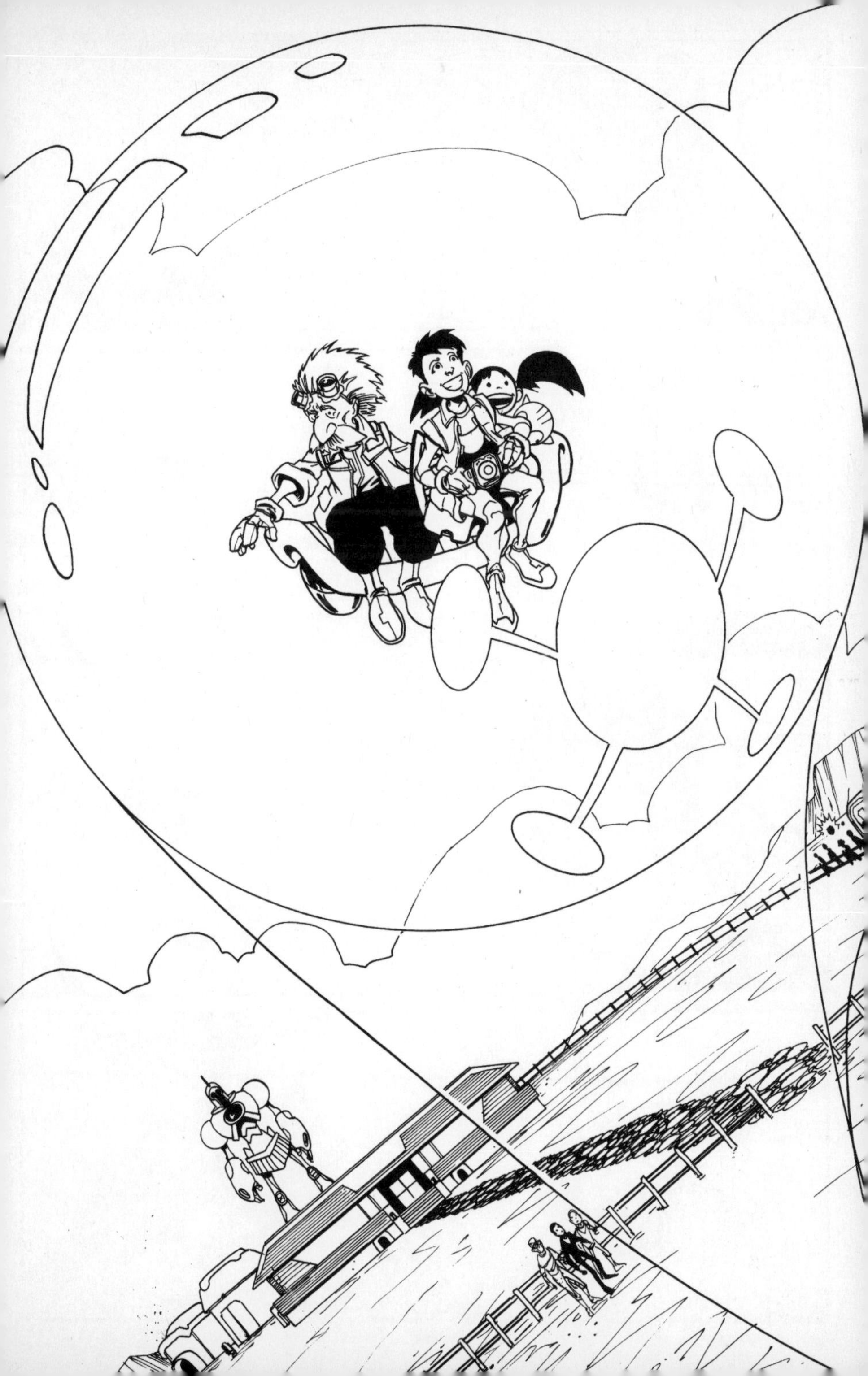

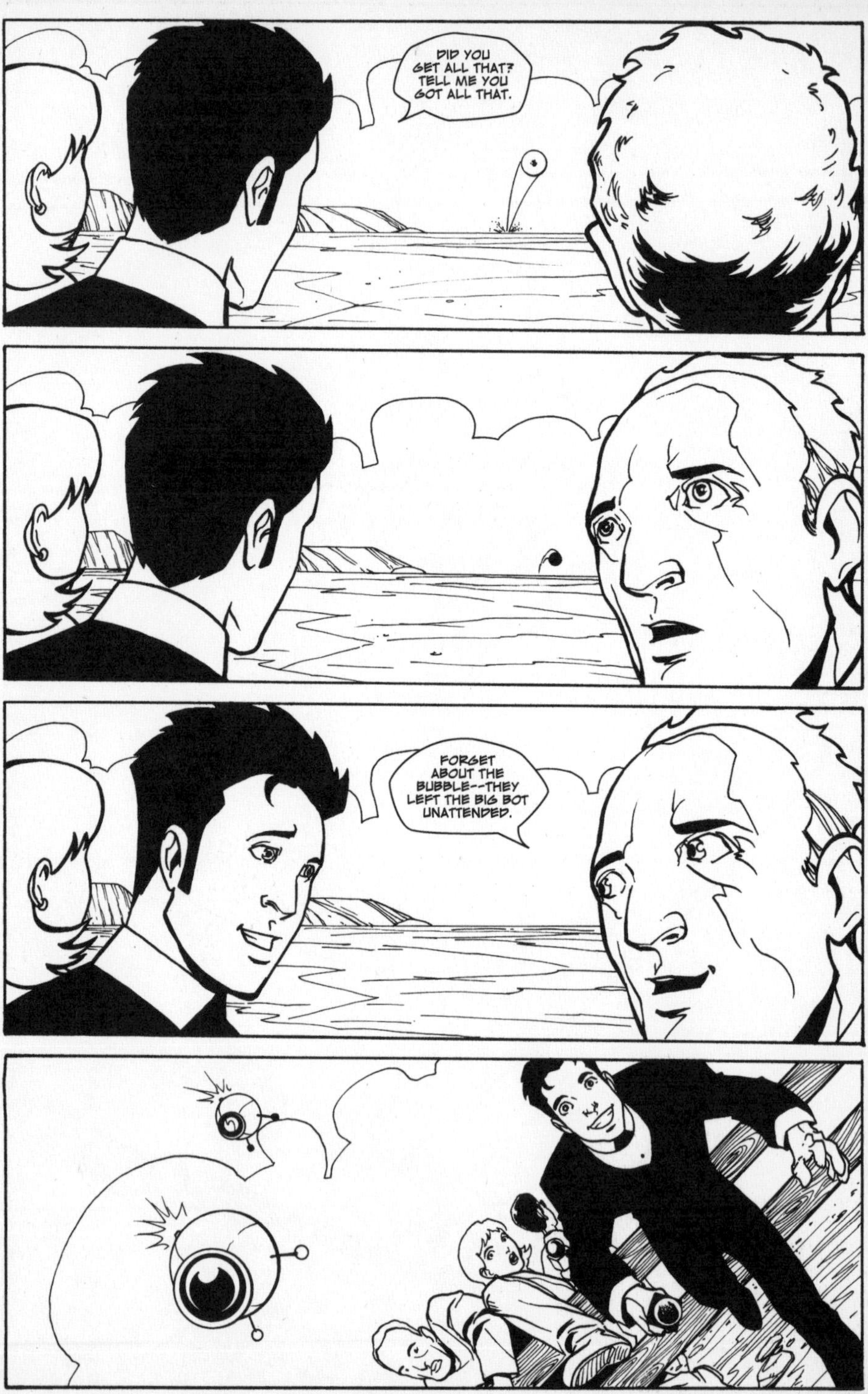
DID YOU GET ALL THAT? TELL ME YOU GOT ALL THAT.
FORGET ABOUT THE BUBBLE--THEY LEFT THE BIG BOT UNATTENDED.

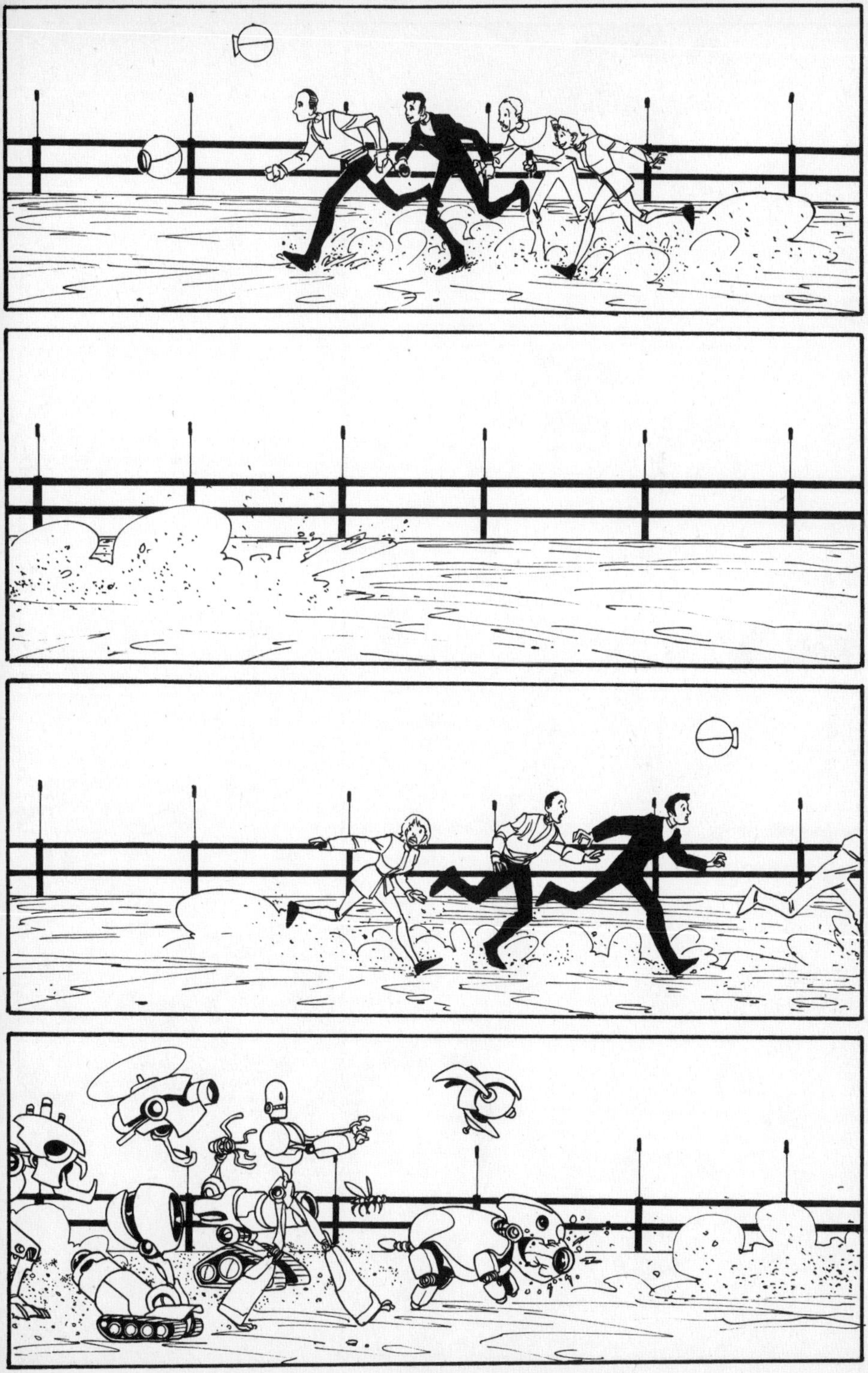

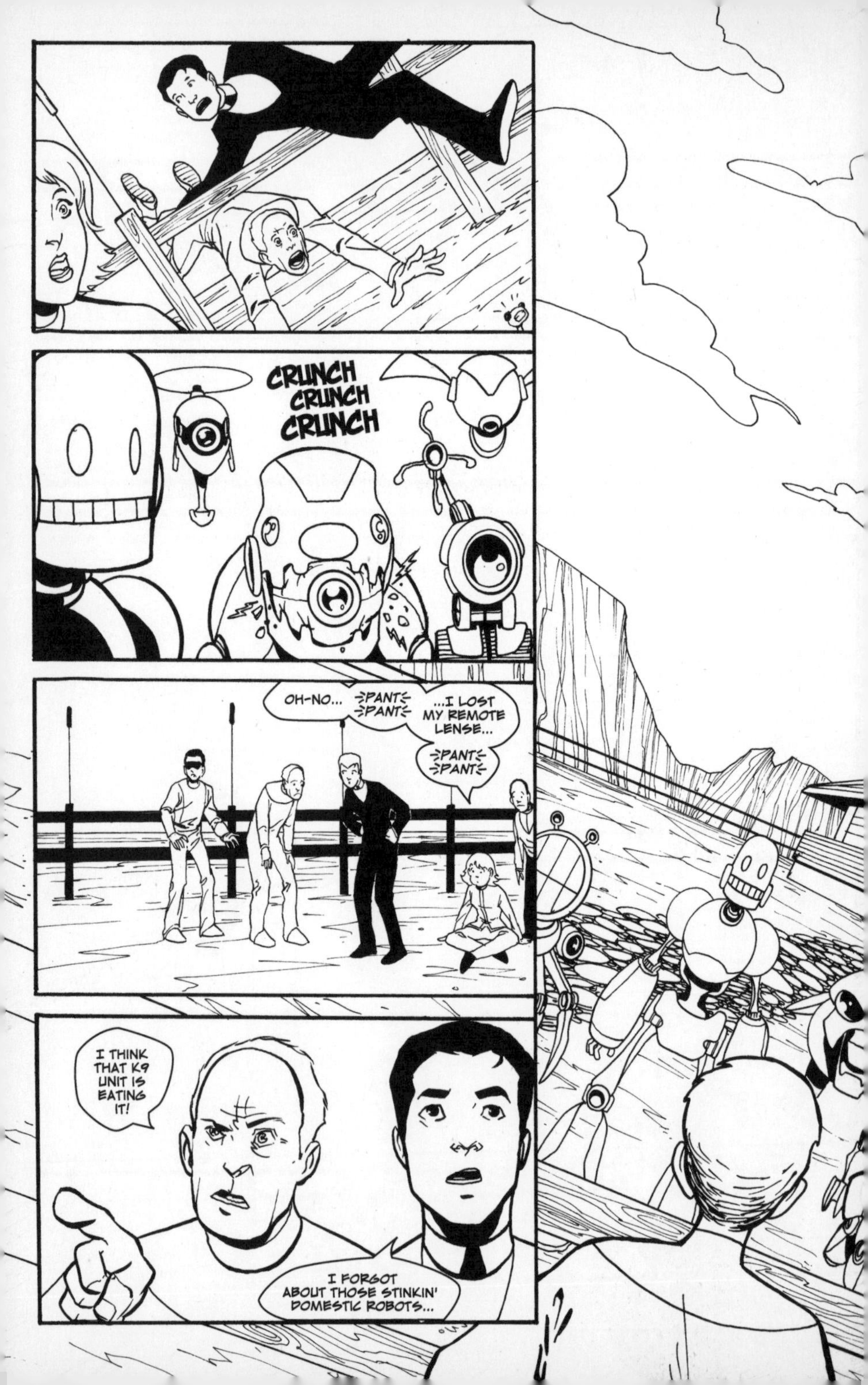
CRUNCH
CRUNCH
CRUNCH
OH-NO... =PANT= =PANT=
...I LOST MY REMOTE LENSE...
=PANT= =PANT=
I THINK THAT K9 UNIT IS EATING IT!
I FORGOT ABOUT THOSE STINKIN' DOMESTIC ROBOTS...

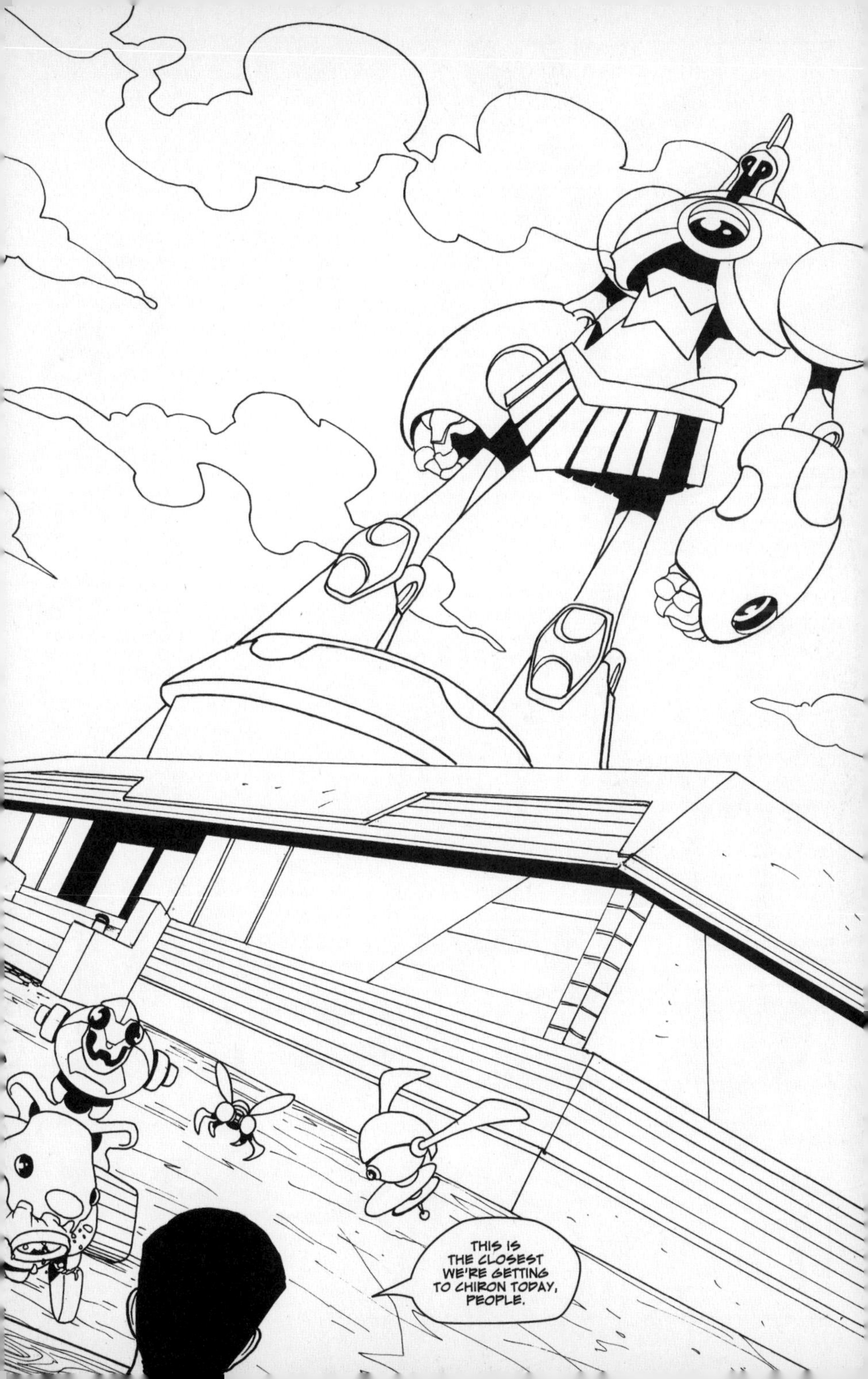
THIS IS THE CLOSEST WE'RE GETTING TO CHIRON TODAY, PEOPLE.

PART 2: LEVERS

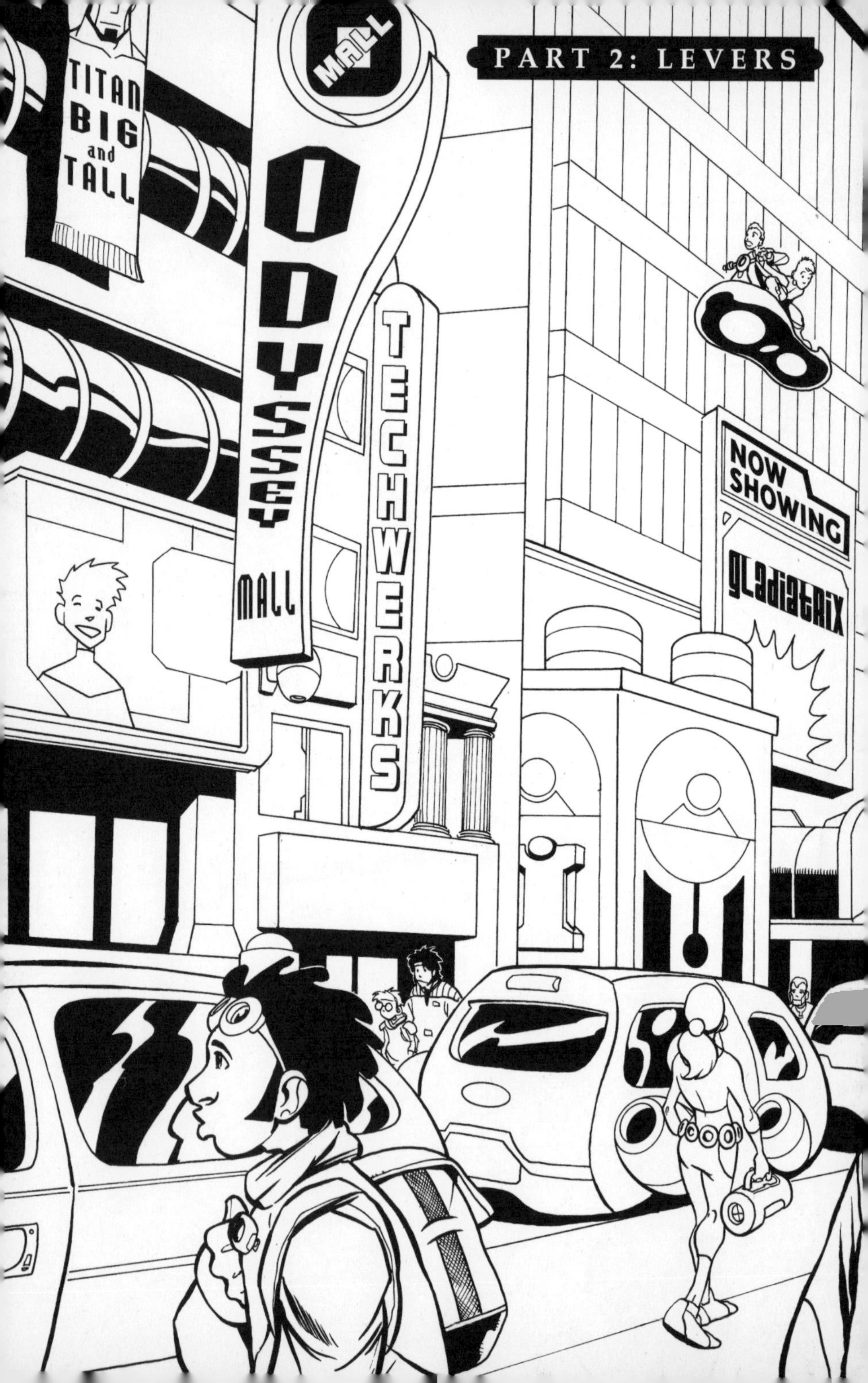
TITAN BIG and TALL
MALL
ODYSSEY
MALL
TECHWERKS
NOW SHOWING
gladiatrix

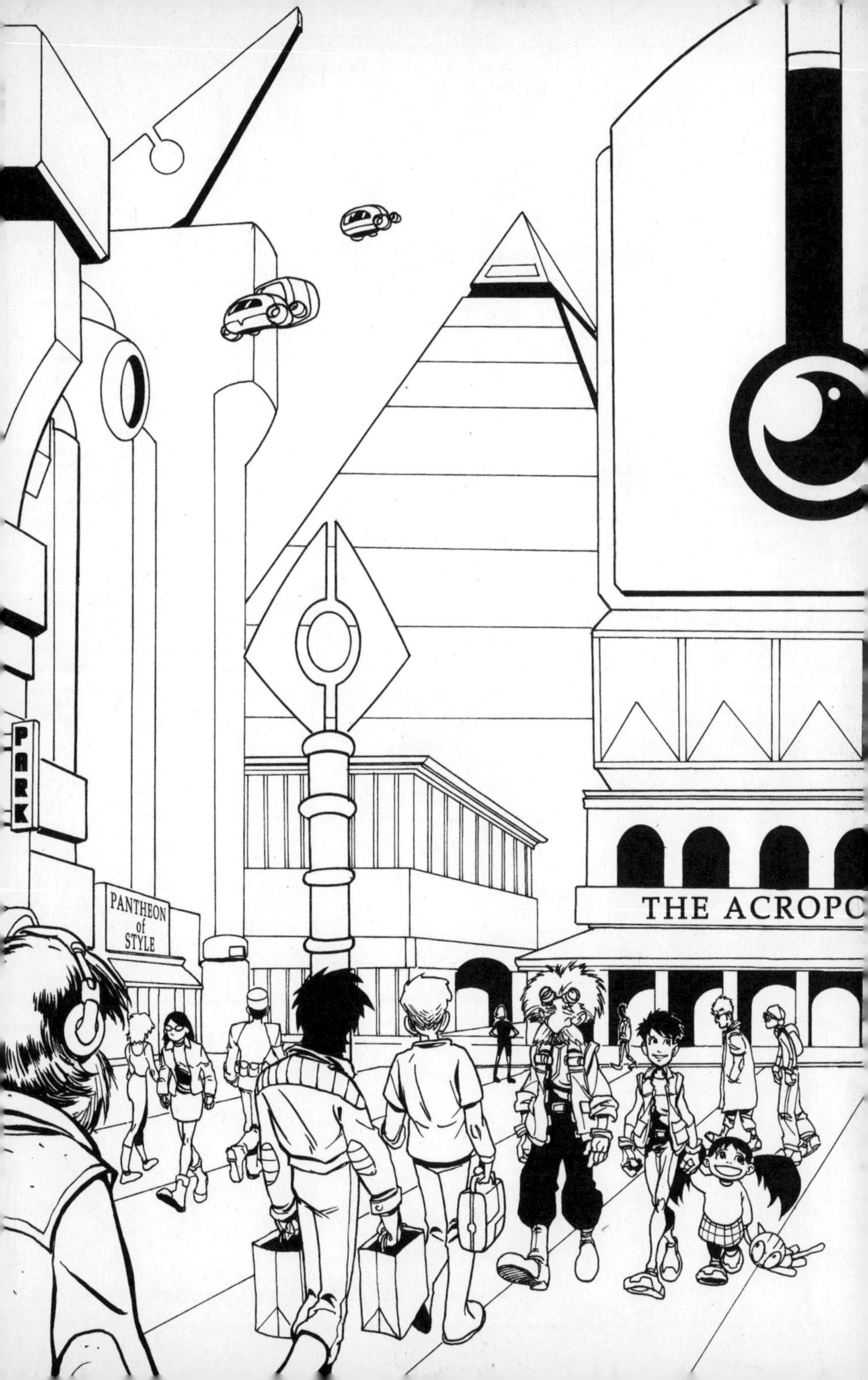
PARK
PANTHEON of STYLE
THE ACROPO

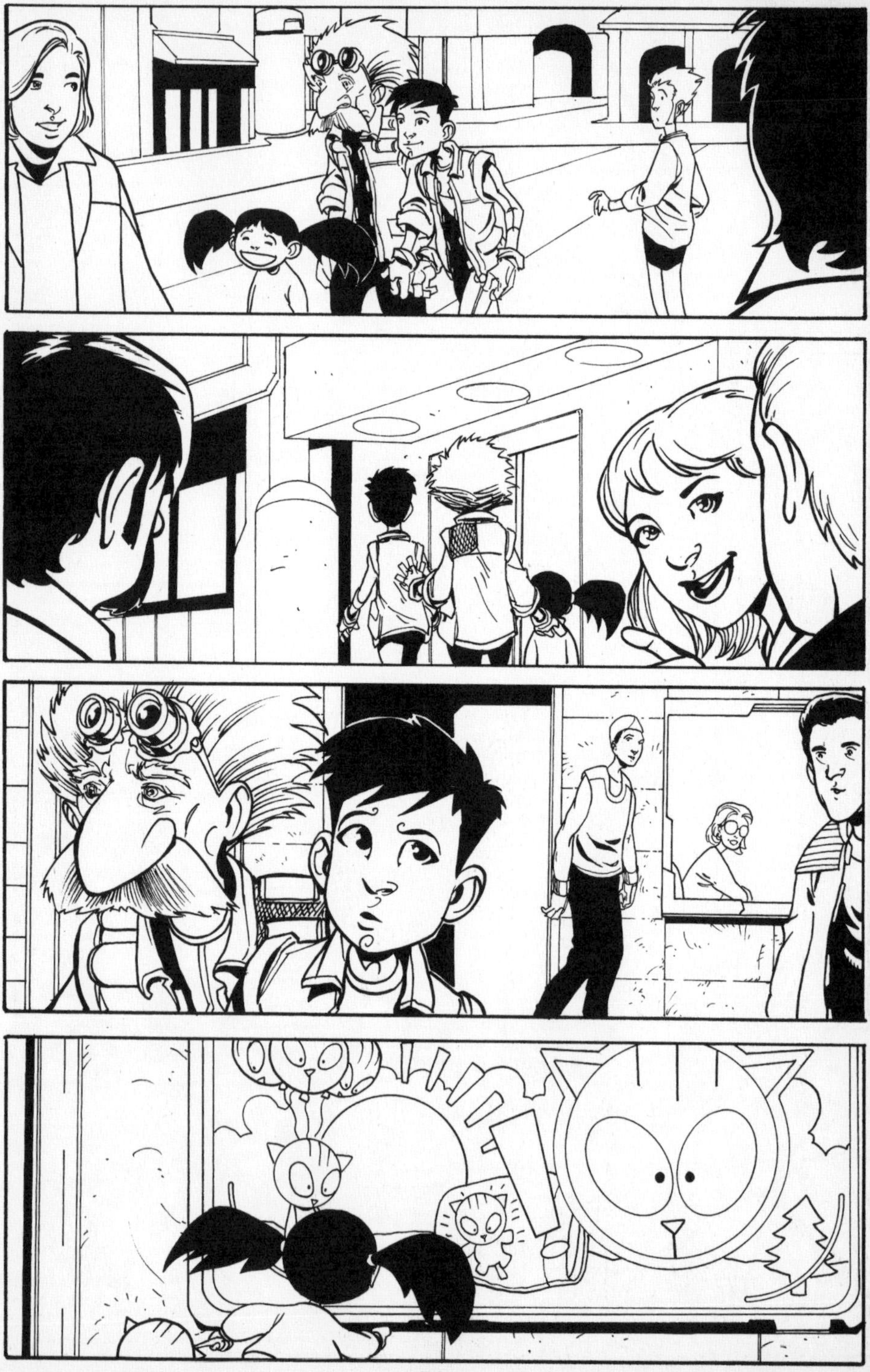

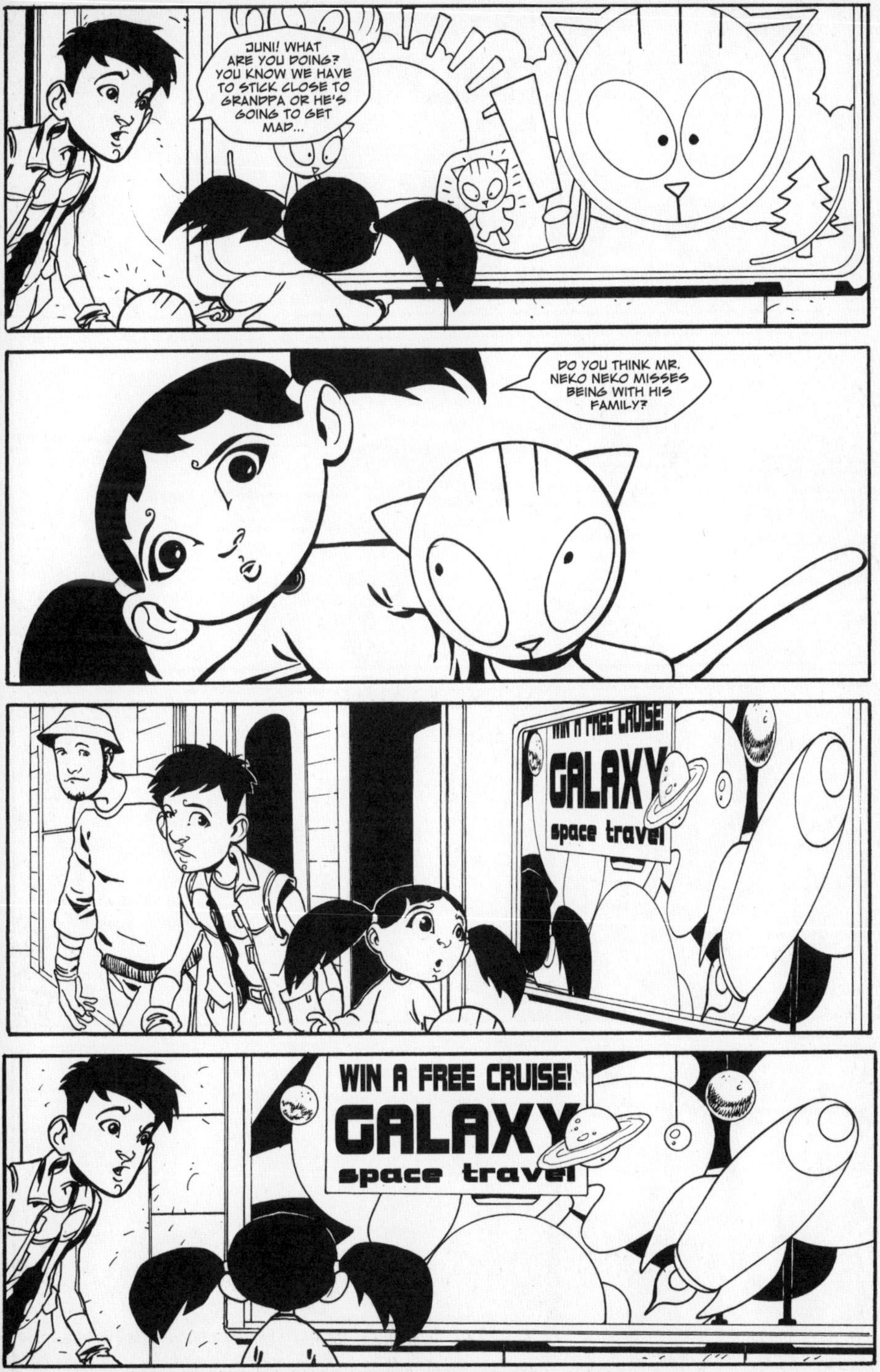
JUNI! WHAT ARE YOU DOING? YOU KNOW WE HAVE TO STICK CLOSE TO GRANDPA OR HE'S GOING TO GET MAD...
DO YOU THINK MR. NEKO NEKO MISSES BEING WITH HIS FAMILY?
WIN A FREE CRUISE!
GALAXY
space travel
WIN A FREE CRUISE!
GALAXY
space travel

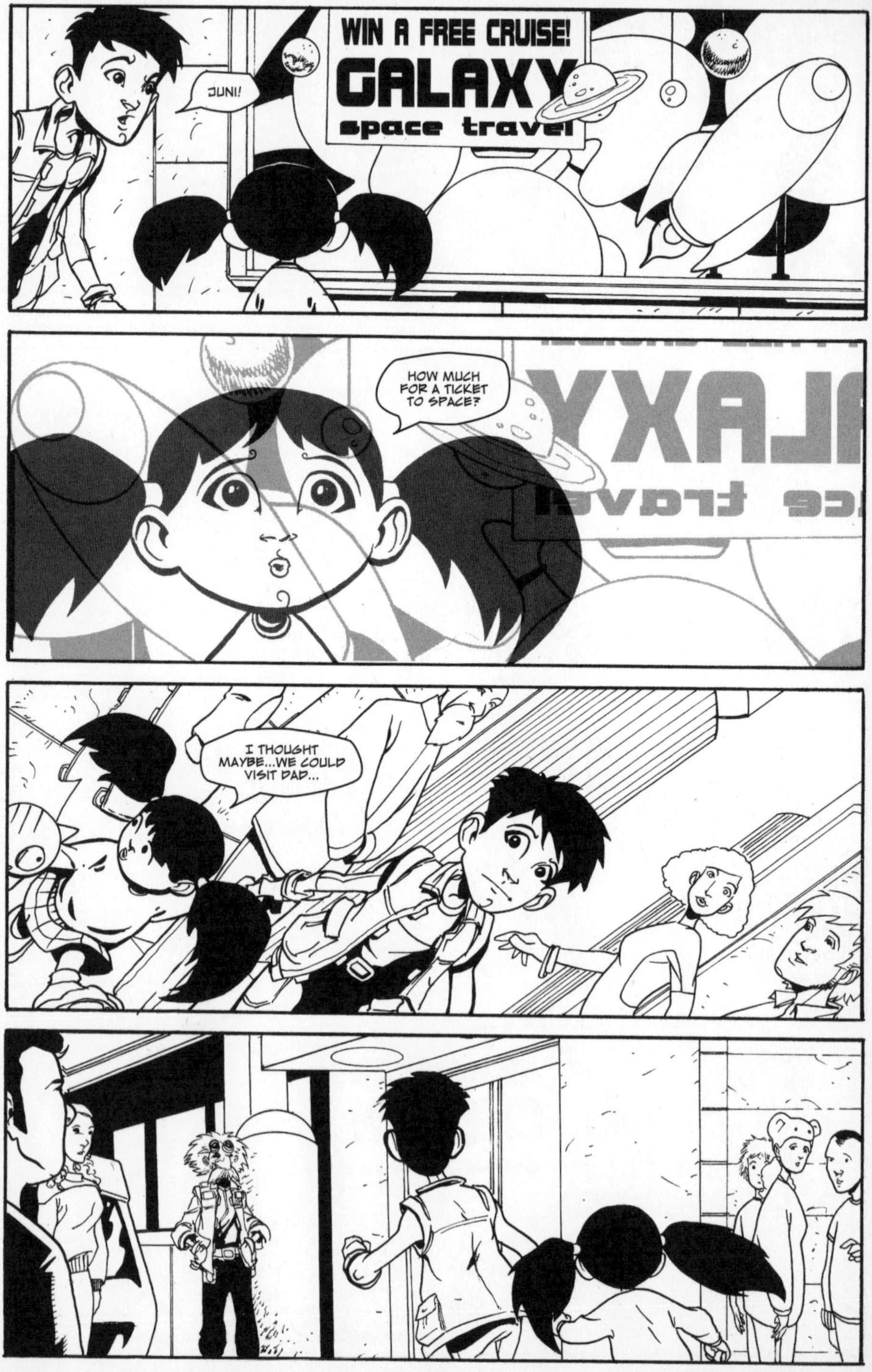
WIN A FREE CRUISE!
GALAXY
space travel
JUNI!
HOW MUCH FOR A TICKET TO SPACE?
I THOUGHT MAYBE...WE COULD VISIT DAD...

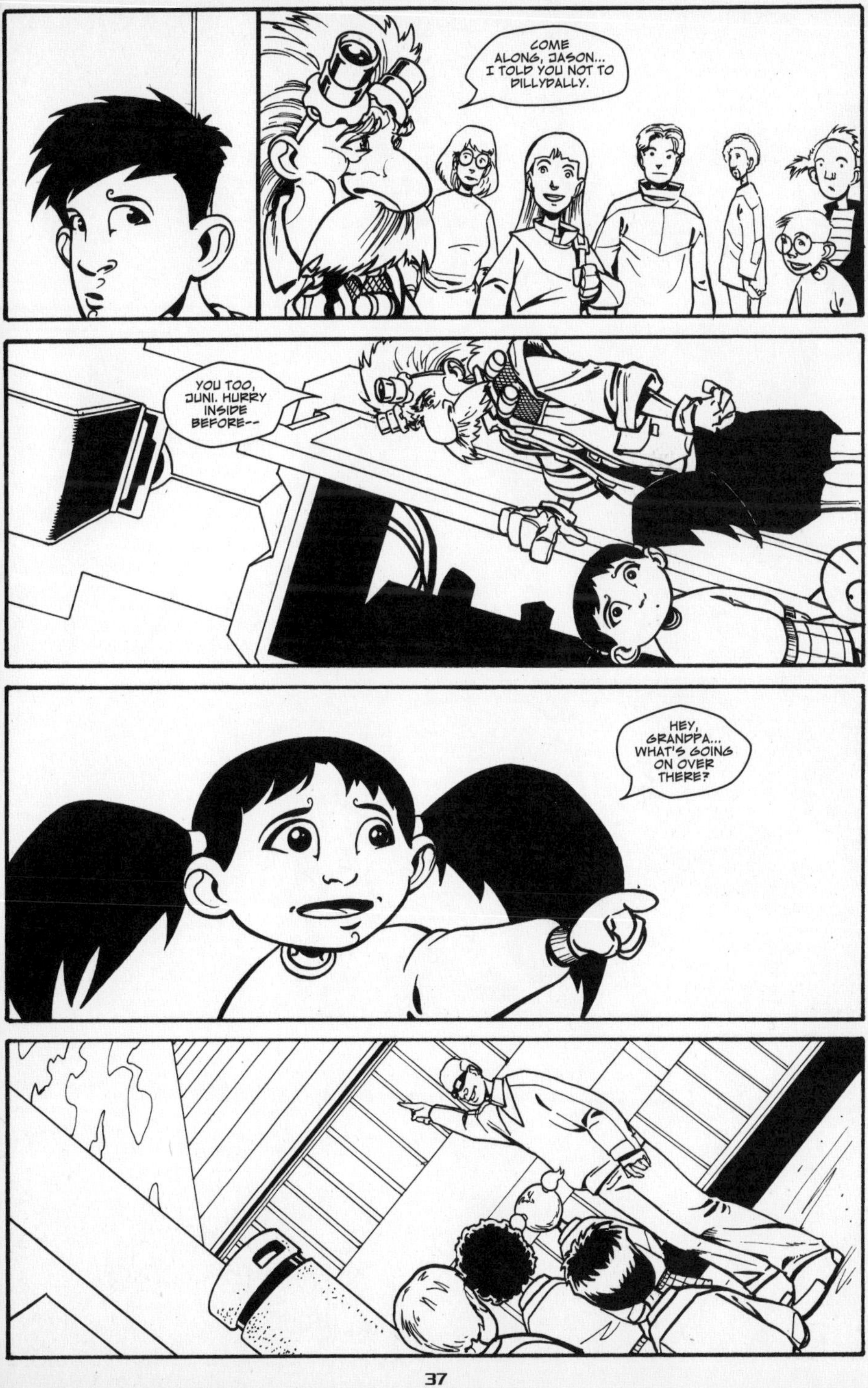
COME ALONG, JASON... I TOLD YOU NOT TO DILLYDALLY.
YOU TOO, JUNI. HURRY INSIDE BEFORE--
HEY, GRANDPA... WHAT'S GOING ON OVER THERE?

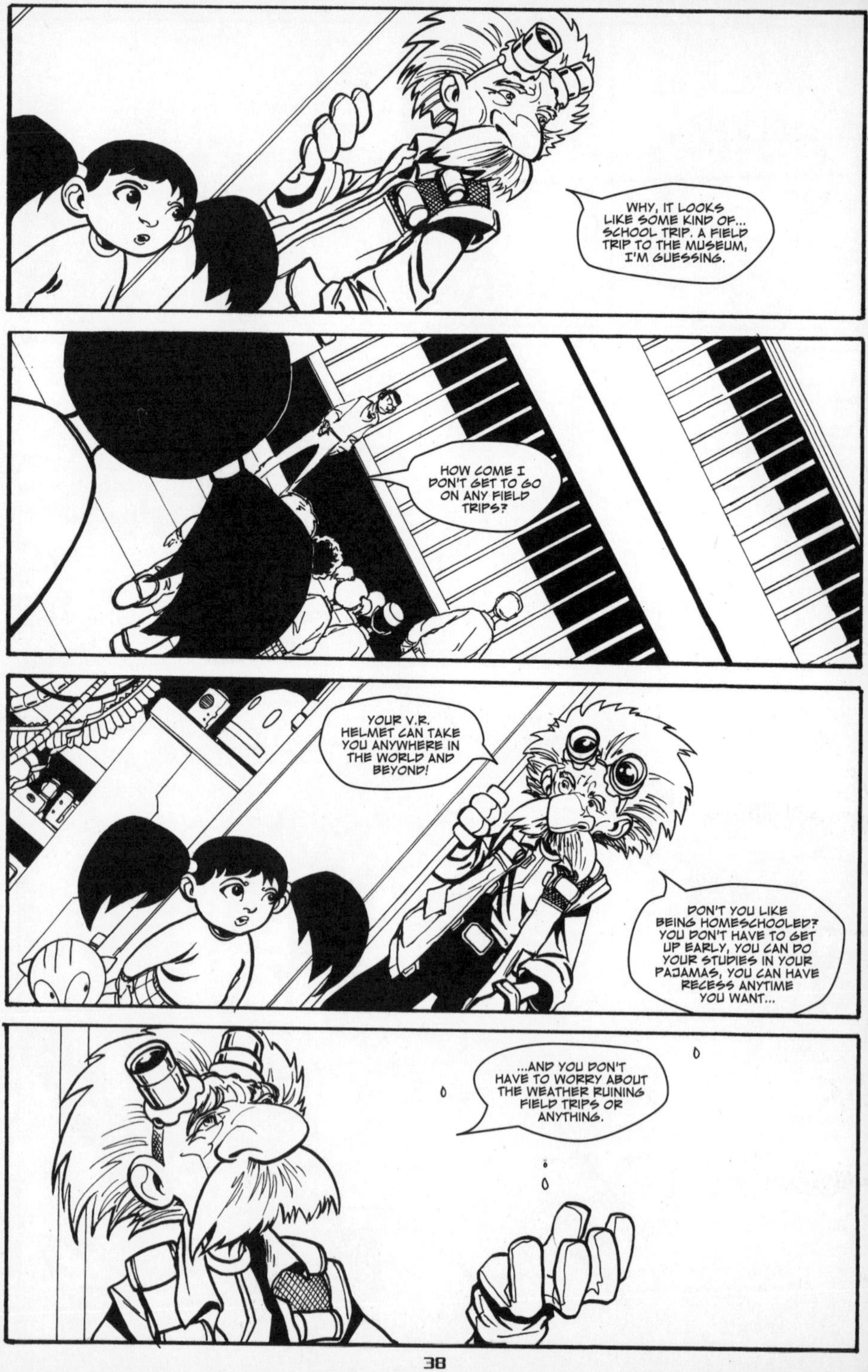
WHY, IT LOOKS LIKE SOME KIND OF... SCHOOL TRIP. A FIELD TRIP TO THE MUSEUM, I'M GUESSING.
HOW COME I DON'T GET TO GO ON ANY FIELD TRIPS?
YOUR V.R. HELMET CAN TAKE YOU ANYWHERE IN THE WORLD AND BEYOND!
DON'T YOU LIKE BEING HOMESCHOOLED? YOU DON'T HAVE TO GET UP EARLY, YOU CAN DO YOUR STUDIES IN YOUR PAJAMAS, YOU CAN HAVE RECESS ANYTIME YOU WANT...
...AND YOU DON'T HAVE TO WORRY ABOUT THE WEATHER RUINING FIELD TRIPS OR ANYTHING.

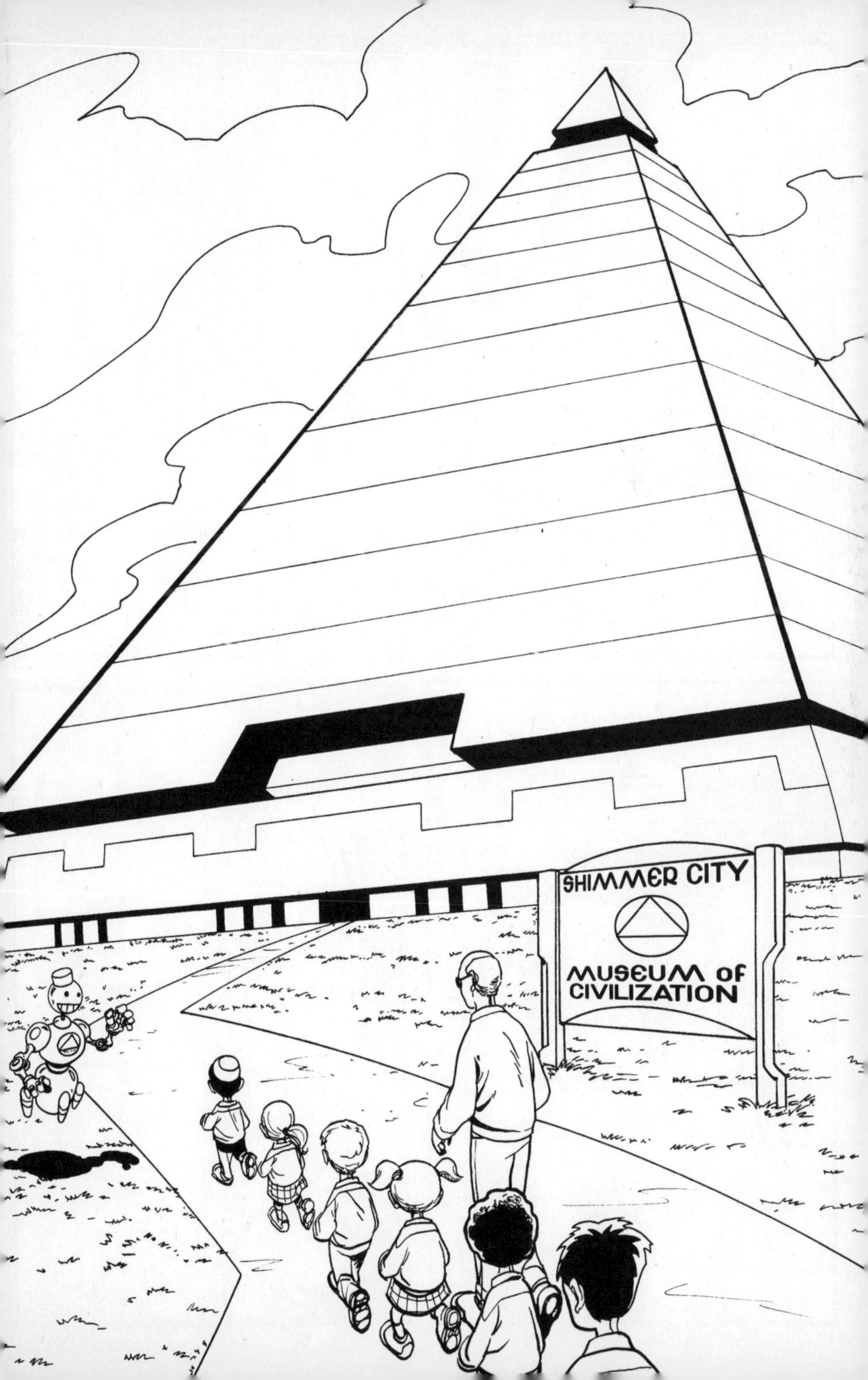
SHIMMER CITY
MUSEUM of CIVILIZATION

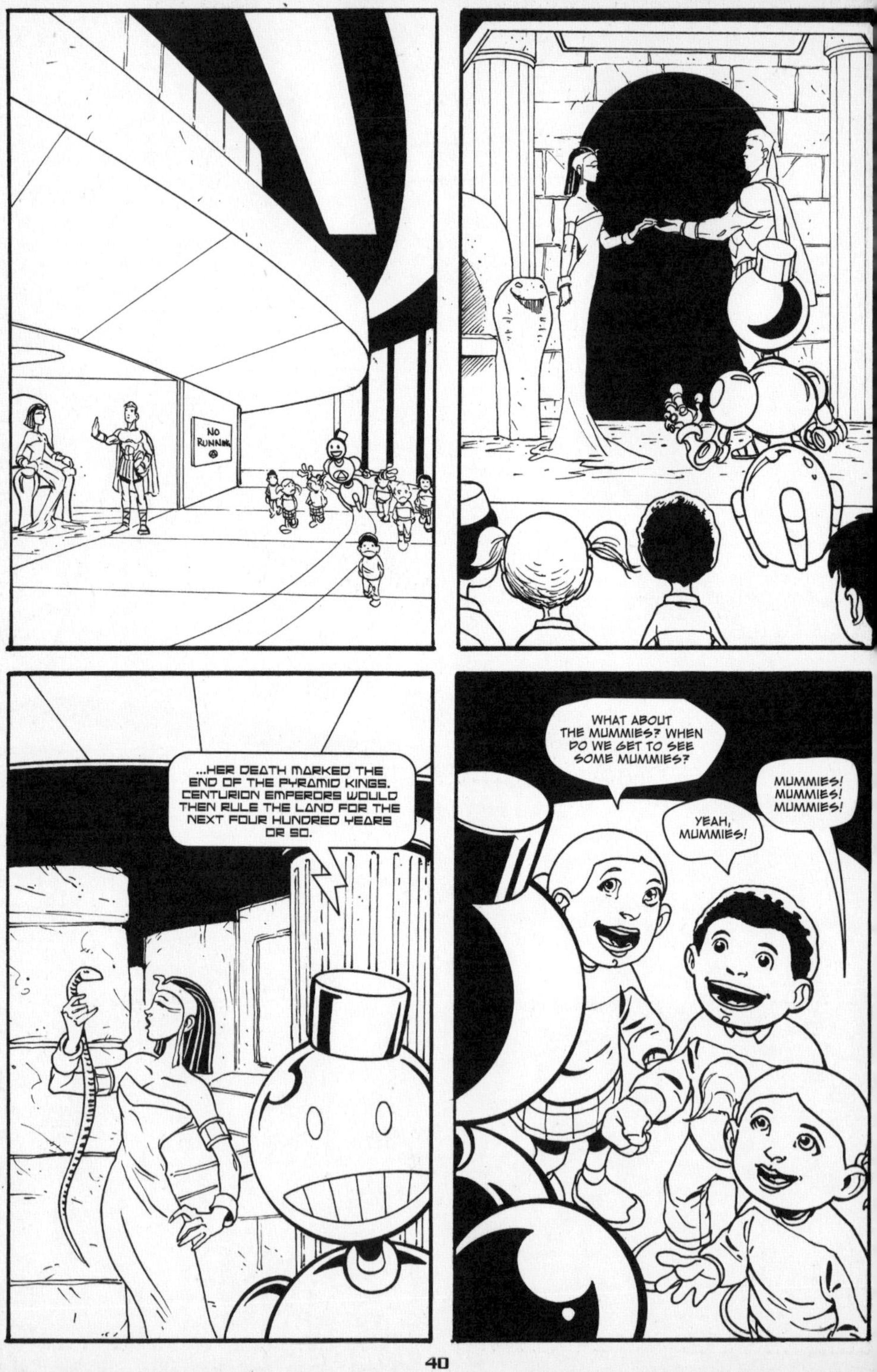
NO RUNNING
...HER DEATH MARKED THE END OF THE PYRAMID KINGS. CENTURION EMPERORS WOULD THEN RULE THE LAND FOR THE NEXT FOUR HUNDRED YEARS OR SO.
WHAT ABOUT THE MUMMIES? WHEN DO WE GET TO SEE SOME MUMMIES?
YEAH, MUMMIES!
MUMMIES! MUMMIES! MUMMIES!

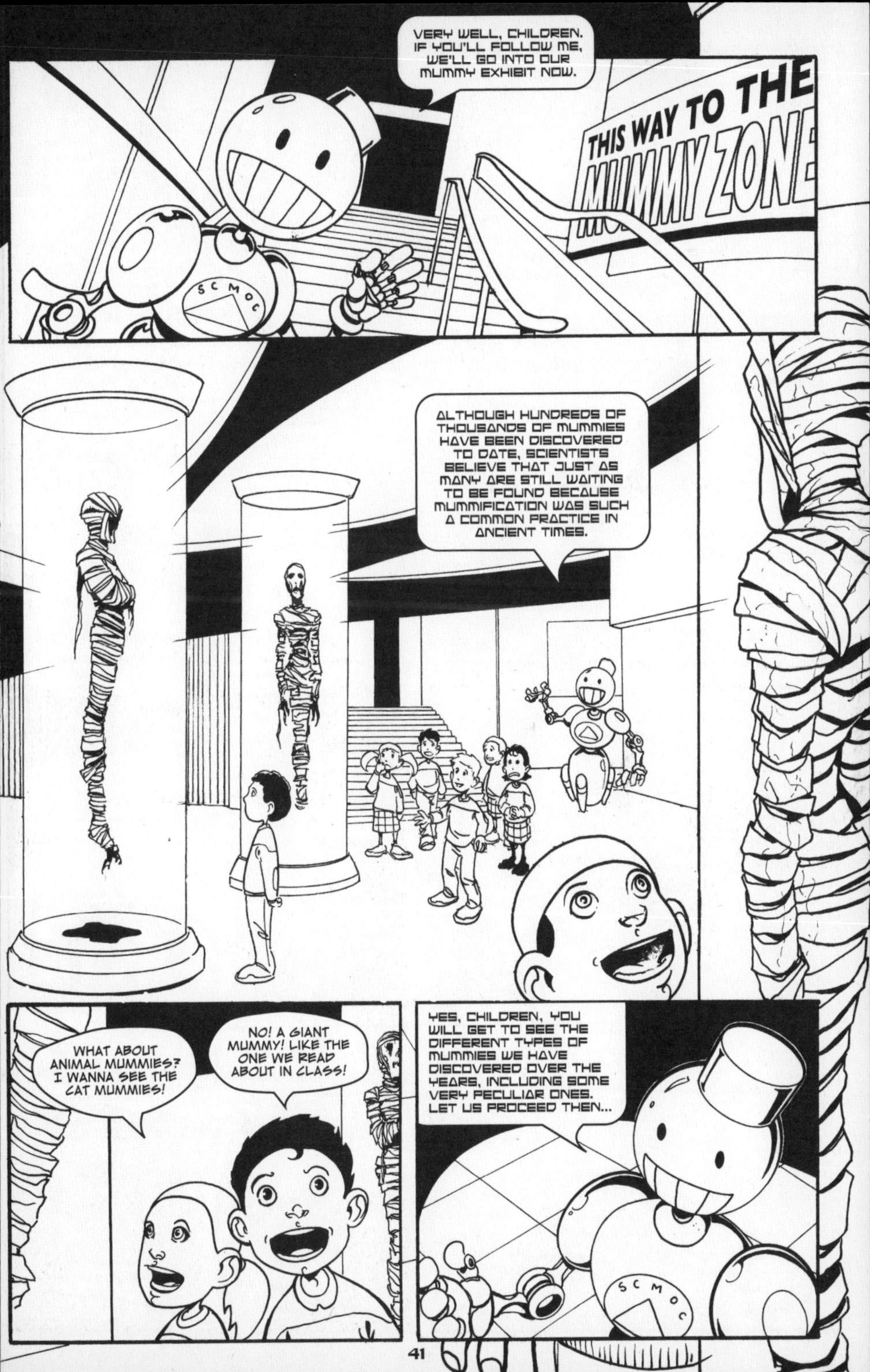
VERY WELL, CHILDREN. IF YOU'LL FOLLOW ME, WE'LL GO INTO OUR MUMMY EXHIBIT NOW.
THIS WAY TO THE MUMMY ZONE
ALTHOUGH HUNDREDS OF THOUSANDS OF MUMMIES HAVE BEEN DISCOVERED TO DATE, SCIENTISTS BELIEVE THAT JUST AS MANY ARE STILL WAITING TO BE FOUND BECAUSE MUMMIFICATION WAS SUCH A COMMON PRACTICE IN ANCIENT TIMES.
WHAT ABOUT ANIMAL MUMMIES? I WANNA SEE THE CAT MUMMIES!
NO! A GIANT MUMMY! LIKE THE ONE WE READ ABOUT IN CLASS!
YES, CHILDREN, YOU WILL GET TO SEE THE DIFFERENT TYPES OF MUMMIES WE HAVE DISCOVERED OVER THE YEARS, INCLUDING SOME VERY PECULIAR ONES. LET US PROCEED THEN...

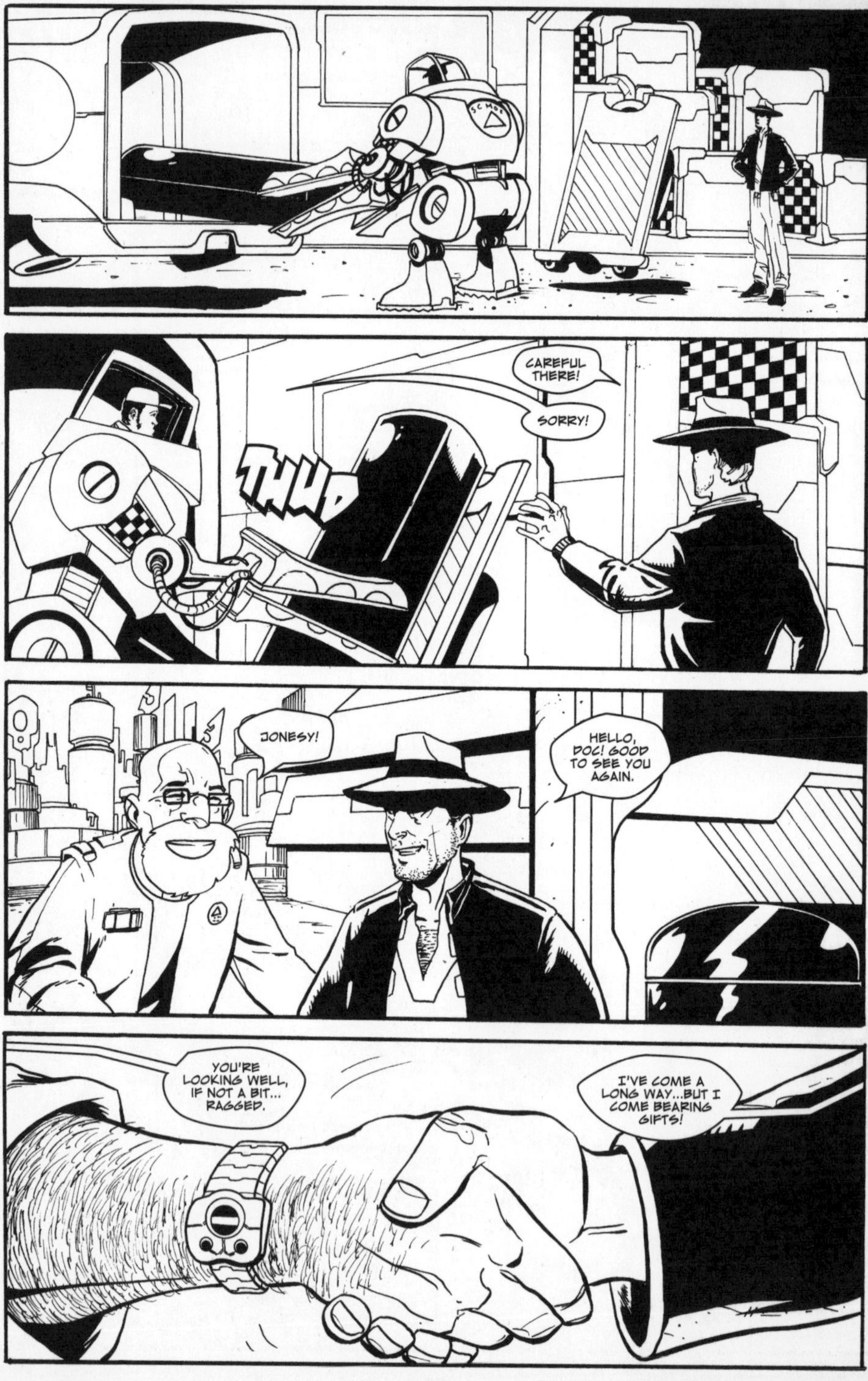
CAREFUL THERE!
SORRY!
THUD
JONESY!
HELLO, DOC! GOOD TO SEE YOU AGAIN.
YOU'RE LOOKING WELL, IF NOT A BIT... RAGGED.
I'VE COME A LONG WAY...BUT I COME BEARING GIFTS!

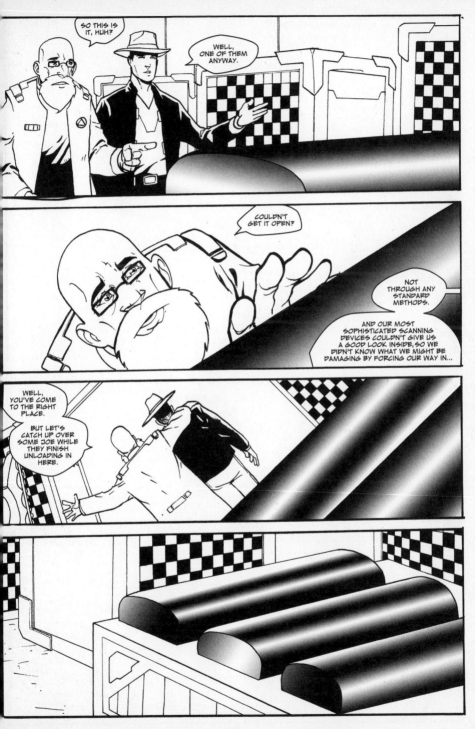

SO THIS IS IT, HUH?

WELL, ONE OF THEM ANYWAY.

COULDN'T GET IT OPEN?

NOT THROUGH ANY STANDARD METHODS.

AND OUR MOST SOPHISTICATED SCANNING DEVICES COULDN'T GIVE US A GOOD LOOK INSIDE, SO WE DIDN'T KNOW WHAT WE MIGHT BE DAMAGING BY FORCING OUR WAY IN...

WELL, YOU'VE COME TO THE RIGHT PLACE.

BUT LET'S CATCH UP OVER SOME JOE WHILE THEY FINISH UNLOADING IN HERE.

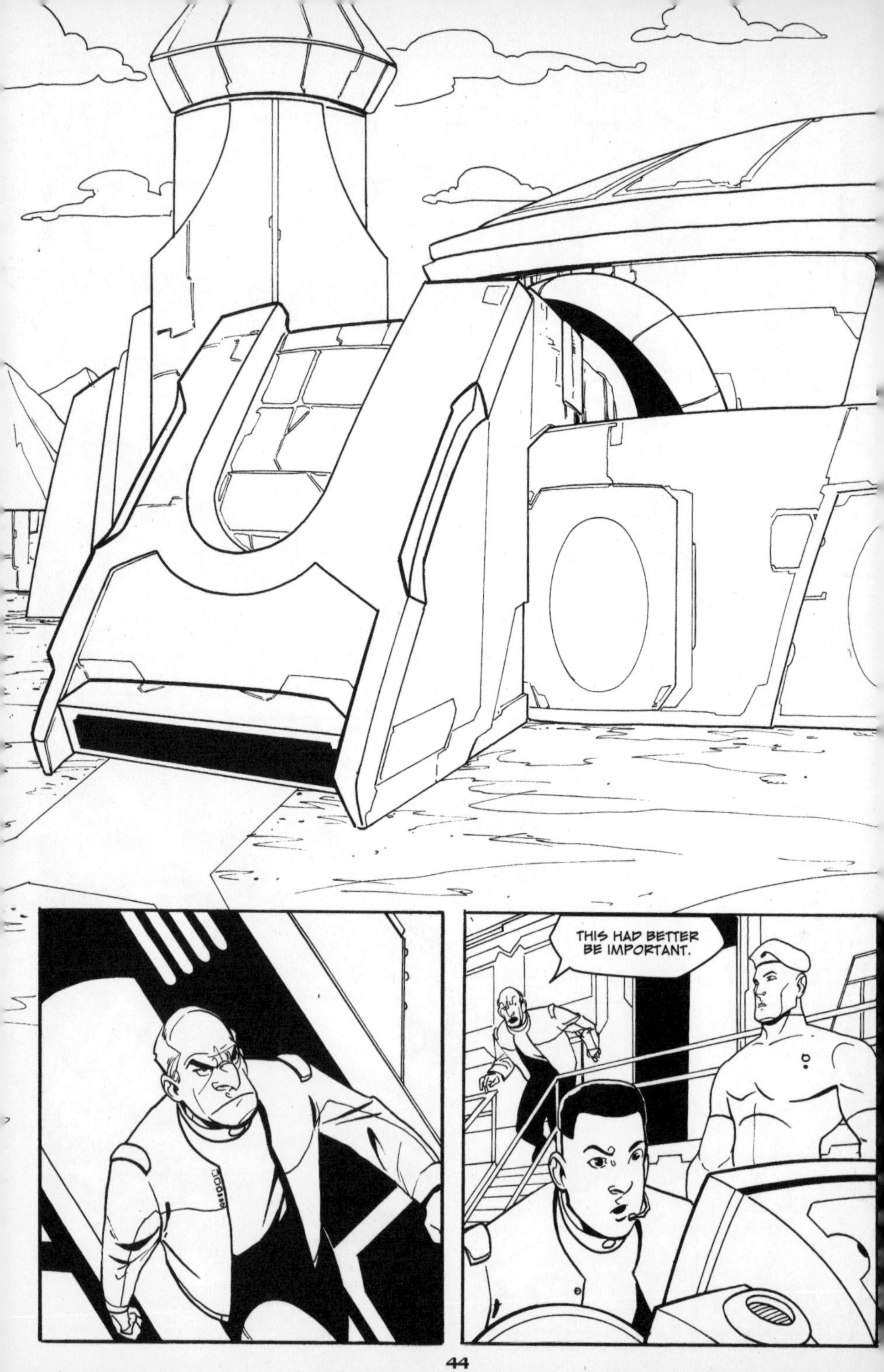
THIS HAD BETTER BE IMPORTANT.

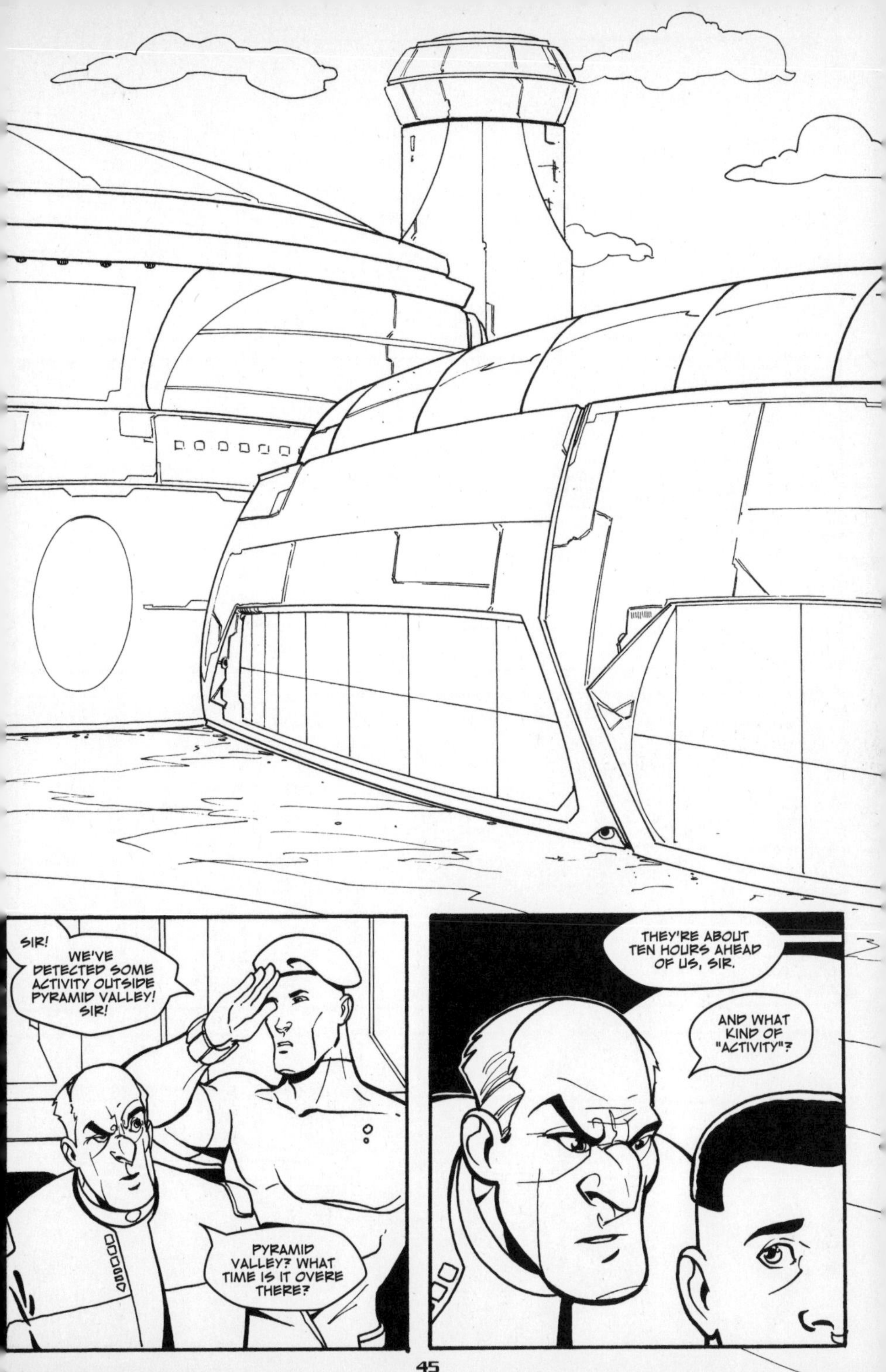
SIR!
WE'VE DETECTED SOME ACTIVITY OUTSIDE PYRAMID VALLEY! SIR!
PYRAMID VALLEY? WHAT TIME IS IT OVERE THERE?
THEY'RE ABOUT TEN HOURS AHEAD OF US, SIR.
AND WHAT KIND OF "ACTIVITY"?

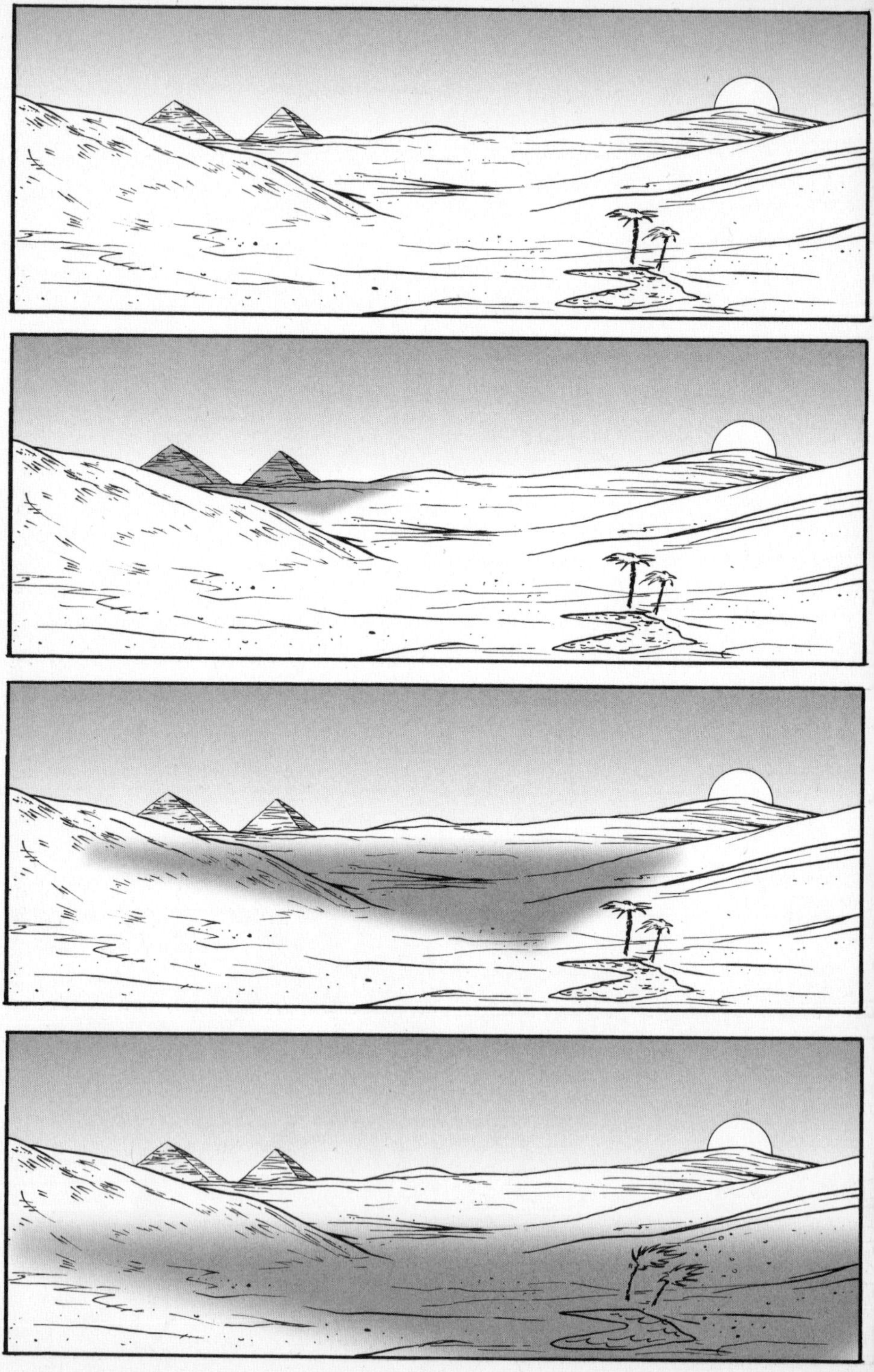

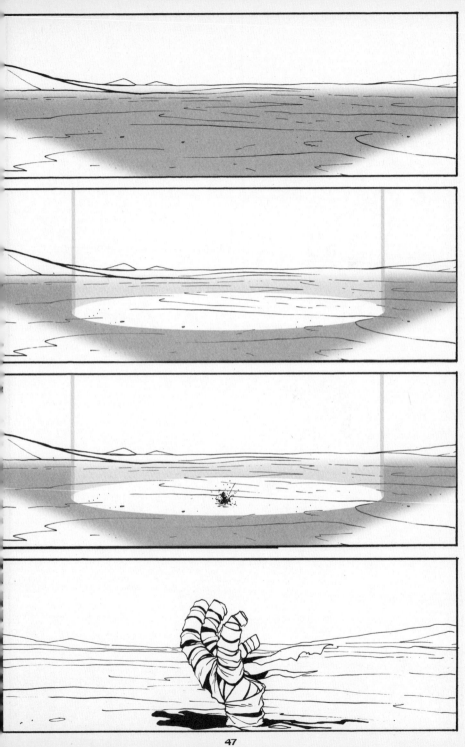

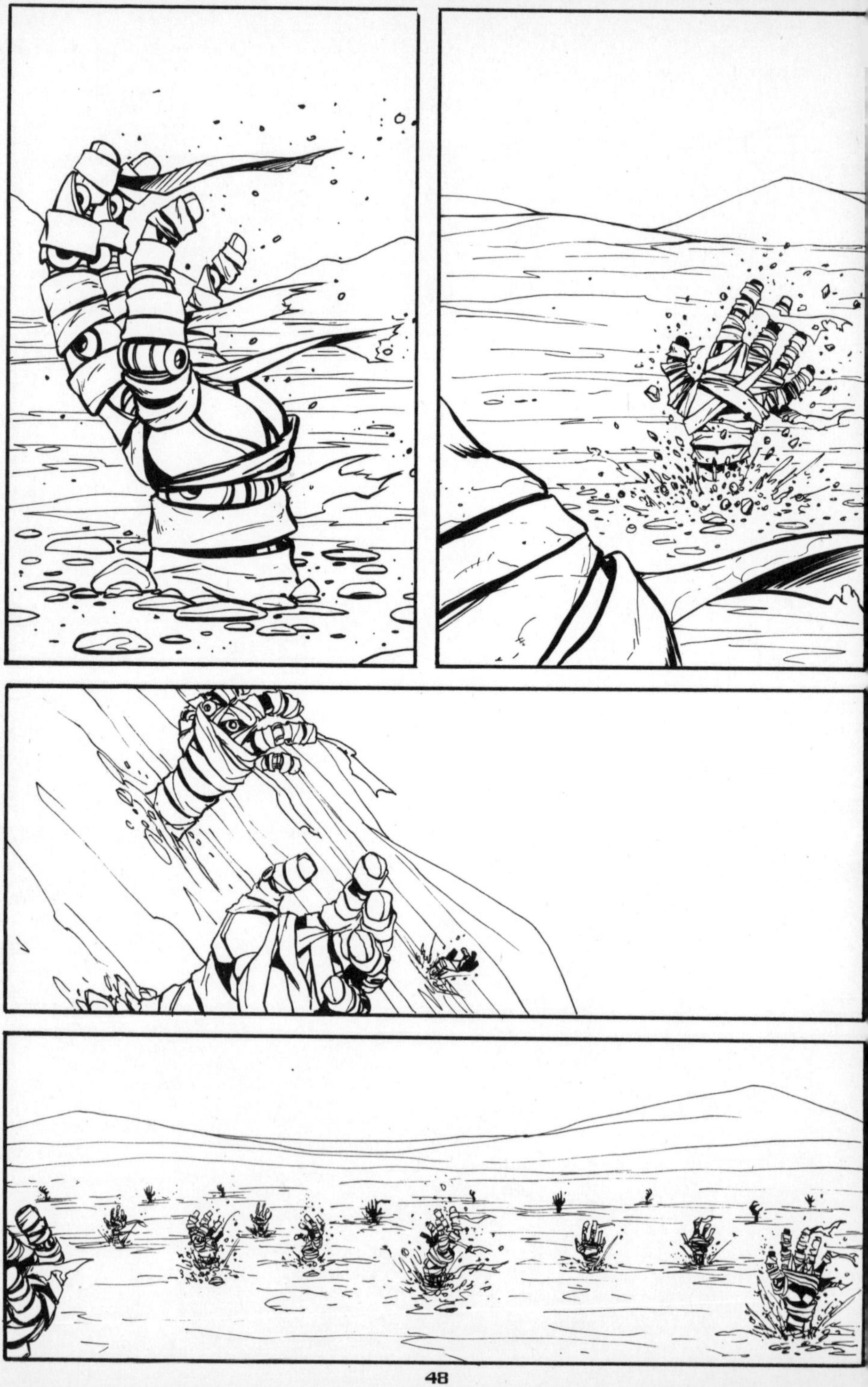

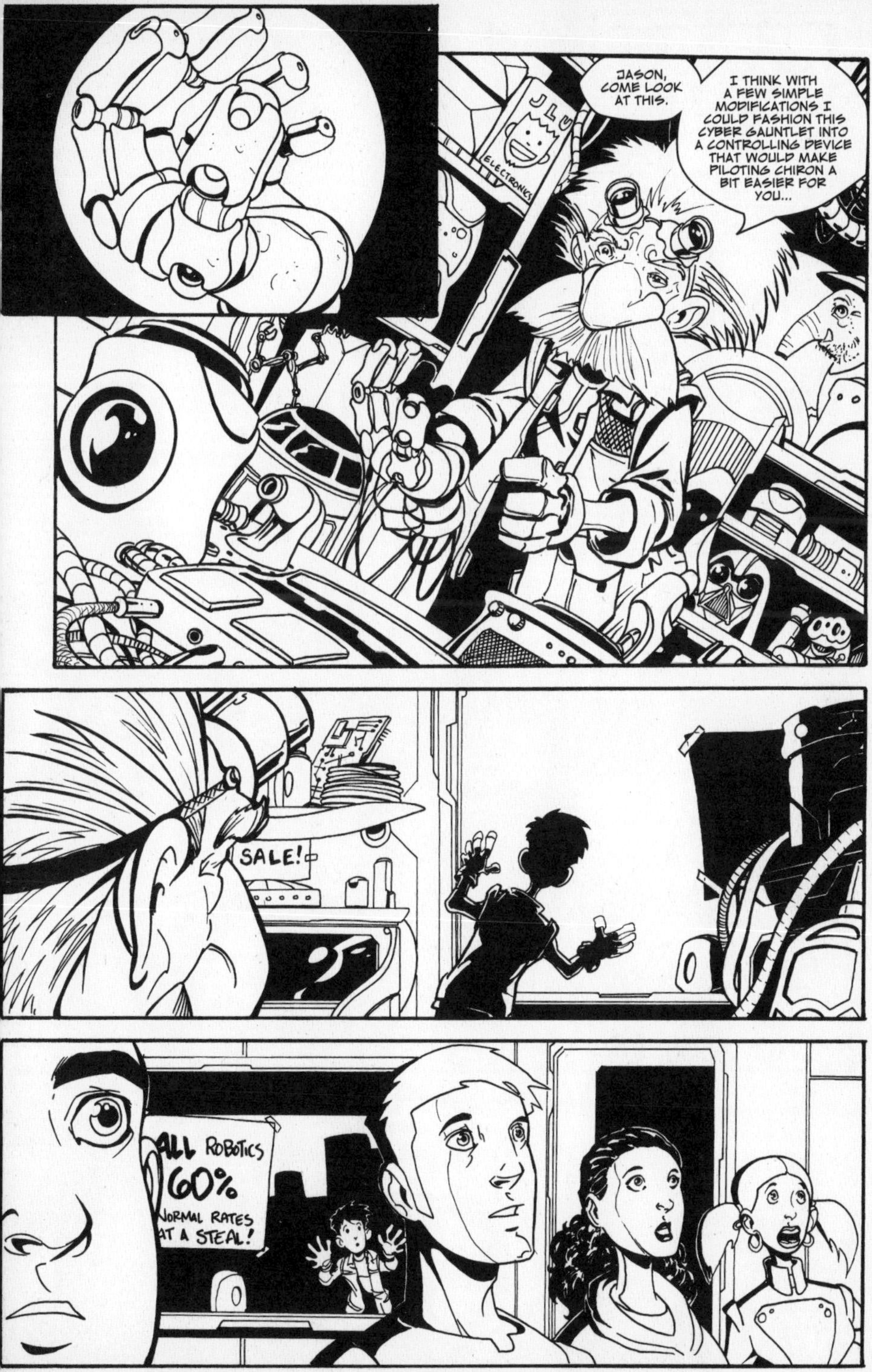
JLU
ELECTRONICS
JASON, COME LOOK AT THIS.
I THINK WITH A FEW SIMPLE MODIFICATIONS I COULD FASHION THIS CYBER GAUNTLET INTO A CONTROLLING DEVICE THAT WOULD MAKE PILOTING CHIRON A BIT EASIER FOR YOU...
SALE!
ALL ROBOTICS 60% NORMAL RATES AT A STEAL!

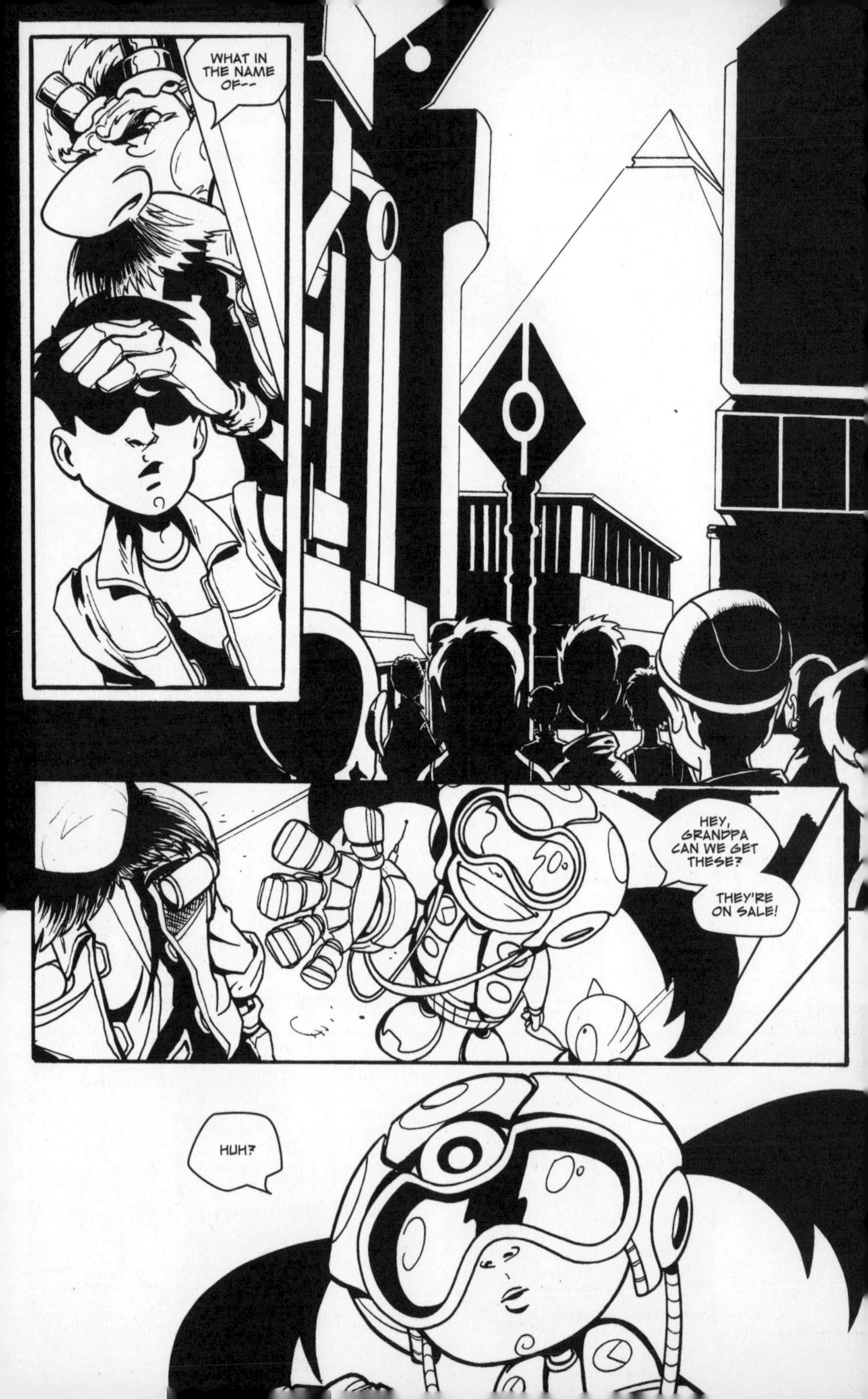
WHAT IN THE NAME OF--
HEY, GRANDPA CAN WE GET THESE?
THEY'RE ON SALE!
HUH?

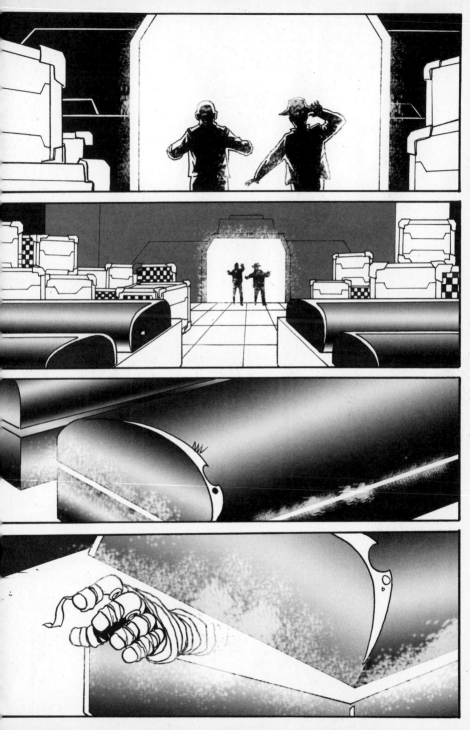

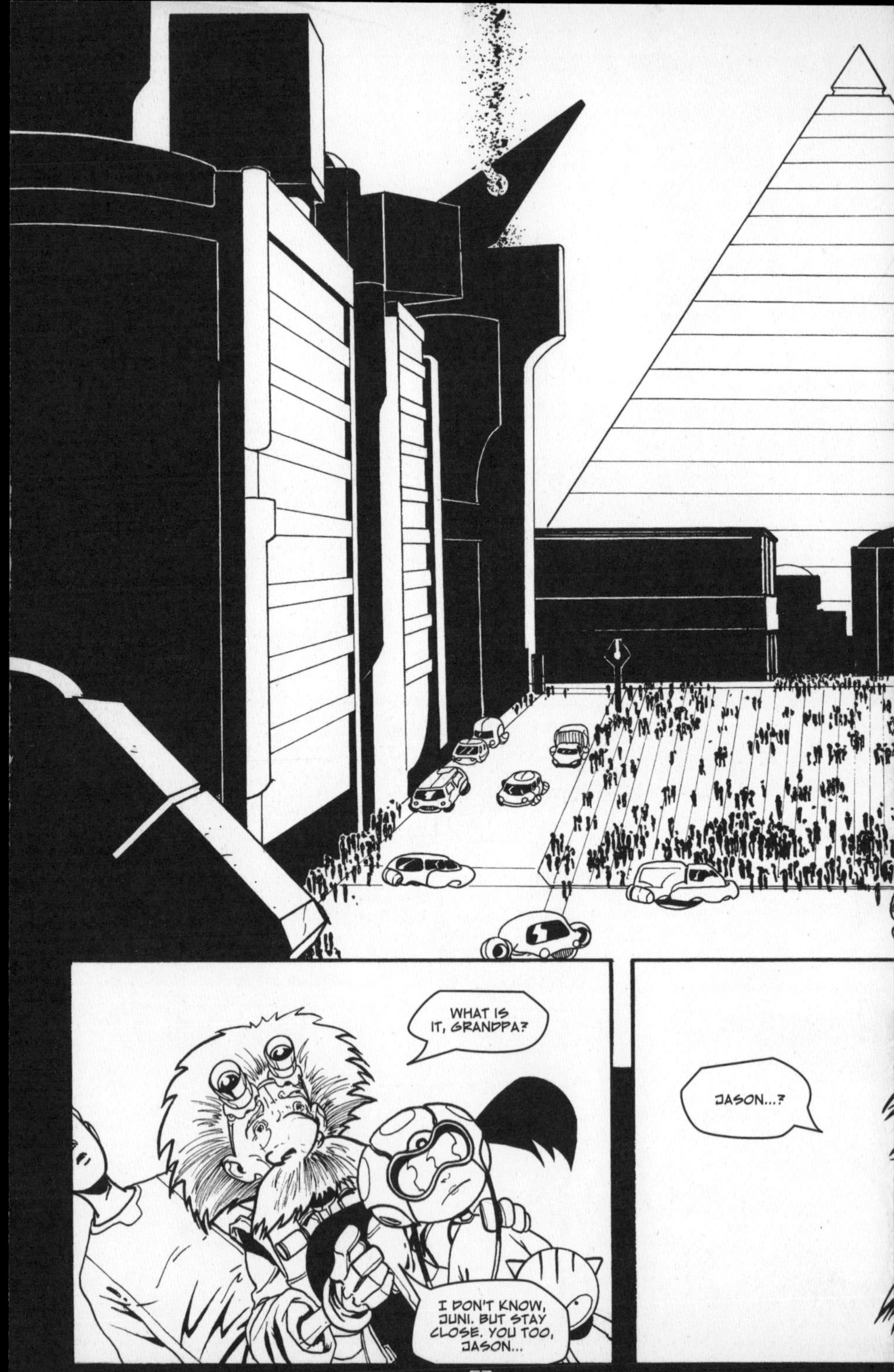
WHAT IS IT, GRANDPA?
I DON'T KNOW, JUNI. BUT STAY CLOSE. YOU TOO, JASON...
JASON...?

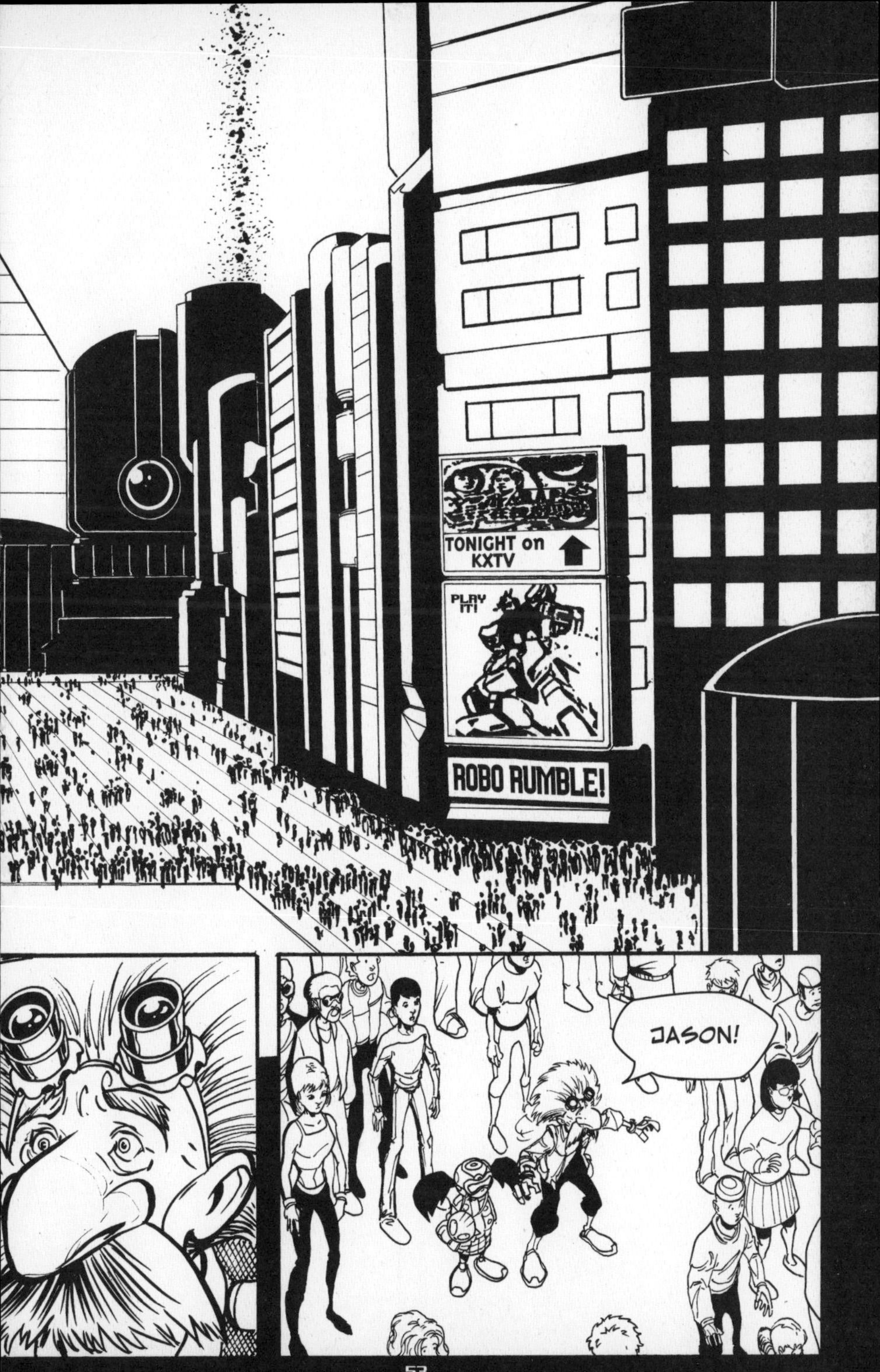
TONIGHT on KXTV
PLAY IT!
ROBO RUMBLE!
JASON!

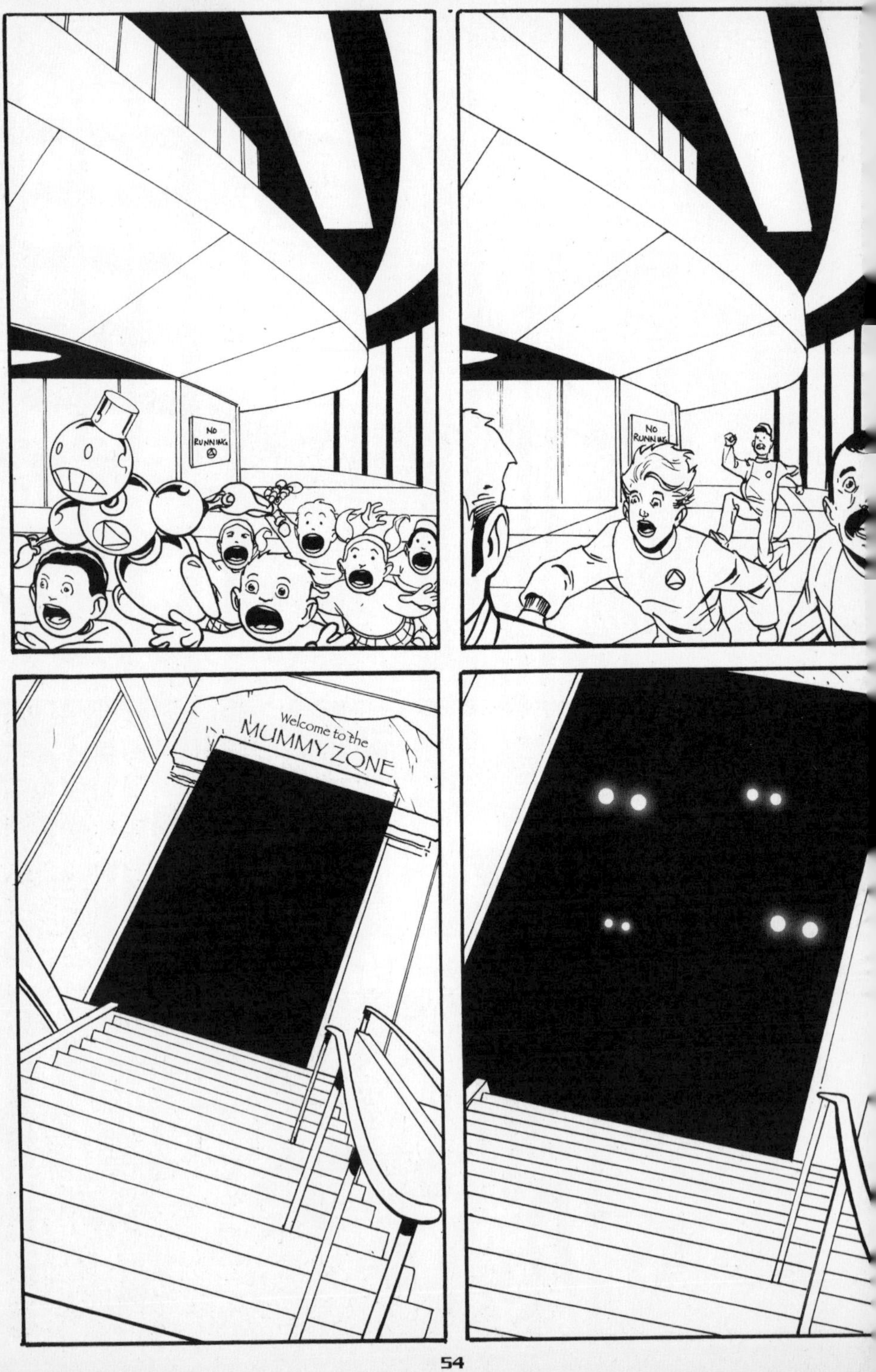

NO RUNNING
NO RUNNING
Welcome to the MUMMY ZONE

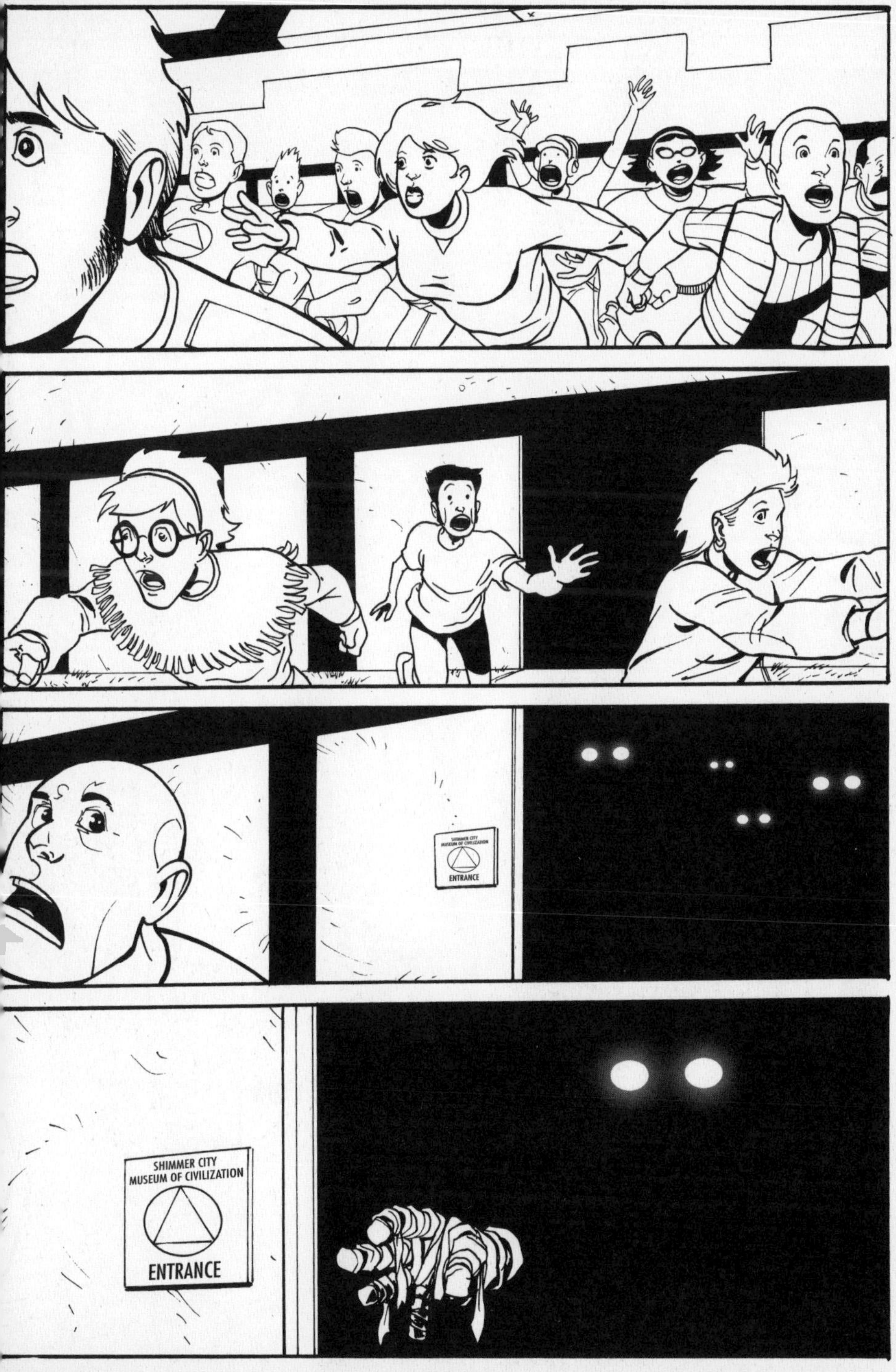
SHIMMER CITY
MUSEUM OF CIVILIZATION
ENTRANCE
SHIMMER CITY
MUSEUM OF CIVILIZATION
ENTRANCE

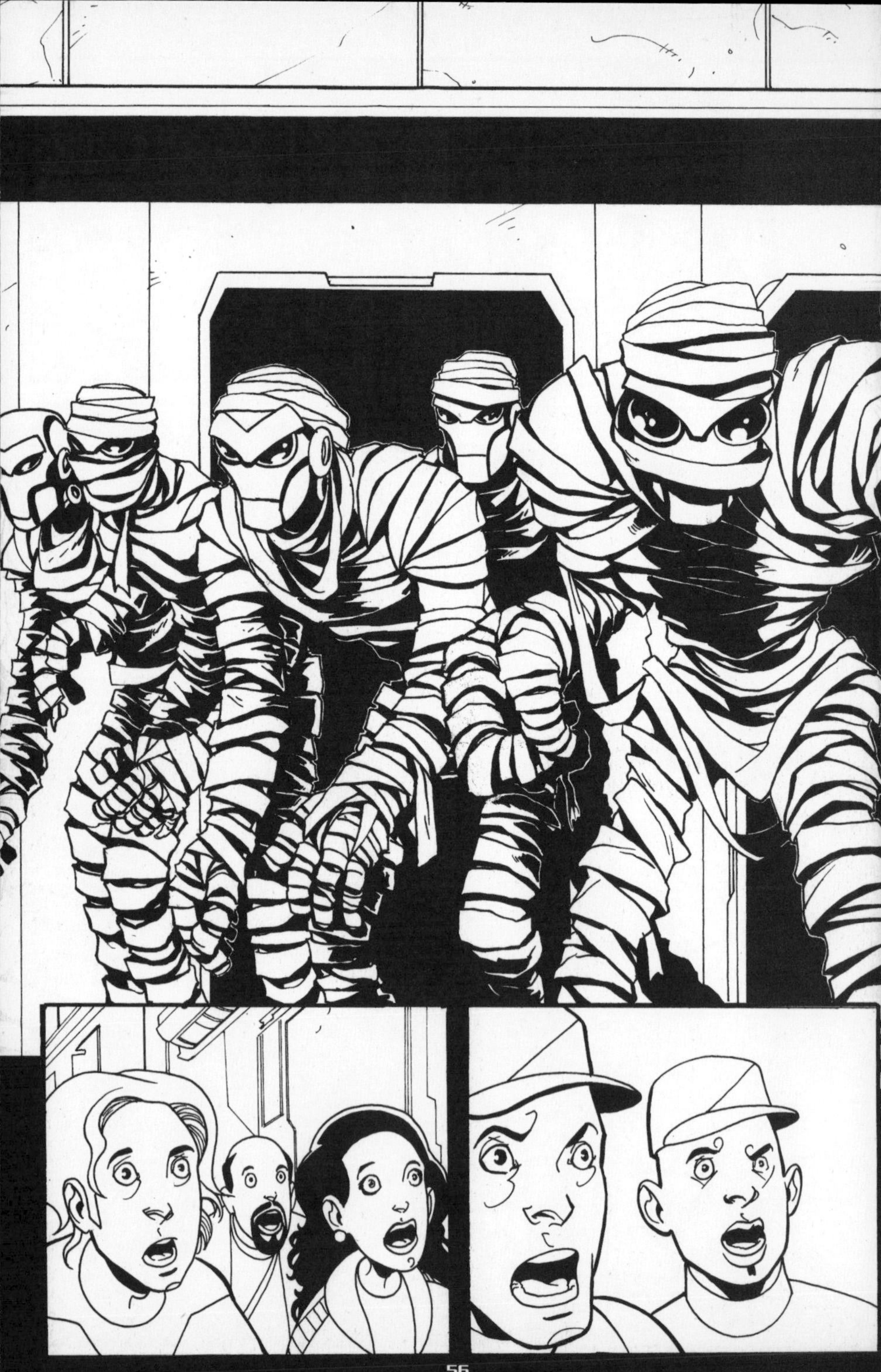

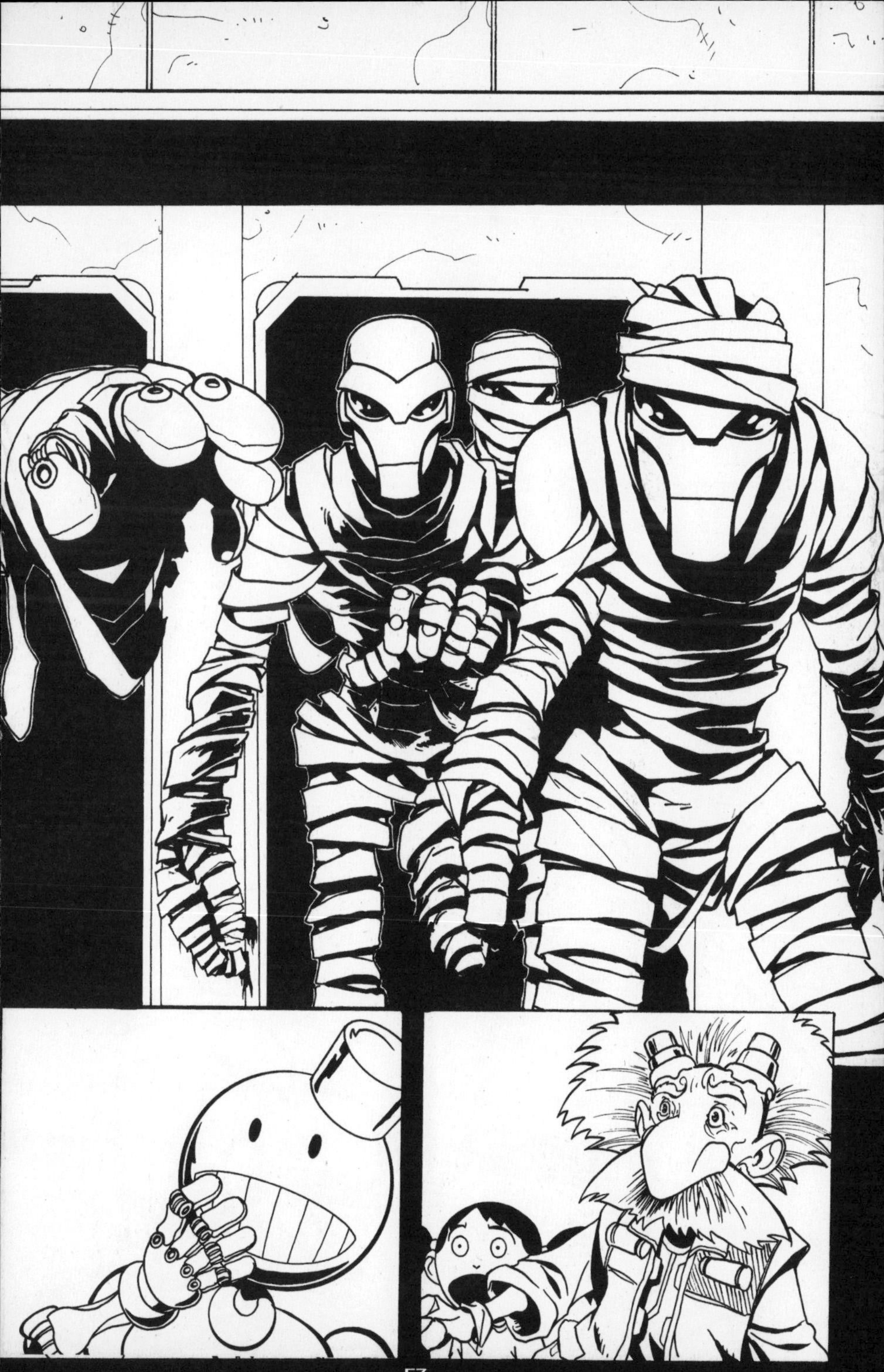

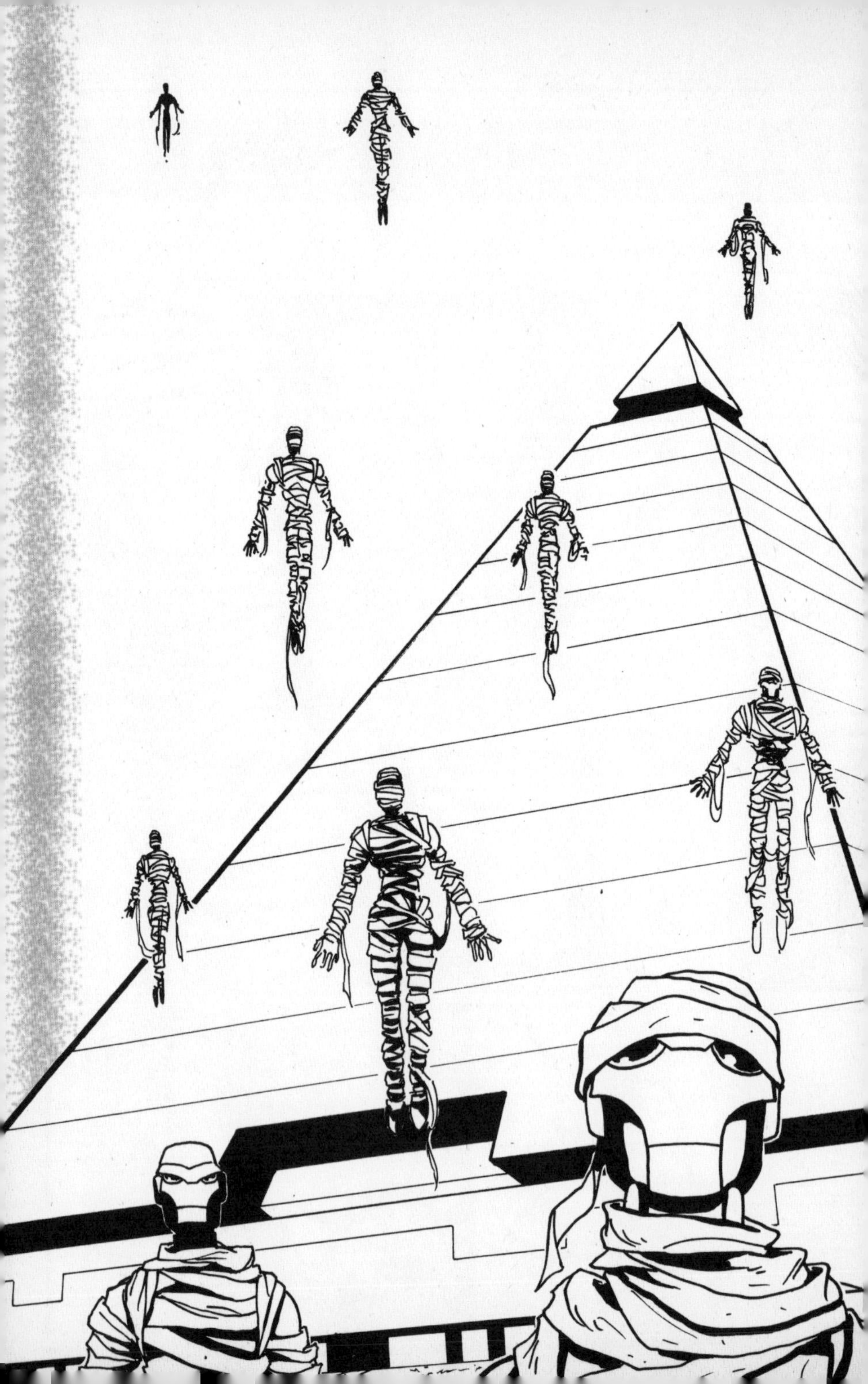

PART 3: ENGINES

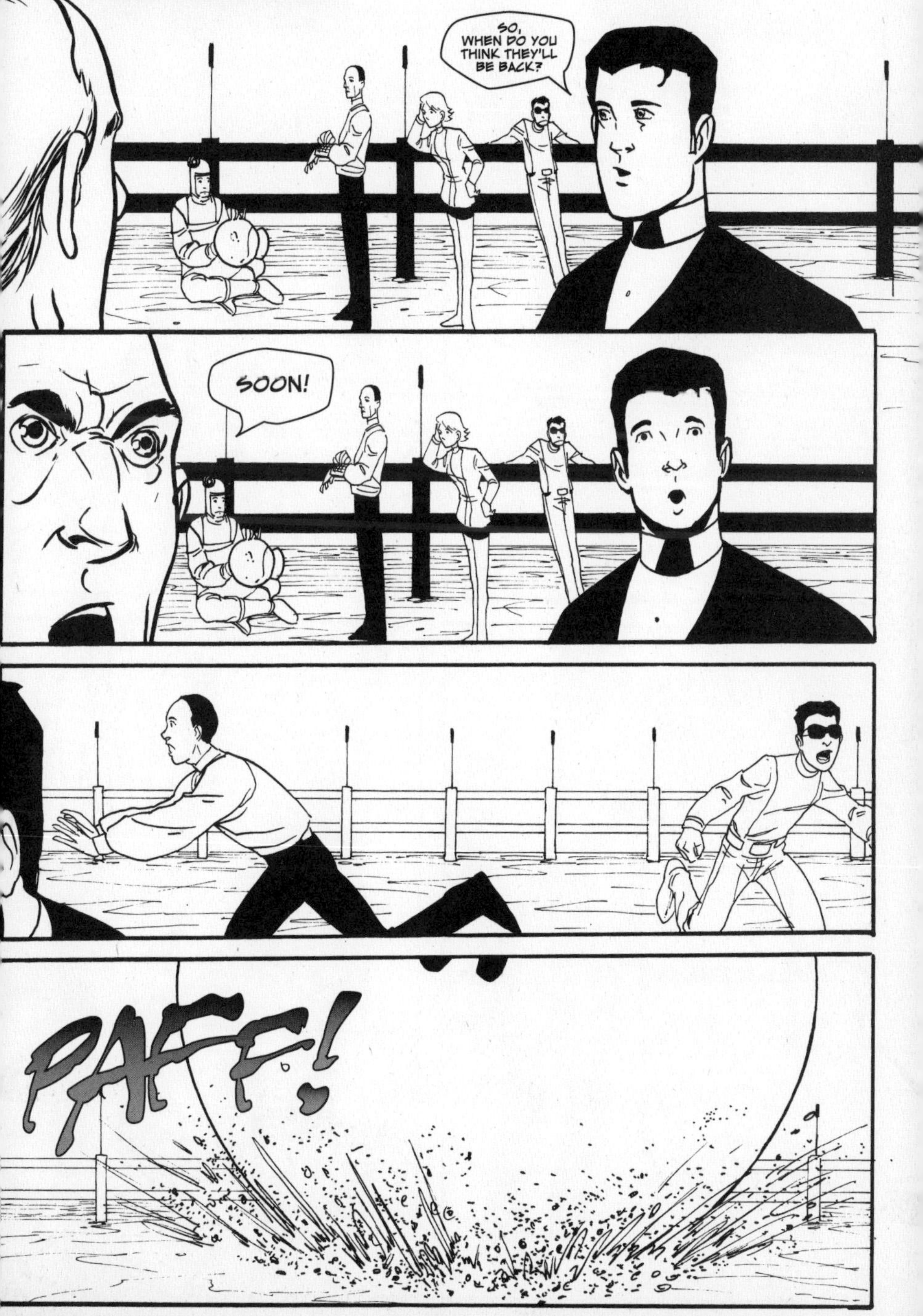
SO, WHEN DO YOU THINK THEY'LL BE BACK?
SOON!
PAFF!

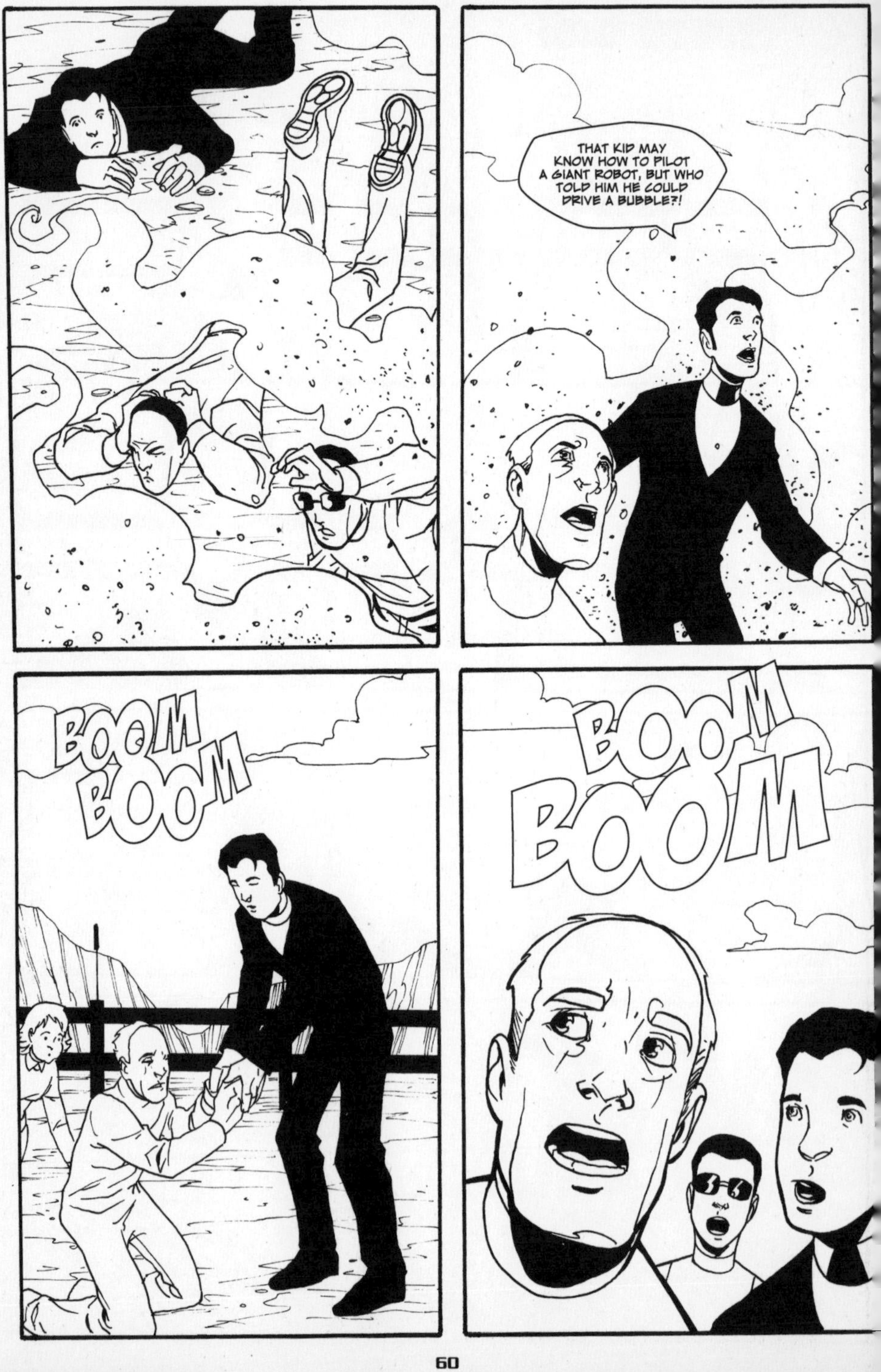
THAT KID MAY KNOW HOW TO PILOT A GIANT ROBOT, BUT WHO TOLD HIM HE COULD DRIVE A BUBBLE?!
BOOM BOOM
BOOM BOOM

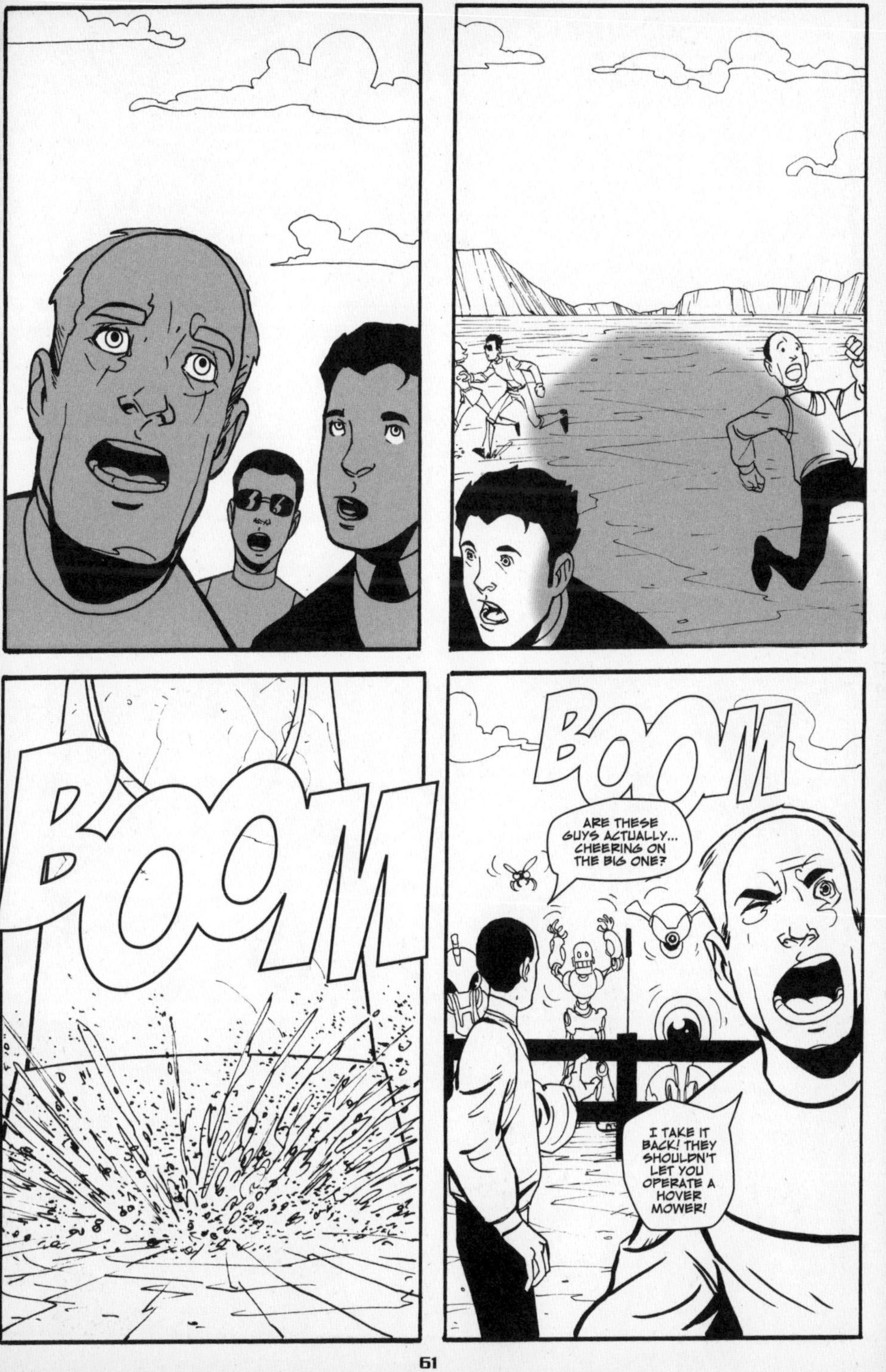
BOOM
BOOM
ARE THESE GUYS ACTUALLY... CHEERING ON THE BIG ONE?
I TAKE IT BACK! THEY SHOULDN'T LET YOU OPERATE A HOVER MOWER!

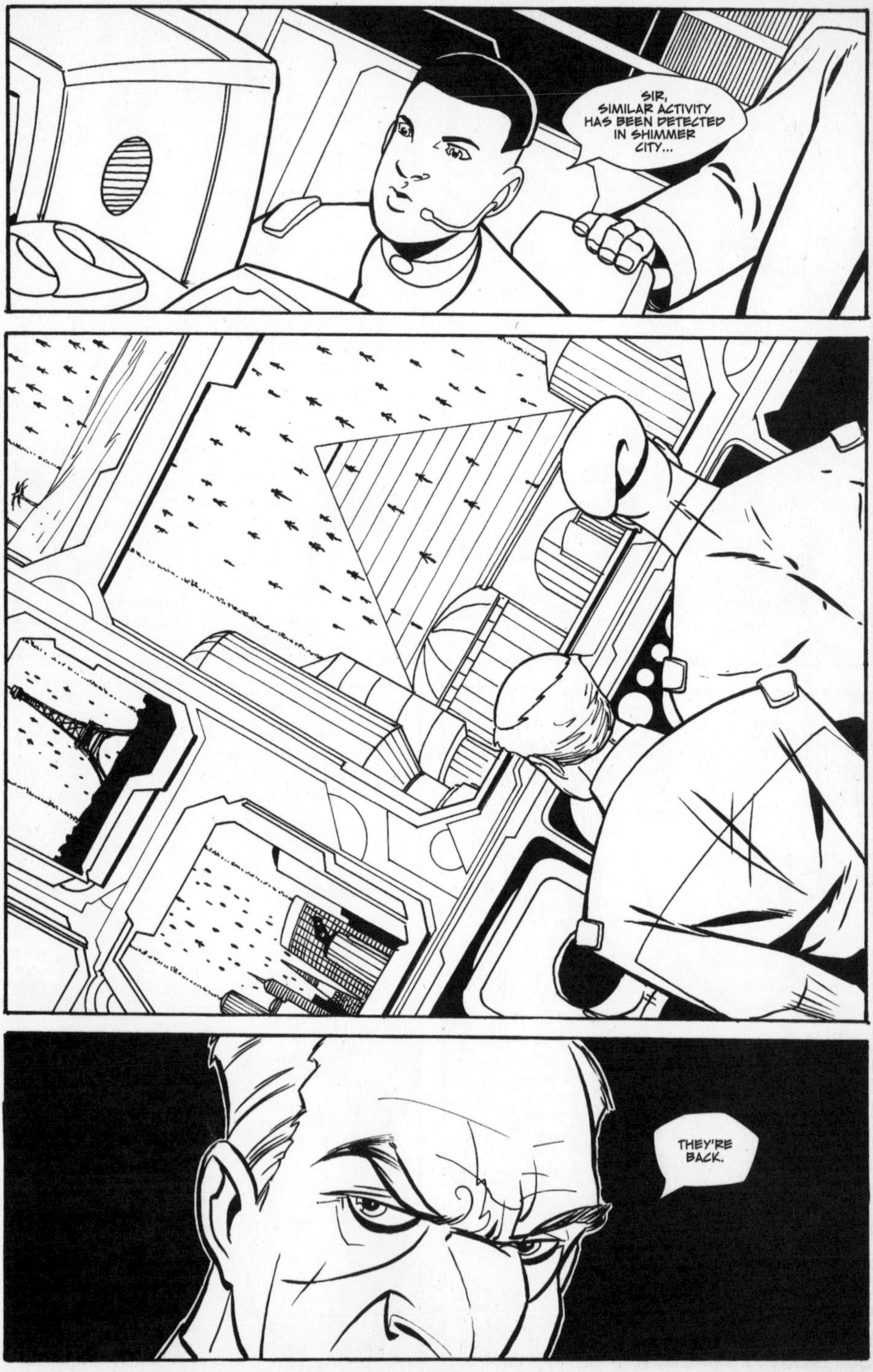
SIR, SIMILAR ACTIVITY HAS BEEN DETECTED IN SHIMMER CITY...
THEY'RE BACK.

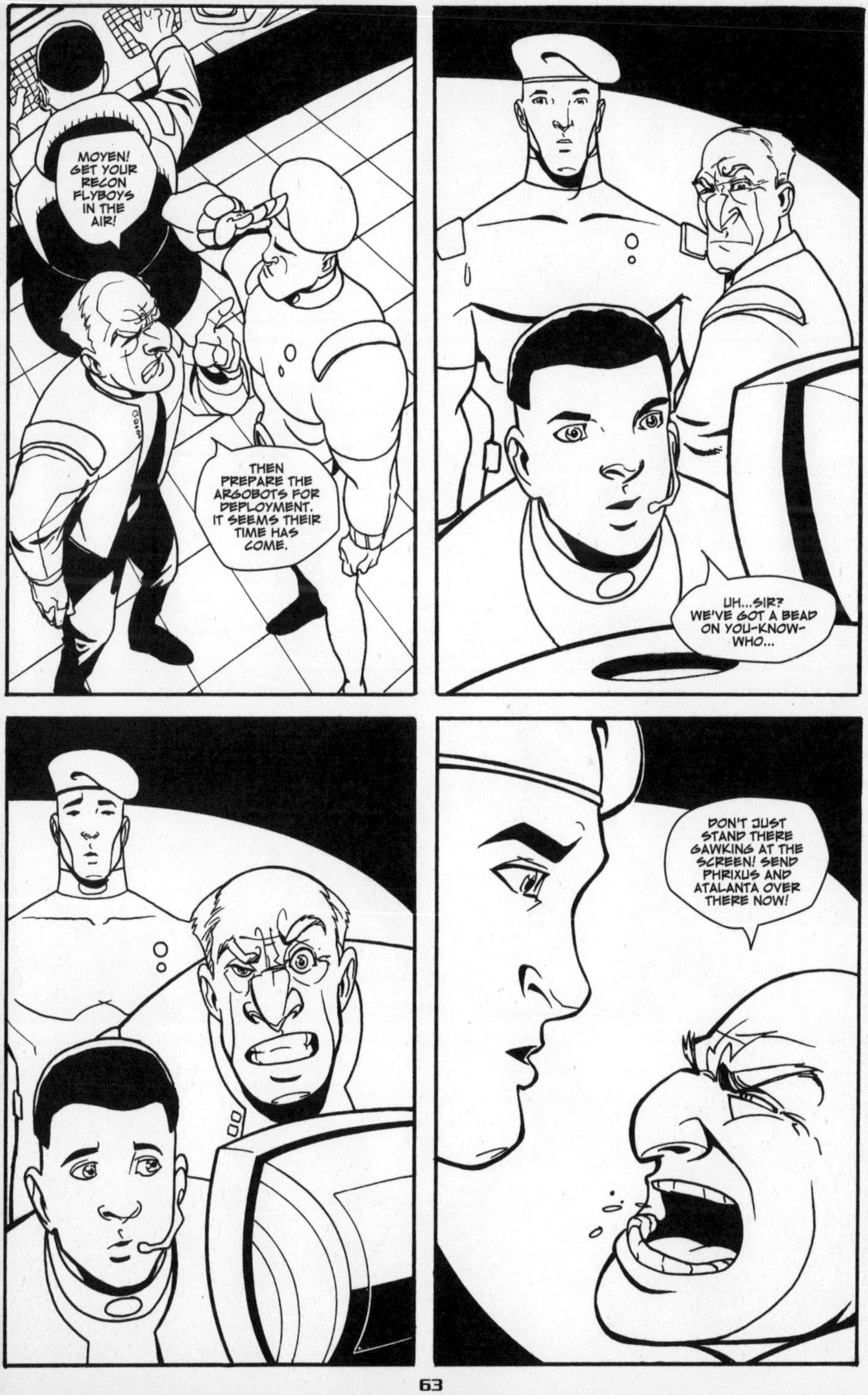
MOYEN! GET YOUR RECON FLYBOYS IN THE AIR!
THEN PREPARE THE ARGOBOTS FOR DEPLOYMENT. IT SEEMS THEIR TIME HAS COME.
UH...SIR? WE'VE GOT A BEAD ON YOU-KNOW-WHO...
DON'T JUST STAND THERE GAWKING AT THE SCREEN! SEND PHRIXUS AND ATALANTA OVER THERE NOW!

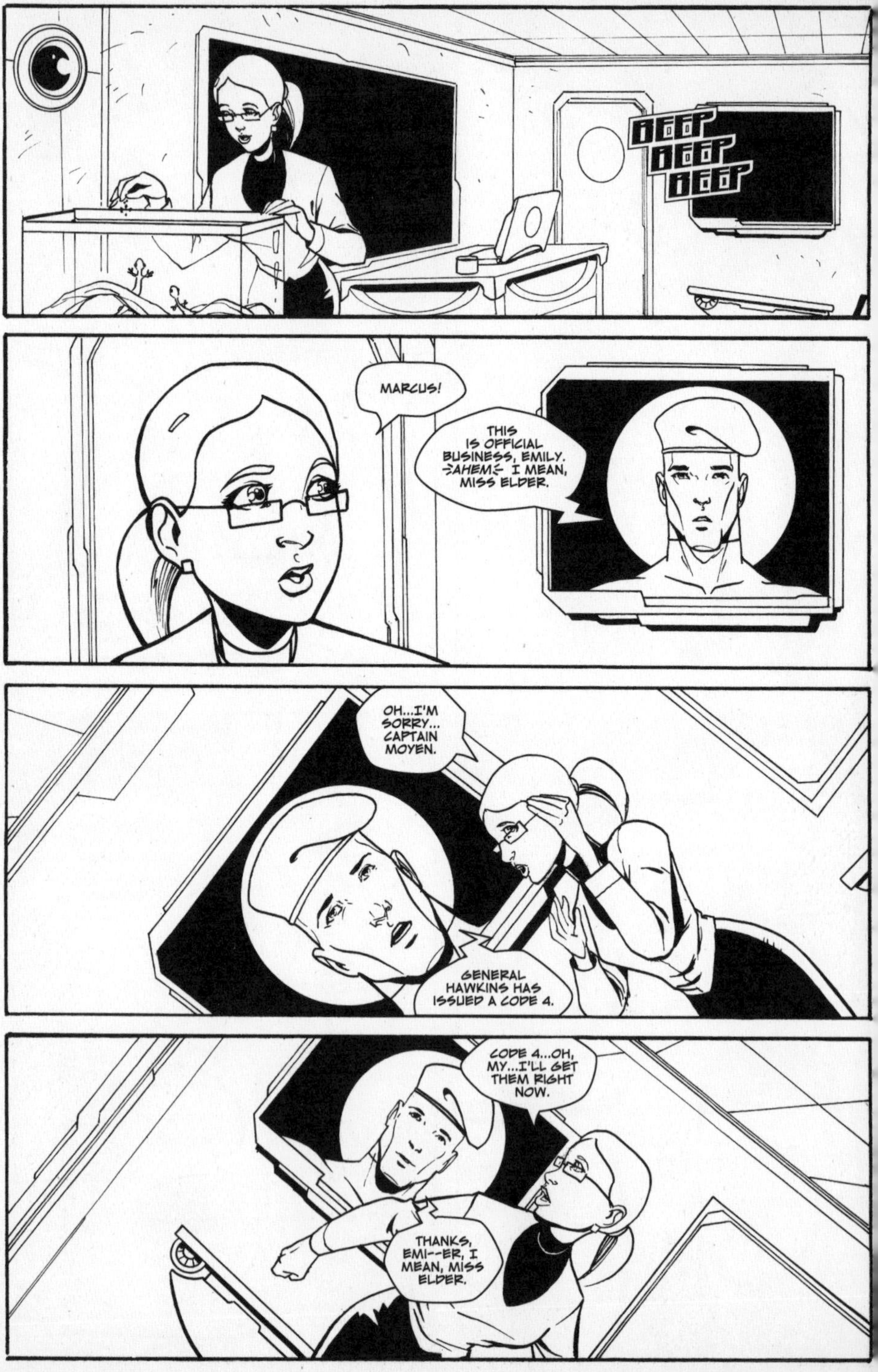
BEEP BEEP BEEP
MARCUS!
THIS IS OFFICIAL BUSINESS, EMILY. ≥AHEM≤ I MEAN, MISS ELDER.
OH...I'M SORRY... CAPTAIN MOYEN.
GENERAL HAWKINS HAS ISSUED A CODE 4.
CODE 4...OH, MY...I'LL GET THEM RIGHT NOW.
THANKS, EMI--ER, I MEAN, MISS ELDER.

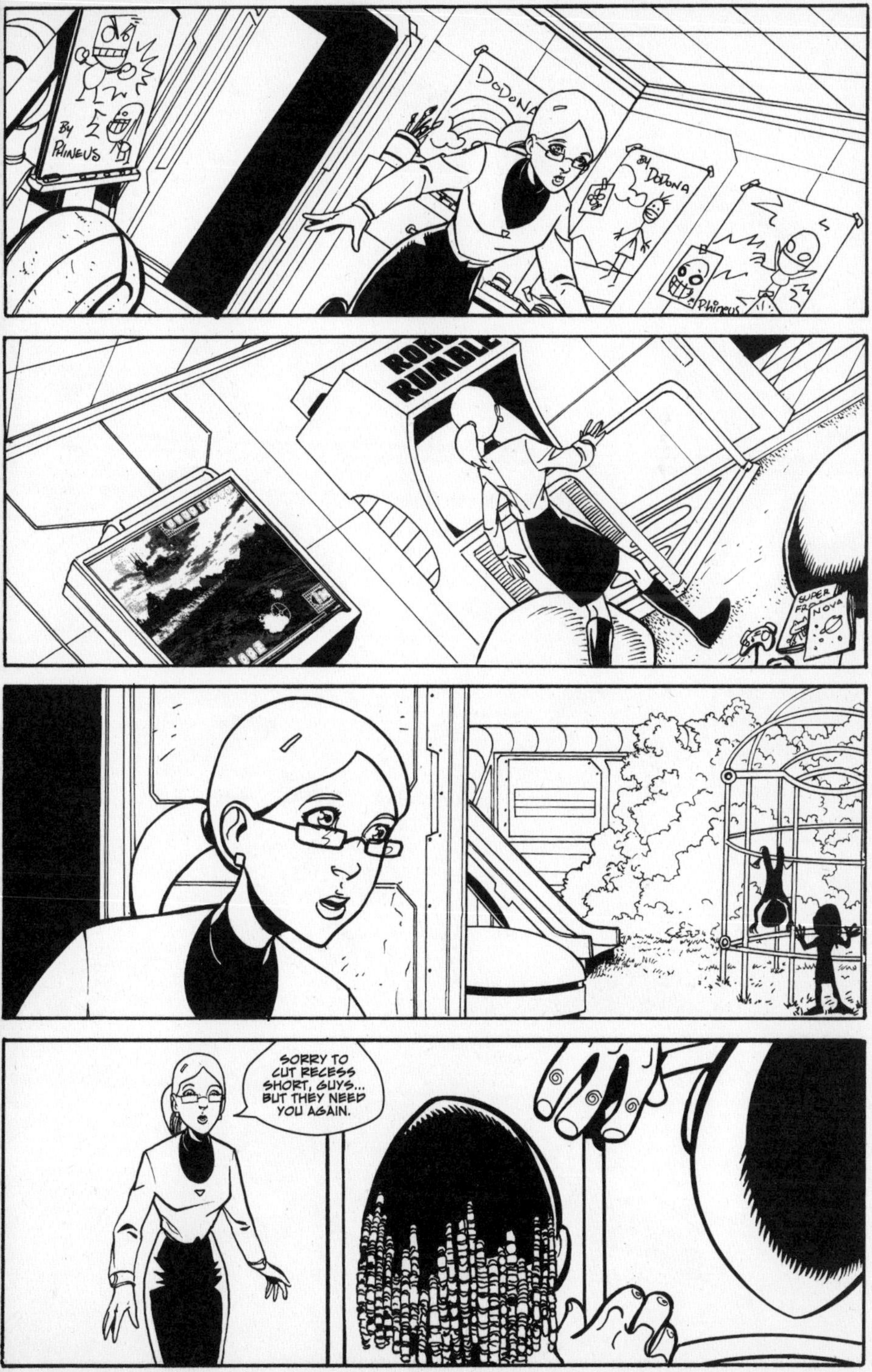
DODONA
BY PHINEUS
BY DODONA
Phineus
RUMBLE
NOVA
SORRY TO CUT RECESS SHORT, GUYS... BUT THEY NEED YOU AGAIN.

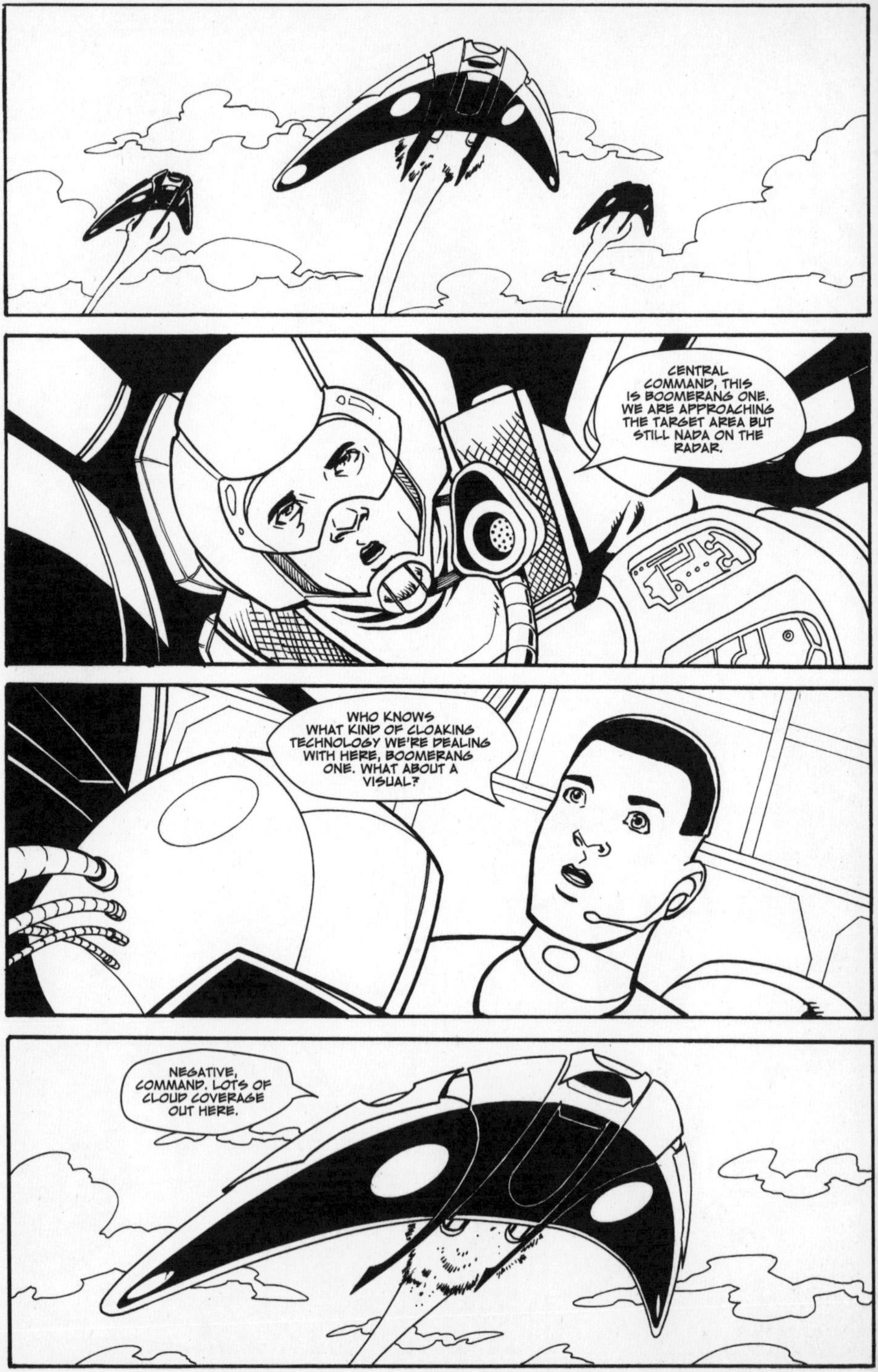
CENTRAL COMMAND, THIS IS BOOMERANG ONE. WE ARE APPROACHING THE TARGET AREA BUT STILL NADA ON THE RADAR.
WHO KNOWS WHAT KIND OF CLOAKING TECHNOLOGY WE'RE DEALING WITH HERE, BOOMERANG ONE. WHAT ABOUT A VISUAL?
NEGATIVE, COMMAND. LOTS OF CLOUD COVERAGE OUT HERE.

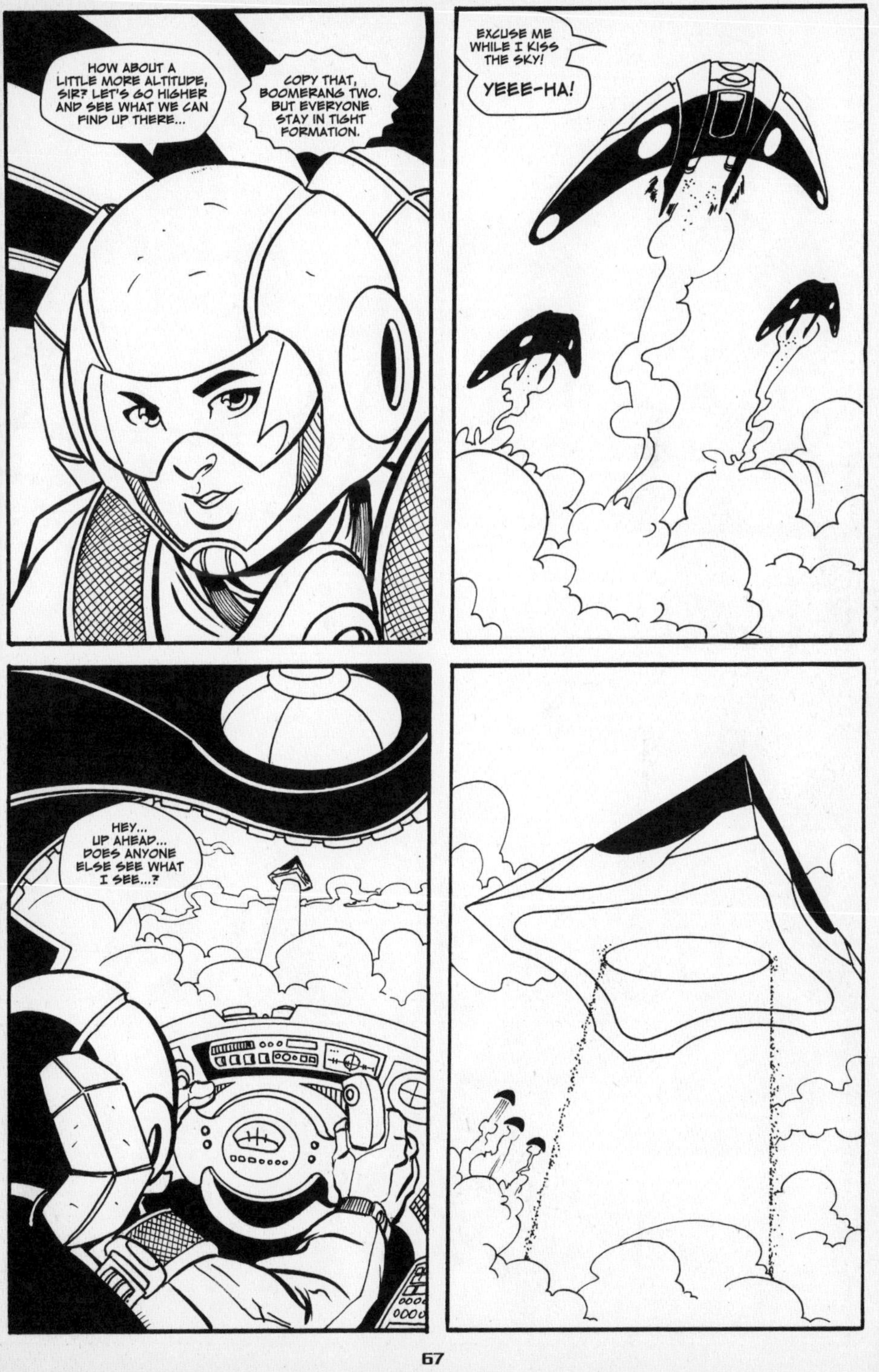
HOW ABOUT A LITTLE MORE ALTITUDE, SIR? LET'S GO HIGHER AND SEE WHAT WE CAN FIND UP THERE...
COPY THAT, BOOMERANG TWO. BUT EVERYONE STAY IN TIGHT FORMATION.
EXCUSE ME WHILE I KISS THE SKY!
YEEE-HA!
HEY... UP AHEAD... DOES ANYONE ELSE SEE WHAT I SEE...?

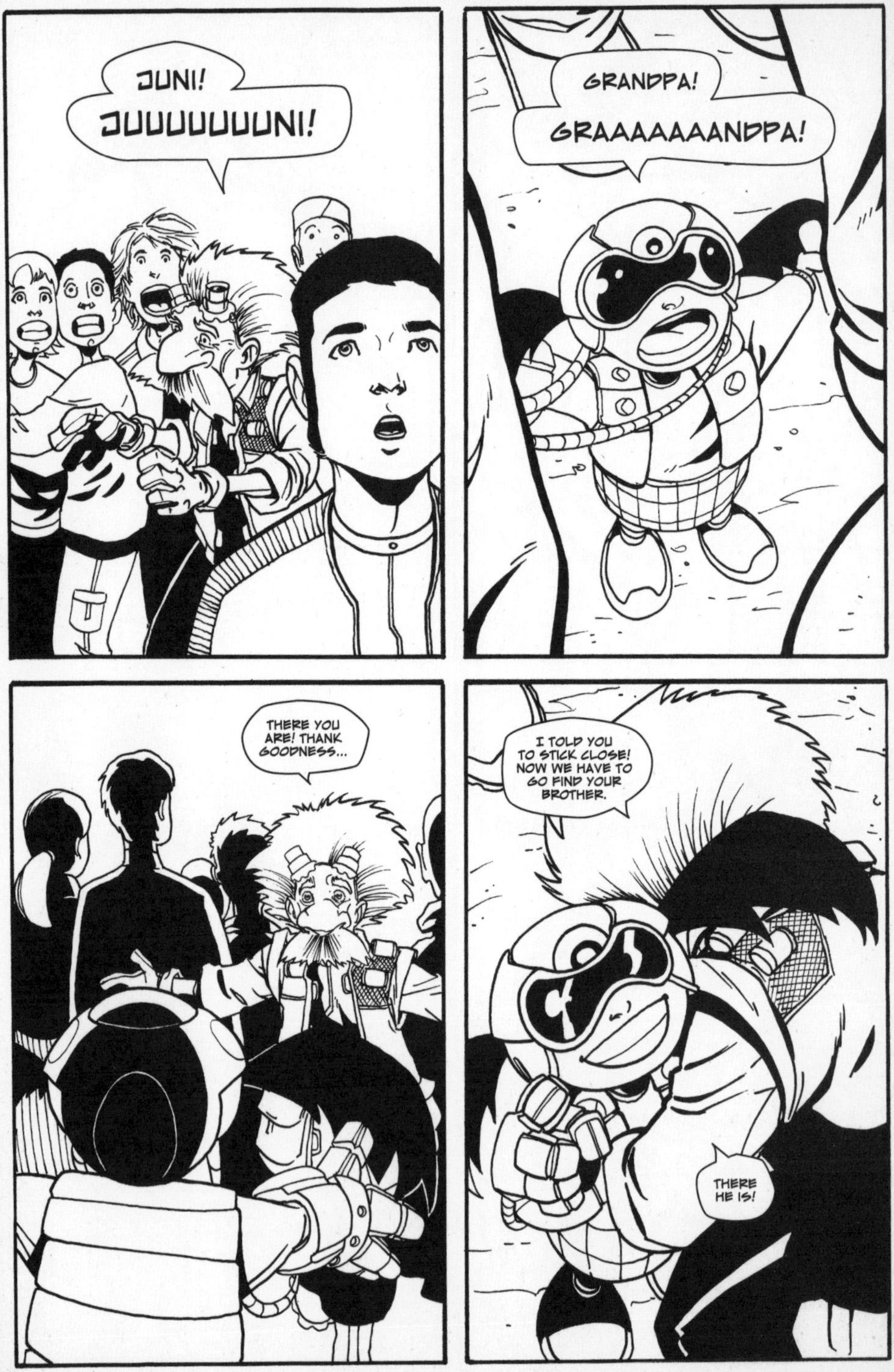
JUNI!
JUUUUUUUUNI!
GRANDPA!
GRAAAAAAAANDPA!
THERE YOU ARE! THANK GOODNESS...
I TOLD YOU TO STICK CLOSE! NOW WE HAVE TO GO FIND YOUR BROTHER.
THERE HE IS!

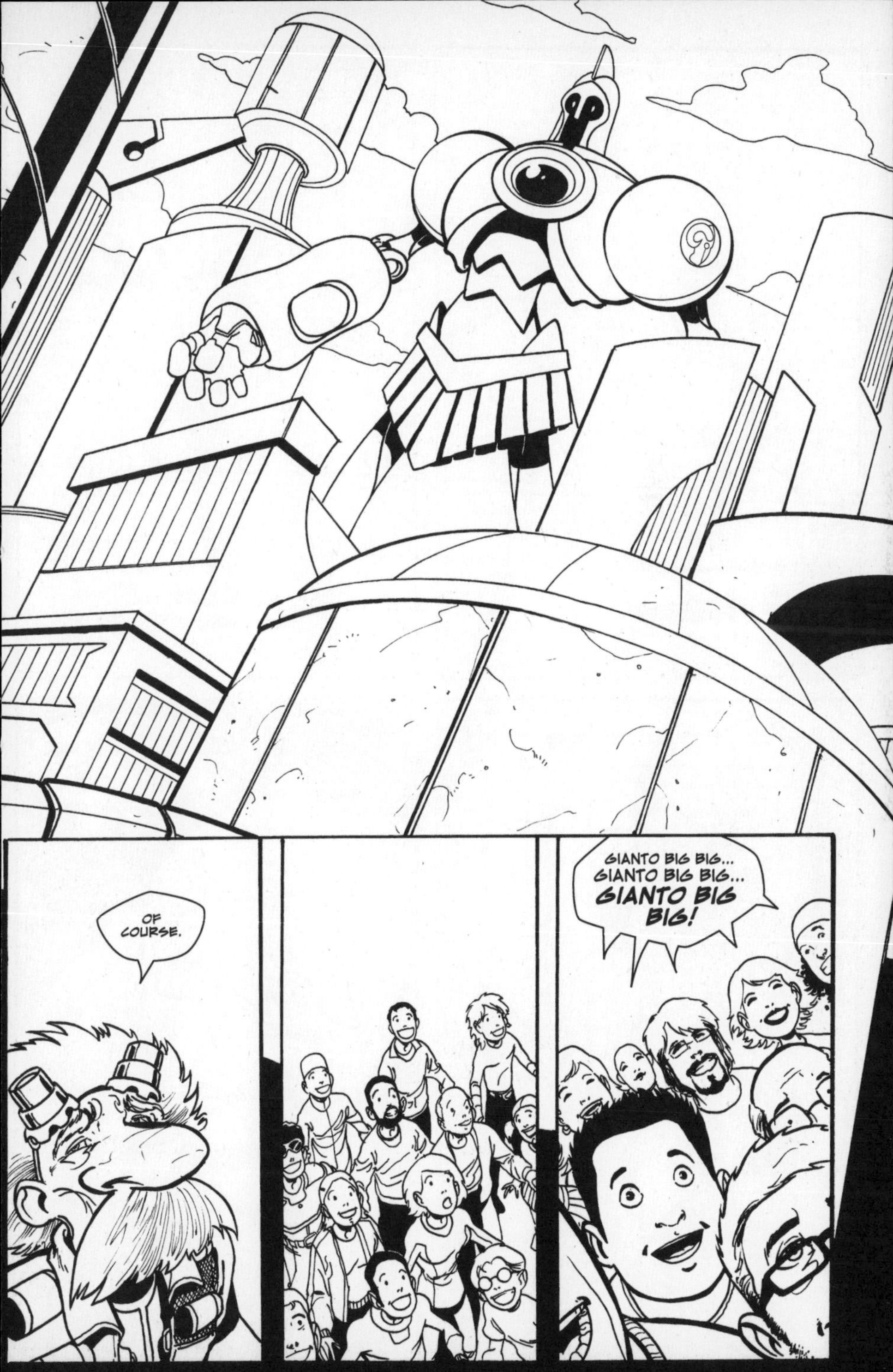
OF COURSE.
GIANTO BIG BIG... GIANTO BIG BIG... GIANTO BIG BIG!

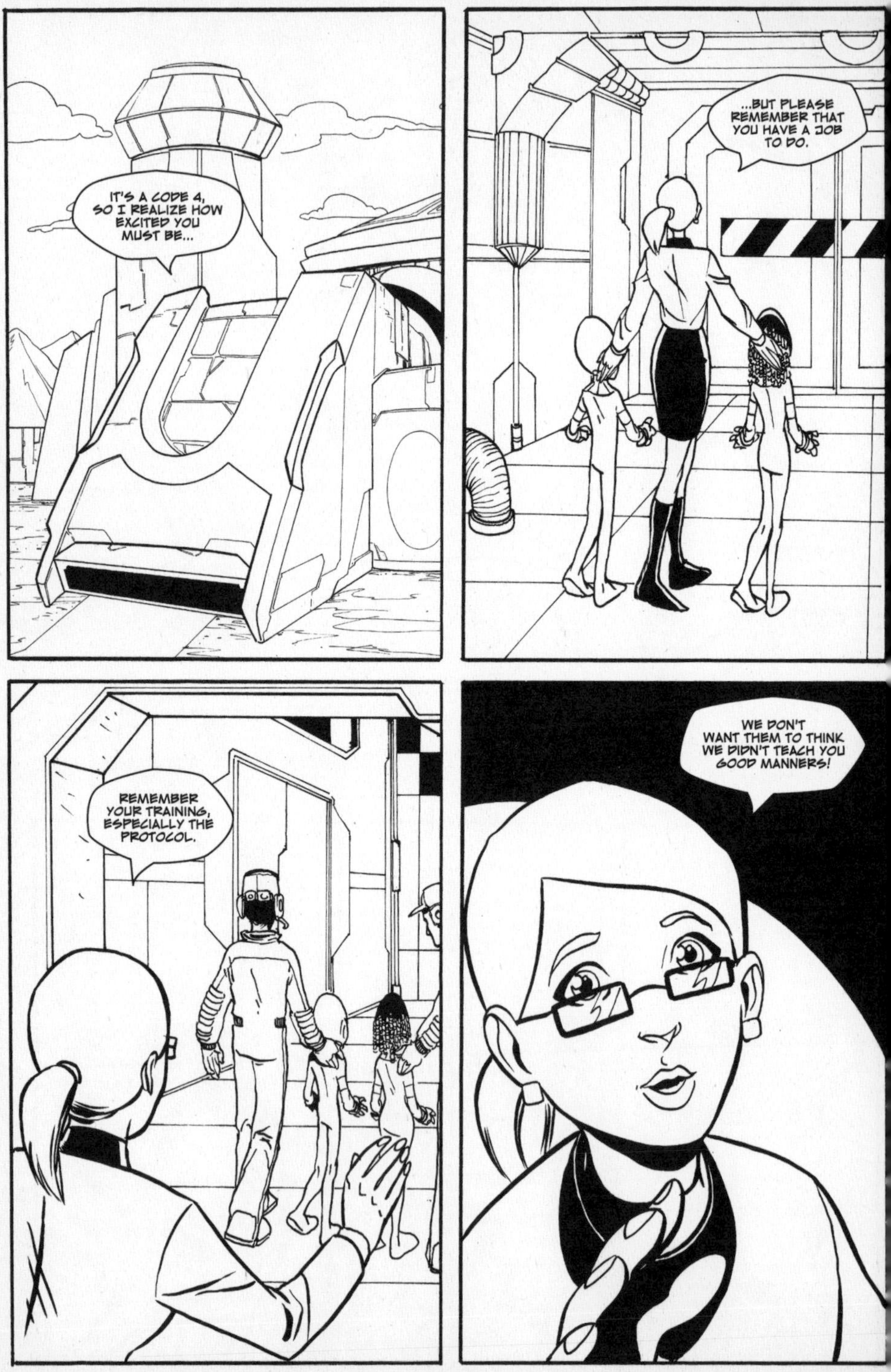
IT'S A CODE 4, SO I REALIZE HOW EXCITED YOU MUST BE...
...BUT PLEASE REMEMBER THAT YOU HAVE A JOB TO DO.
REMEMBER YOUR TRAINING, ESPECIALLY THE PROTOCOL.
WE DON'T WANT THEM TO THINK WE DIDN'T TEACH YOU GOOD MANNERS!

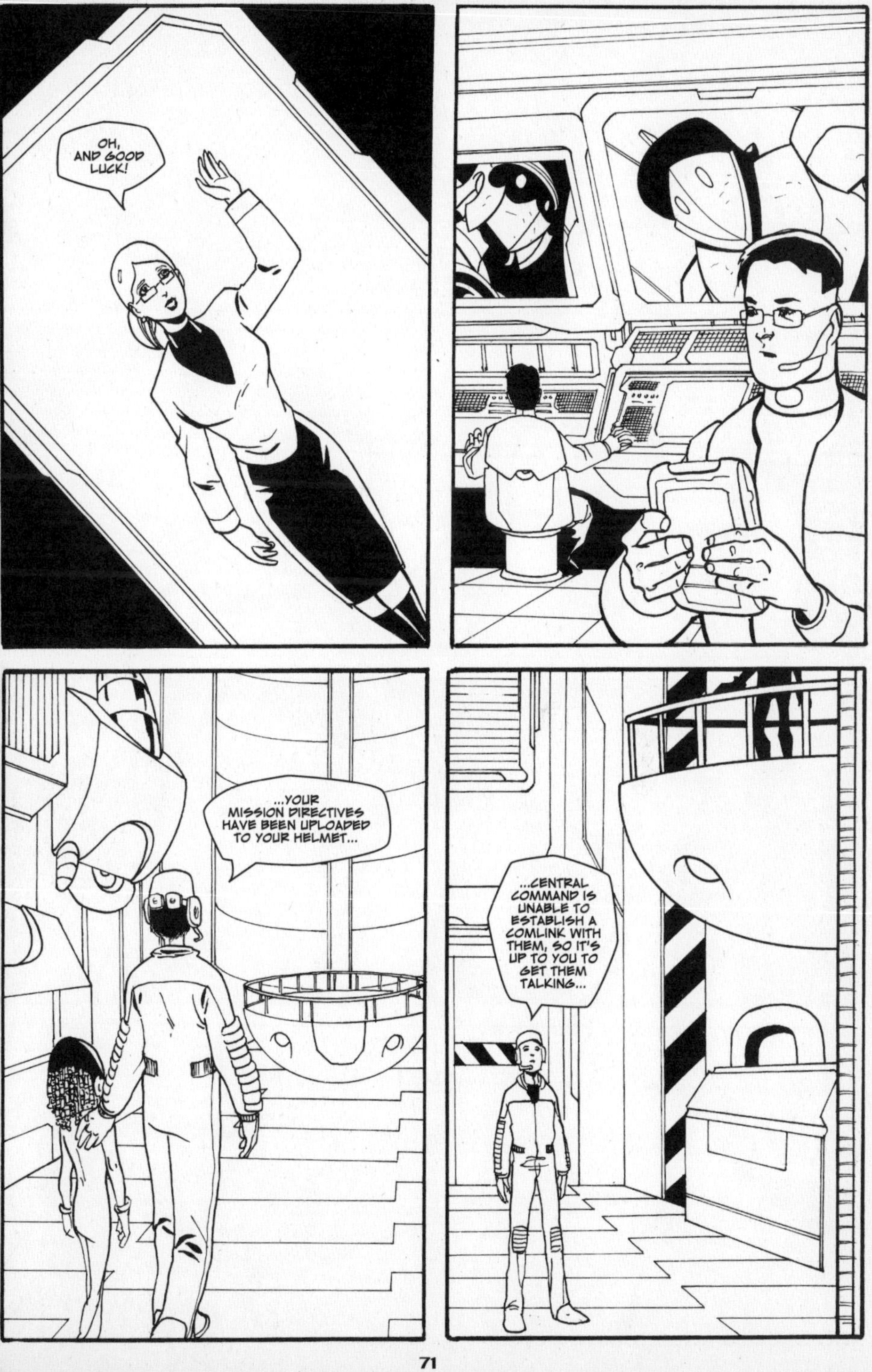
OH, AND GOOD LUCK!
...YOUR MISSION DIRECTIVES HAVE BEEN UPLOADED TO YOUR HELMET...
...CENTRAL COMMAND IS UNABLE TO ESTABLISH A COMLINK WITH THEM, SO IT'S UP TO YOU TO GET THEM TALKING...

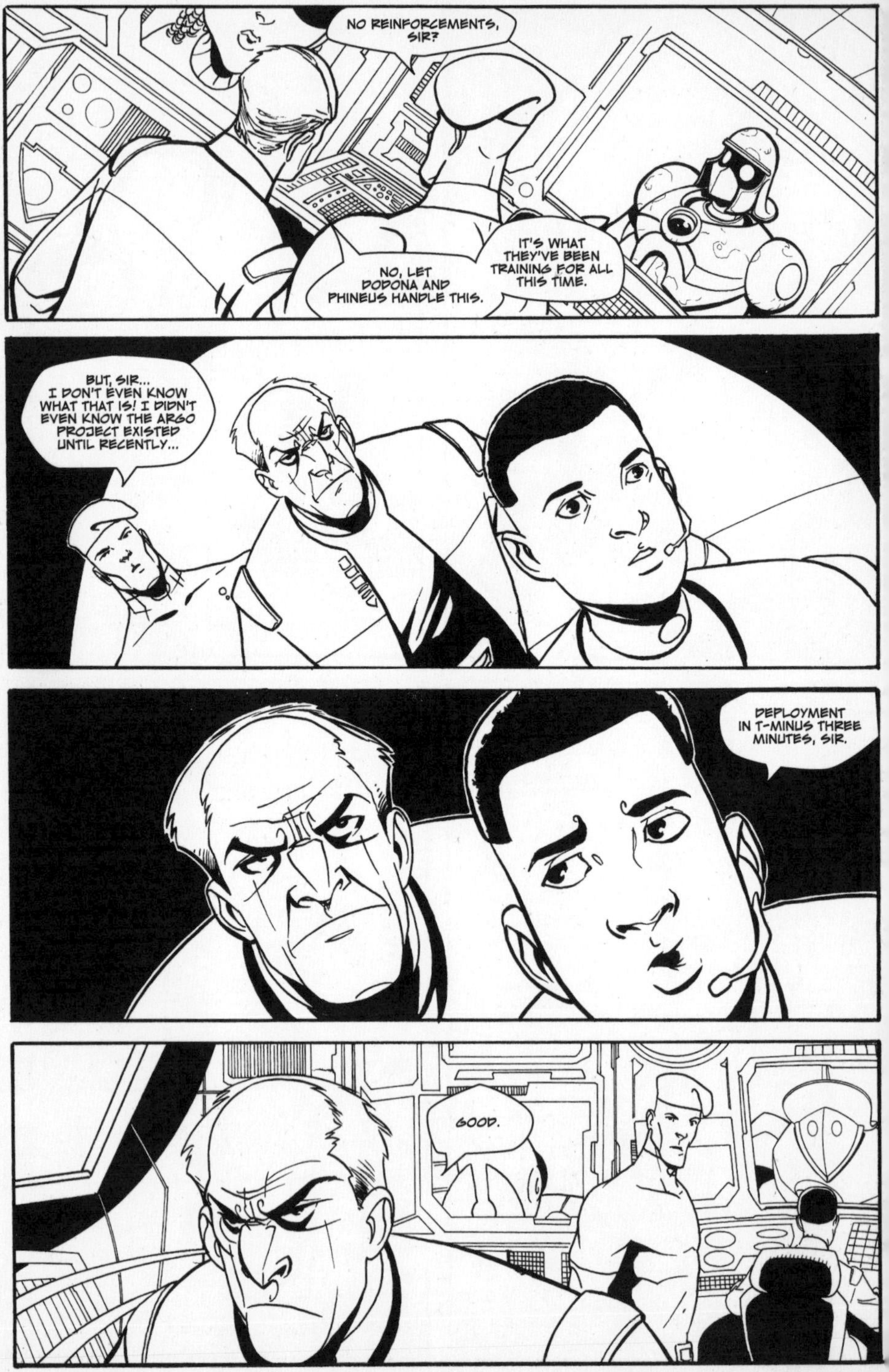
NO REINFORCEMENTS, SIR?
NO, LET DODONA AND PHINEUS HANDLE THIS.
IT'S WHAT THEY'VE BEEN TRAINING FOR ALL THIS TIME.
BUT, SIR... I DON'T EVEN KNOW WHAT THAT IS! I DIDN'T EVEN KNOW THE ARGO PROJECT EXISTED UNTIL RECENTLY...
DEPLOYMENT IN T-MINUS THREE MINUTES, SIR.
GOOD.

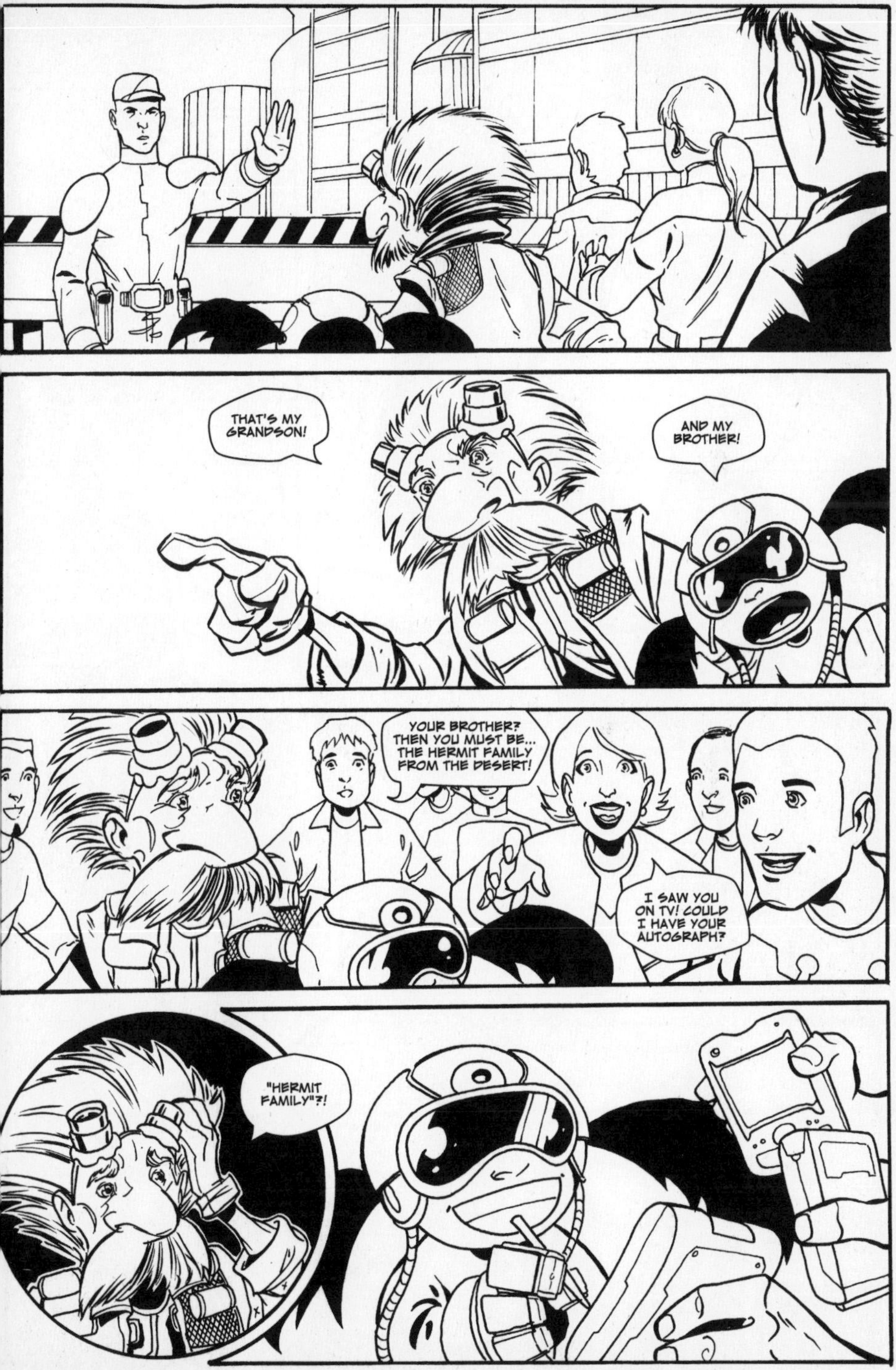
THAT'S MY GRANDSON!
AND MY BROTHER!
YOUR BROTHER? THEN YOU MUST BE... THE HERMIT FAMILY FROM THE DESERT!
I SAW YOU ON TV! COULD I HAVE YOUR AUTOGRAPH?
"HERMIT FAMILY"?!

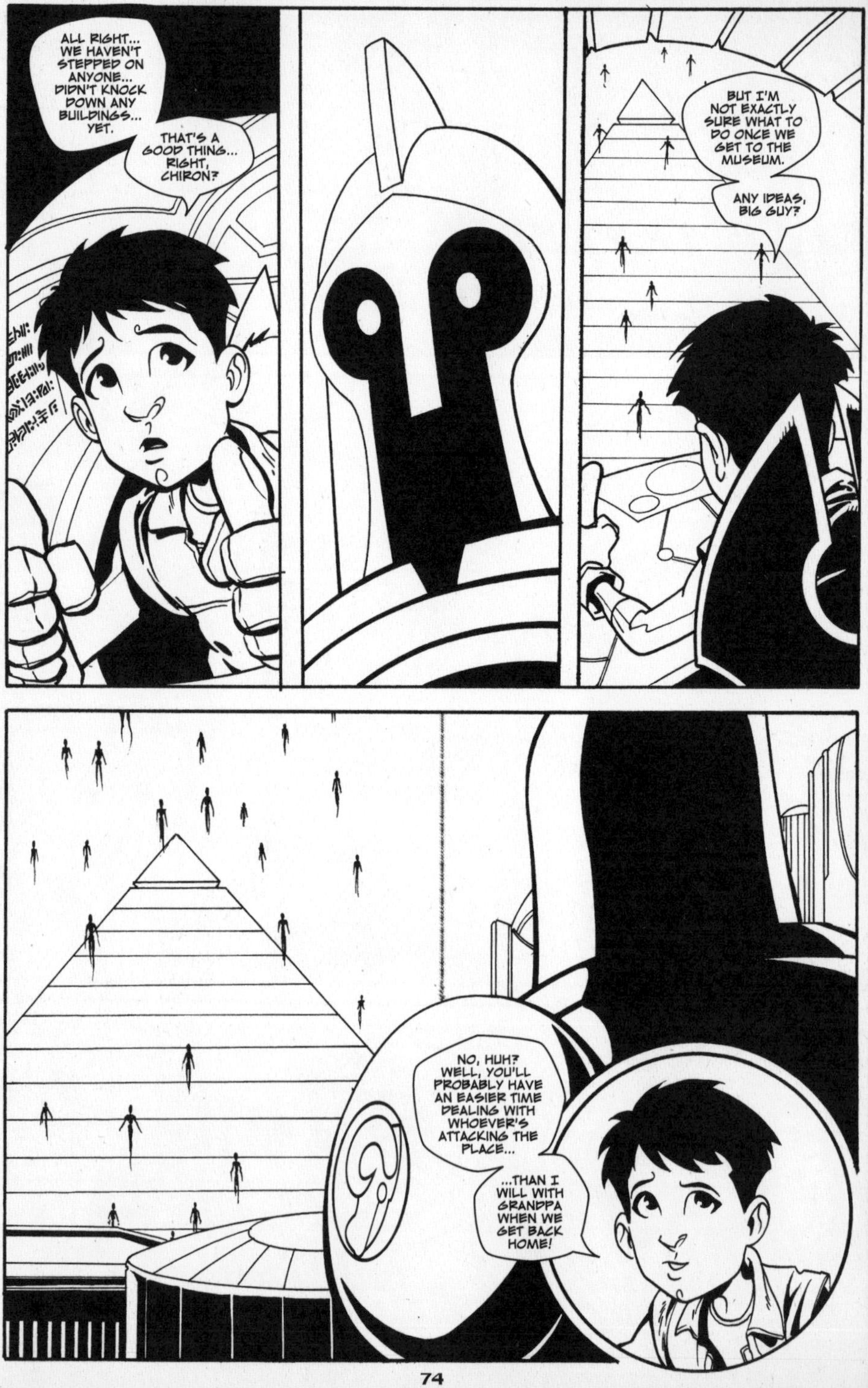
ALL RIGHT... WE HAVEN'T STEPPED ON ANYONE... DIDN'T KNOCK DOWN ANY BUILDINGS... YET.
THAT'S A GOOD THING... RIGHT, CHIRON?
BUT I'M NOT EXACTLY SURE WHAT TO DO ONCE WE GET TO THE MUSEUM.
ANY IDEAS, BIG GUY?
NO, HUH? WELL, YOU'LL PROBABLY HAVE AN EASIER TIME DEALING WITH WHOEVER'S ATTACKING THE PLACE...
...THAN I WILL WITH GRANDPA WHEN WE GET BACK HOME!

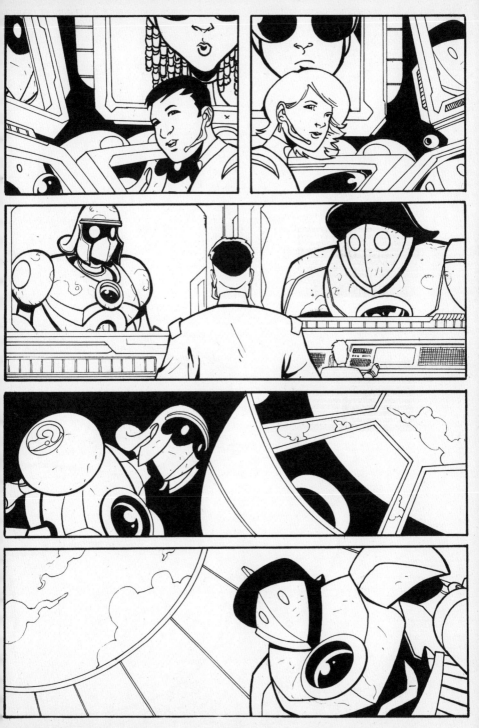

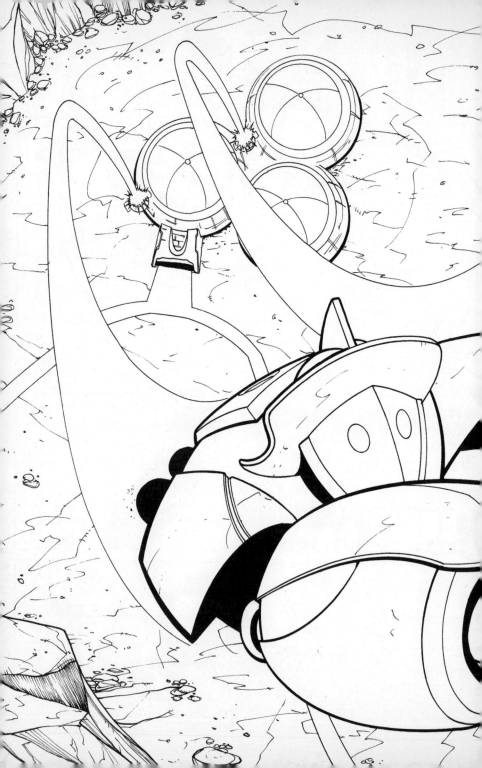

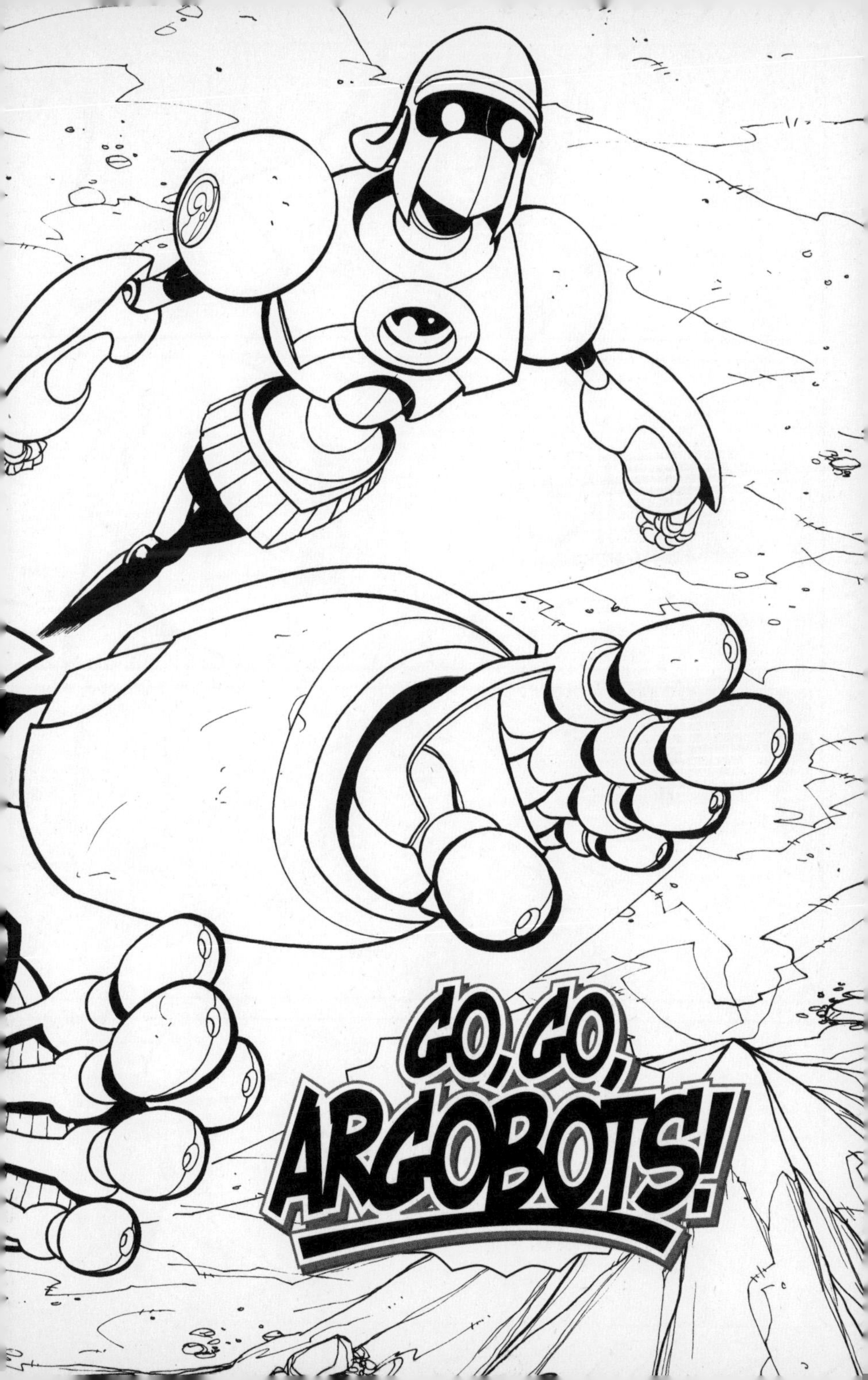
GO, GO, ARGOBOTS!

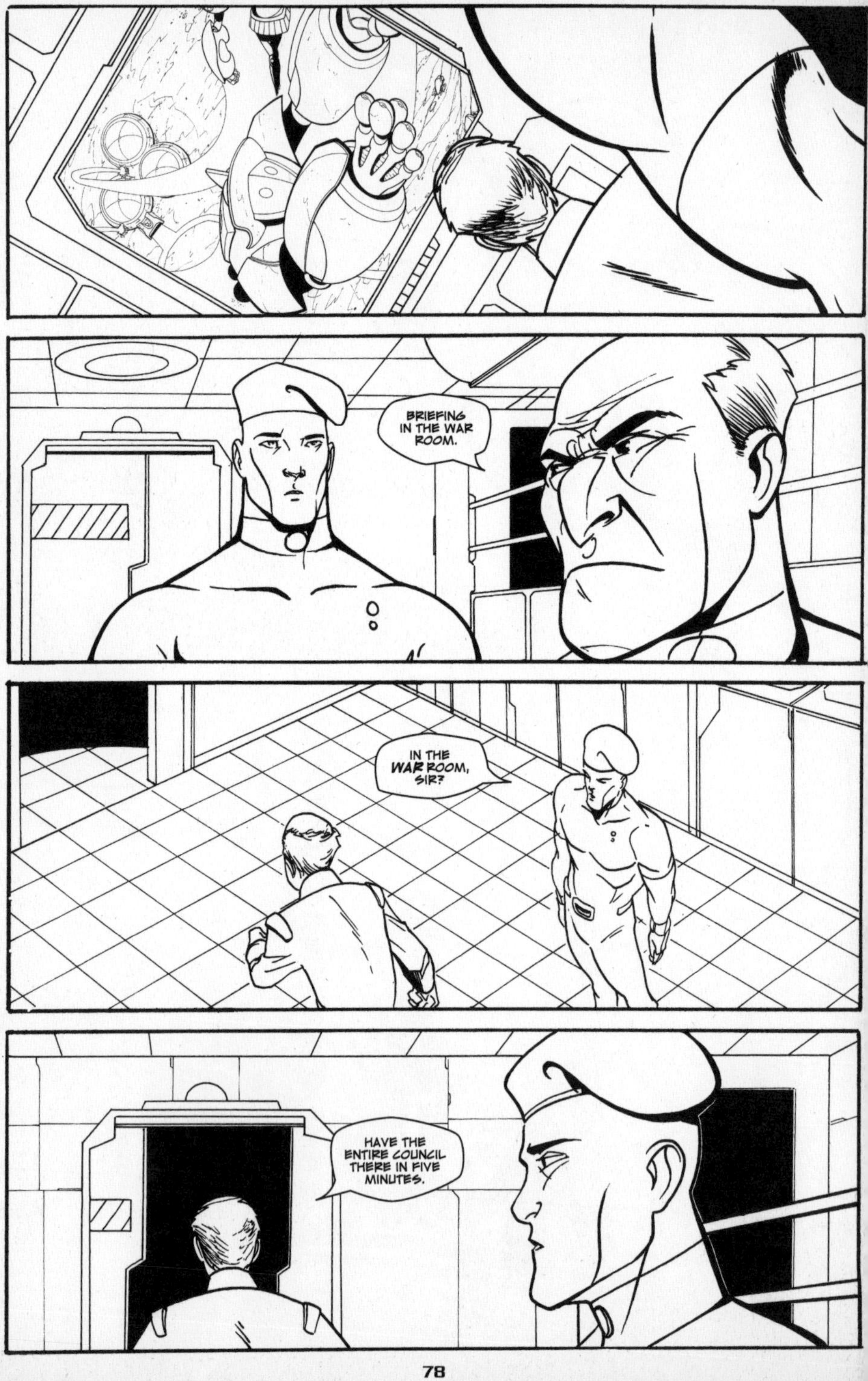
BRIEFING IN THE WAR ROOM.
IN THE WAR ROOM, SIR?
HAVE THE ENTIRE COUNCIL THERE IN FIVE MINUTES.

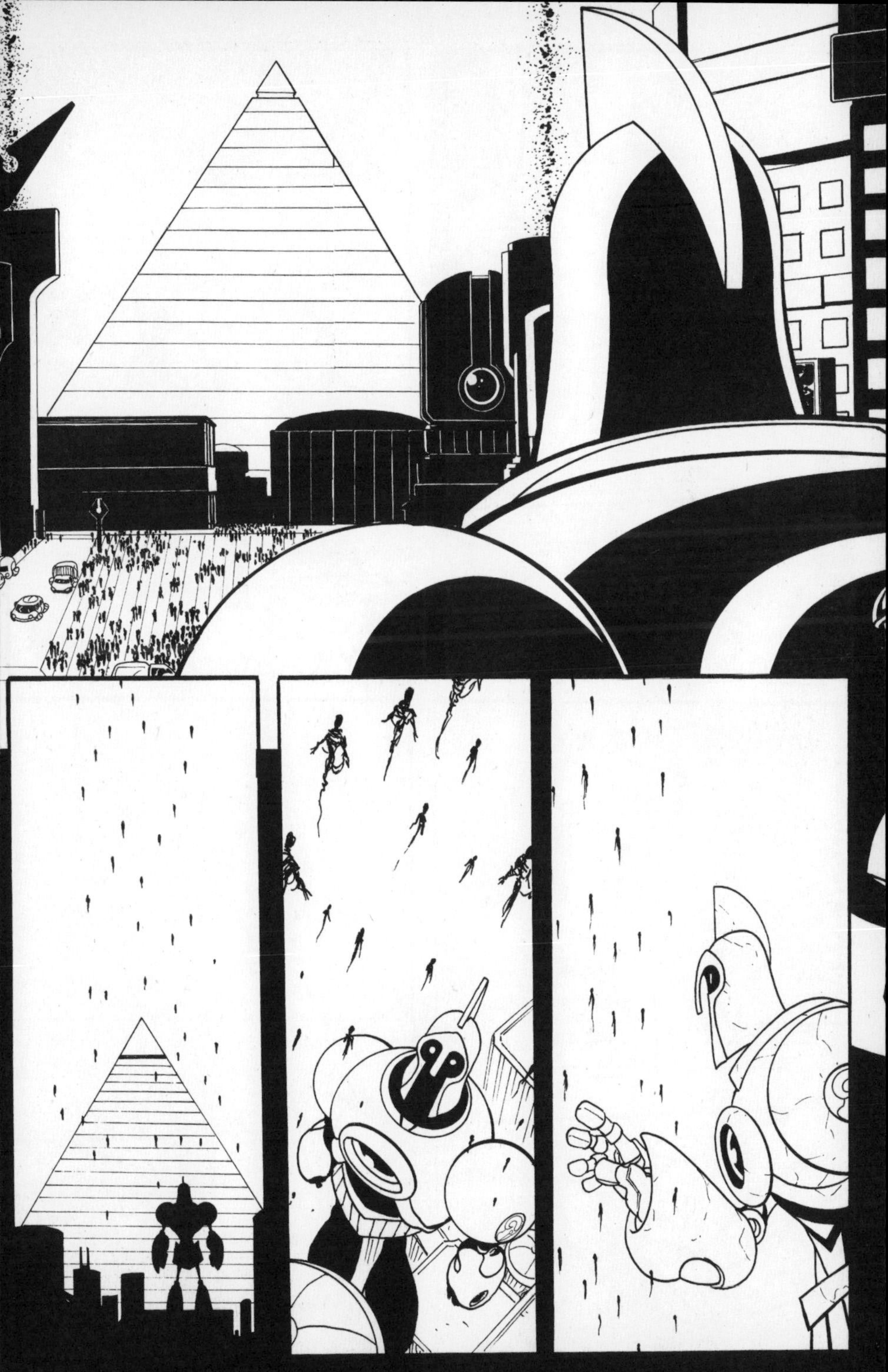

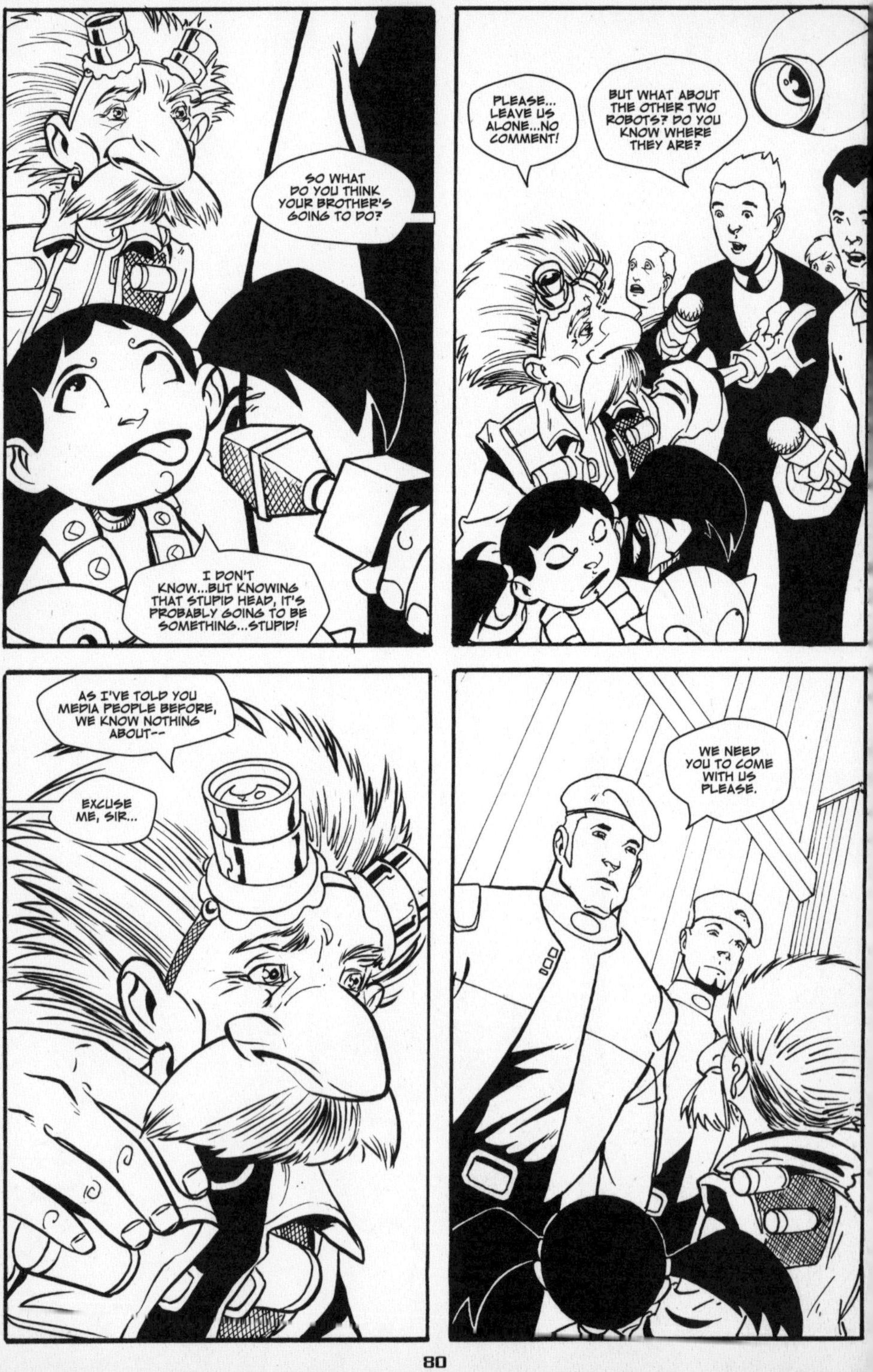
SO WHAT DO YOU THINK YOUR BROTHER'S GOING TO DO?
I DON'T KNOW...BUT KNOWING THAT STUPID HEAD, IT'S PROBABLY GOING TO BE SOMETHING...STUPID!
PLEASE... LEAVE US ALONE...NO COMMENT!
BUT WHAT ABOUT THE OTHER TWO ROBOTS? DO YOU KNOW WHERE THEY ARE?
AS I'VE TOLD YOU MEDIA PEOPLE BEFORE, WE KNOW NOTHING ABOUT--
EXCUSE ME, SIR...
WE NEED YOU TO COME WITH US PLEASE.

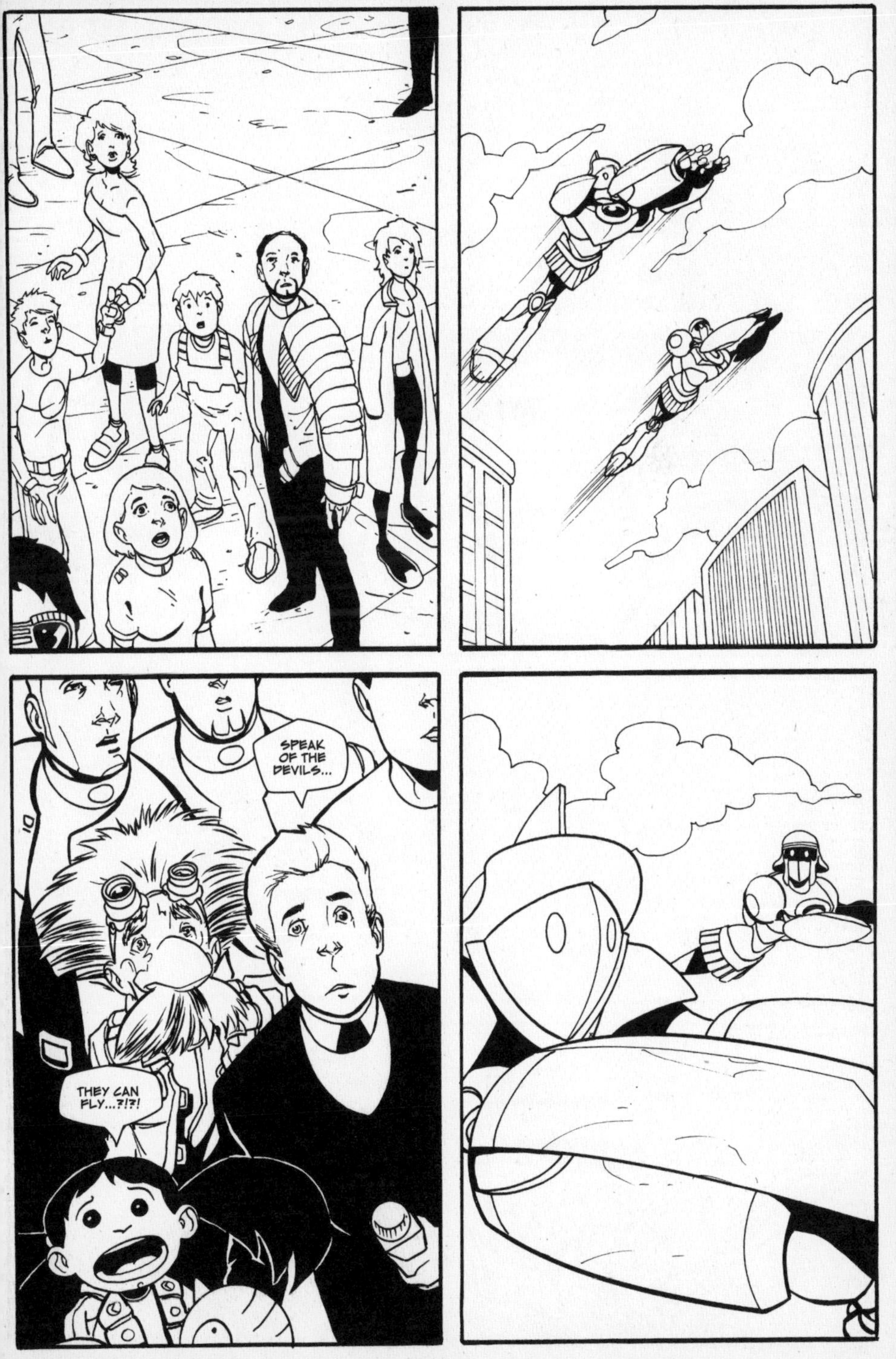
SPEAK OF THE DEVILS...
THEY CAN FLY...?!?!

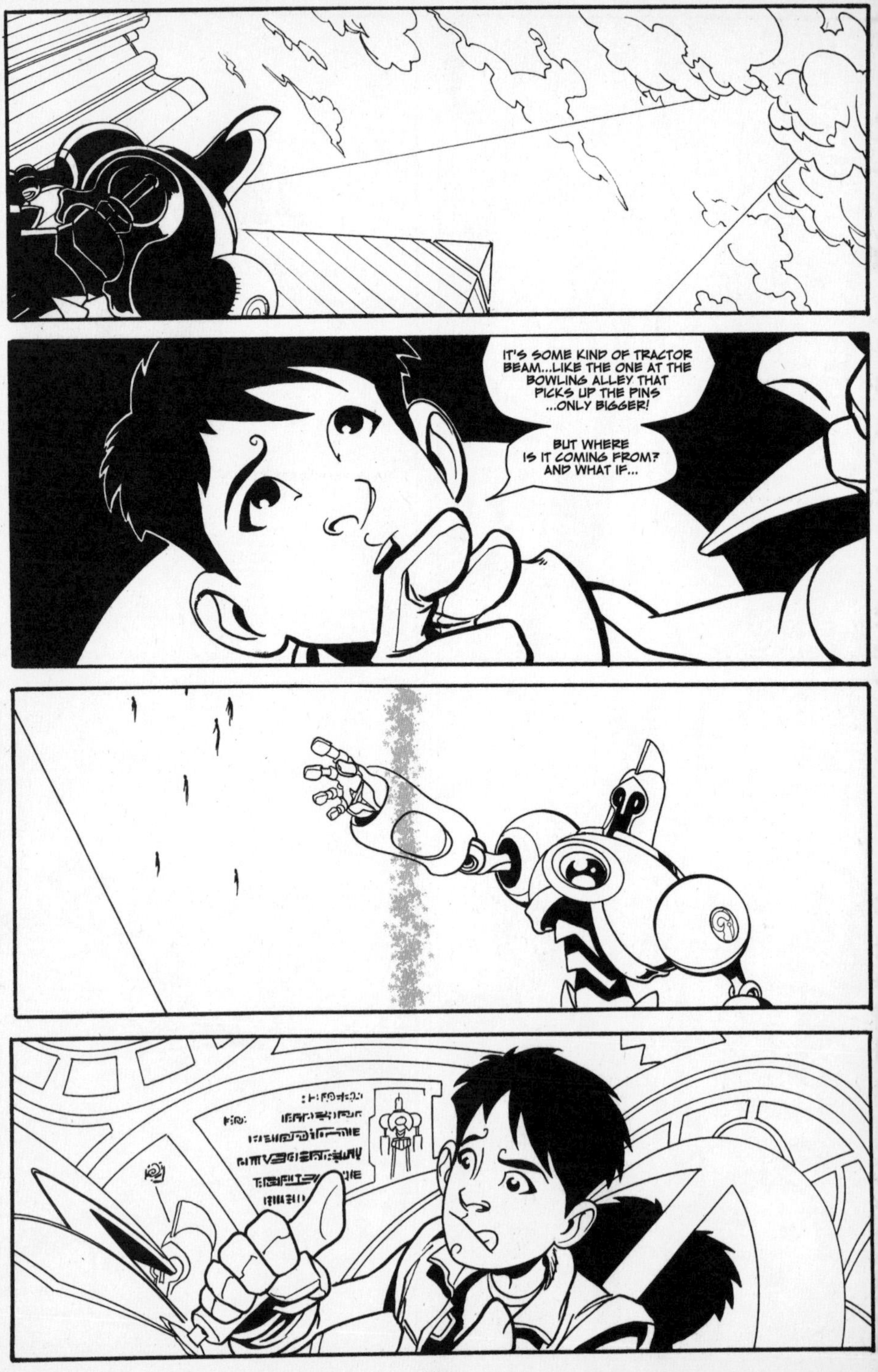
IT'S SOME KIND OF TRACTOR BEAM...LIKE THE ONE AT THE BOWLING ALLEY THAT PICKS UP THE PINS ...ONLY BIGGER!
BUT WHERE IS IT COMING FROM? AND WHAT IF...

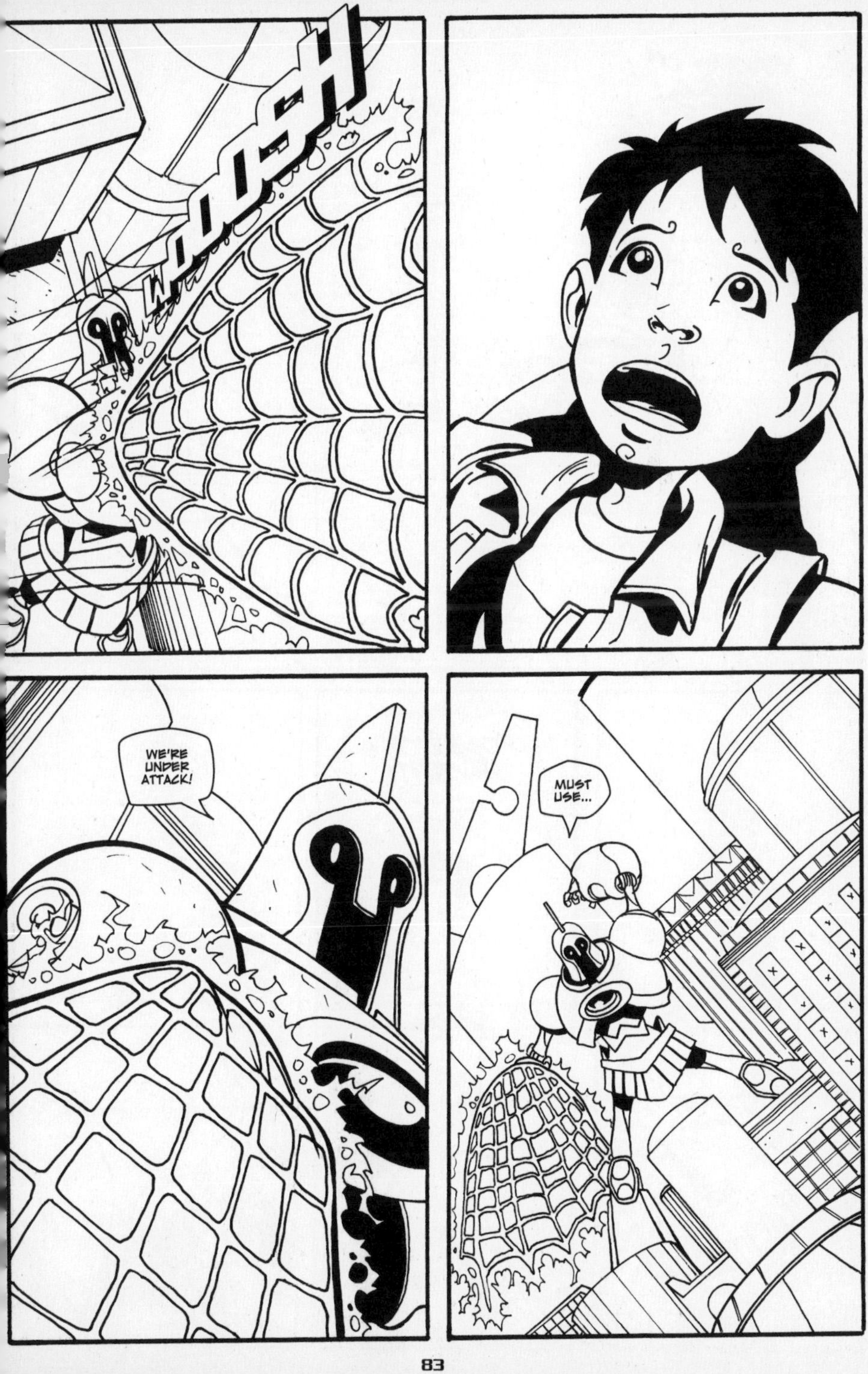
WE'RE UNDER ATTACK!
MUST USE...

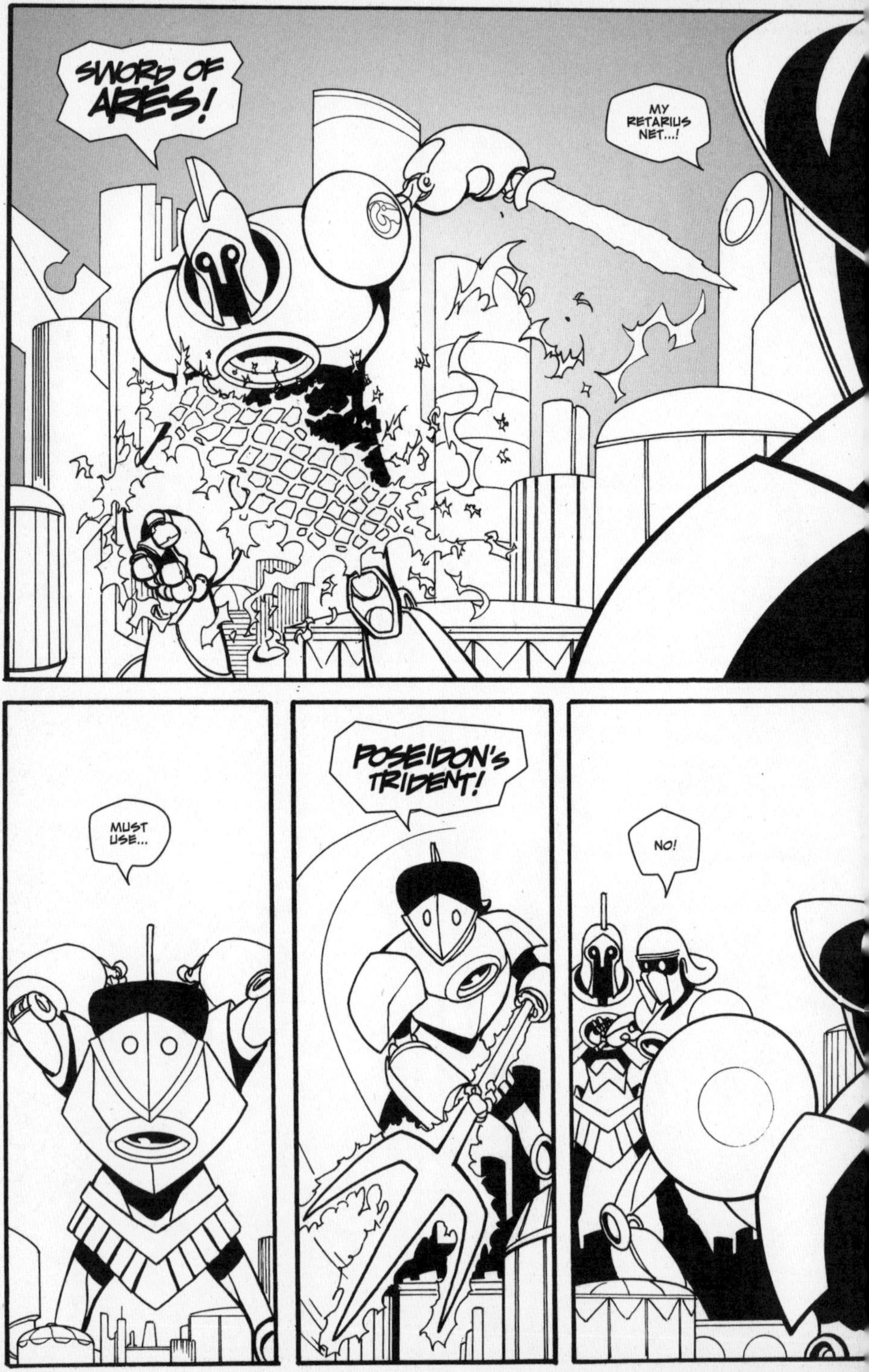
SWORD OF ARÈS!
MY RETARIUS NET...!
MUST USE...
POSEIDON'S TRIDENT!
NO!

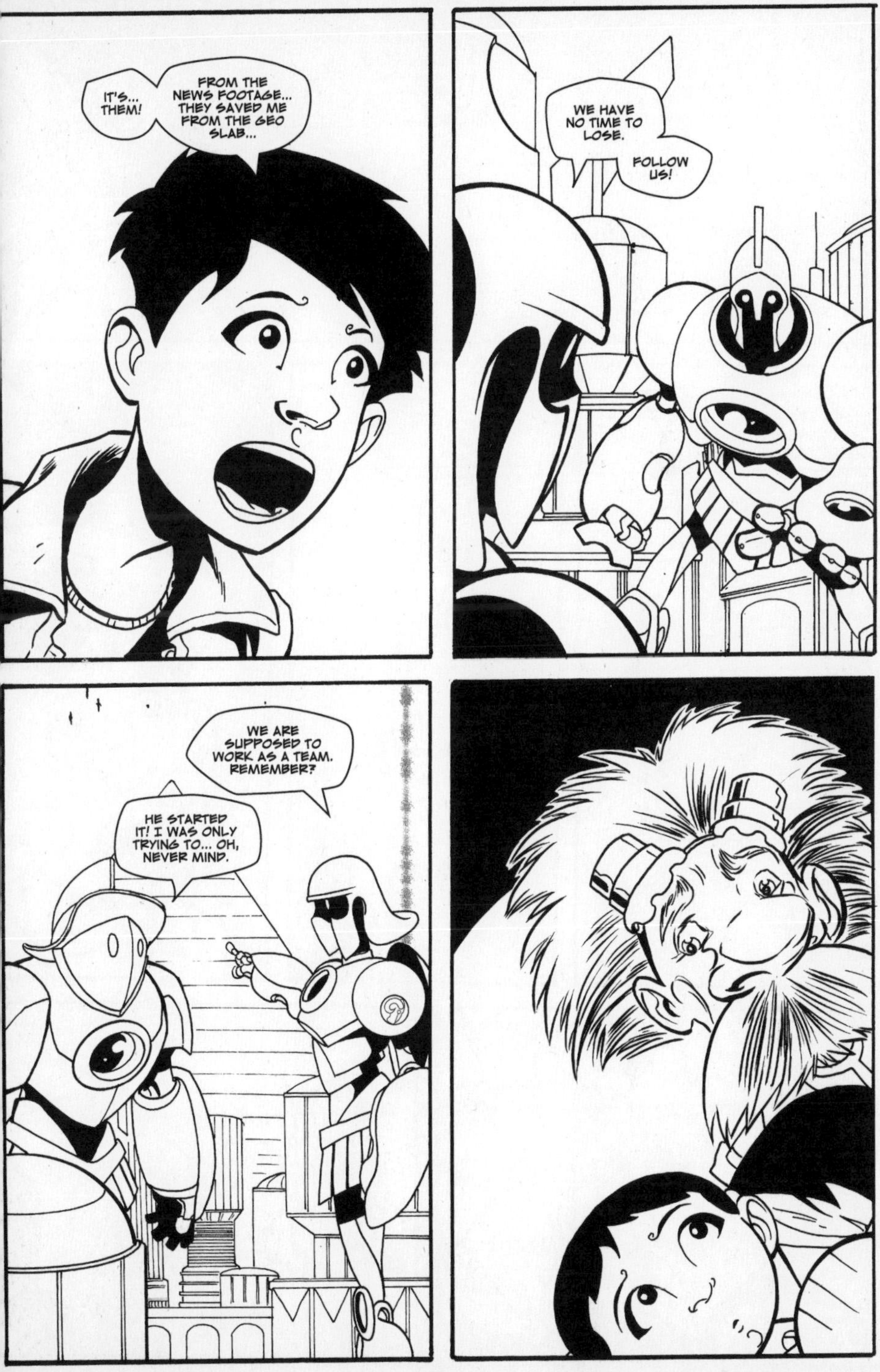
IT'S... THEM!
FROM THE NEWS FOOTAGE... THEY SAVED ME FROM THE GEO SLAB...
WE HAVE NO TIME TO LOSE.
FOLLOW US!
WE ARE SUPPOSED TO WORK AS A TEAM. REMEMBER?
HE STARTED IT! I WAS ONLY TRYING TO... OH, NEVER MIND.

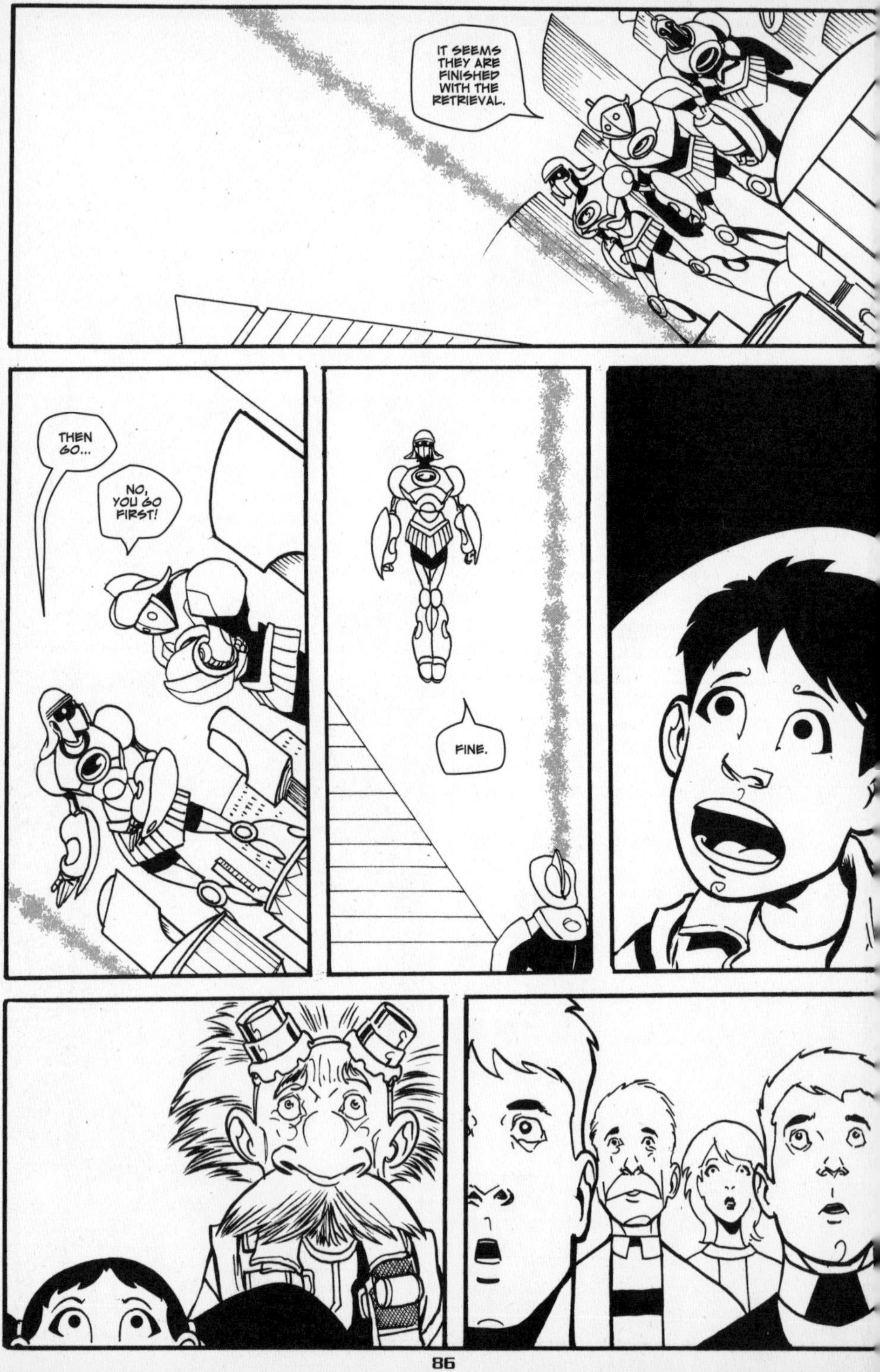
IT SEEMS THEY ARE FINISHED WITH THE RETRIEVAL.
THEN GO...
NO, YOU GO FIRST!
FINE.

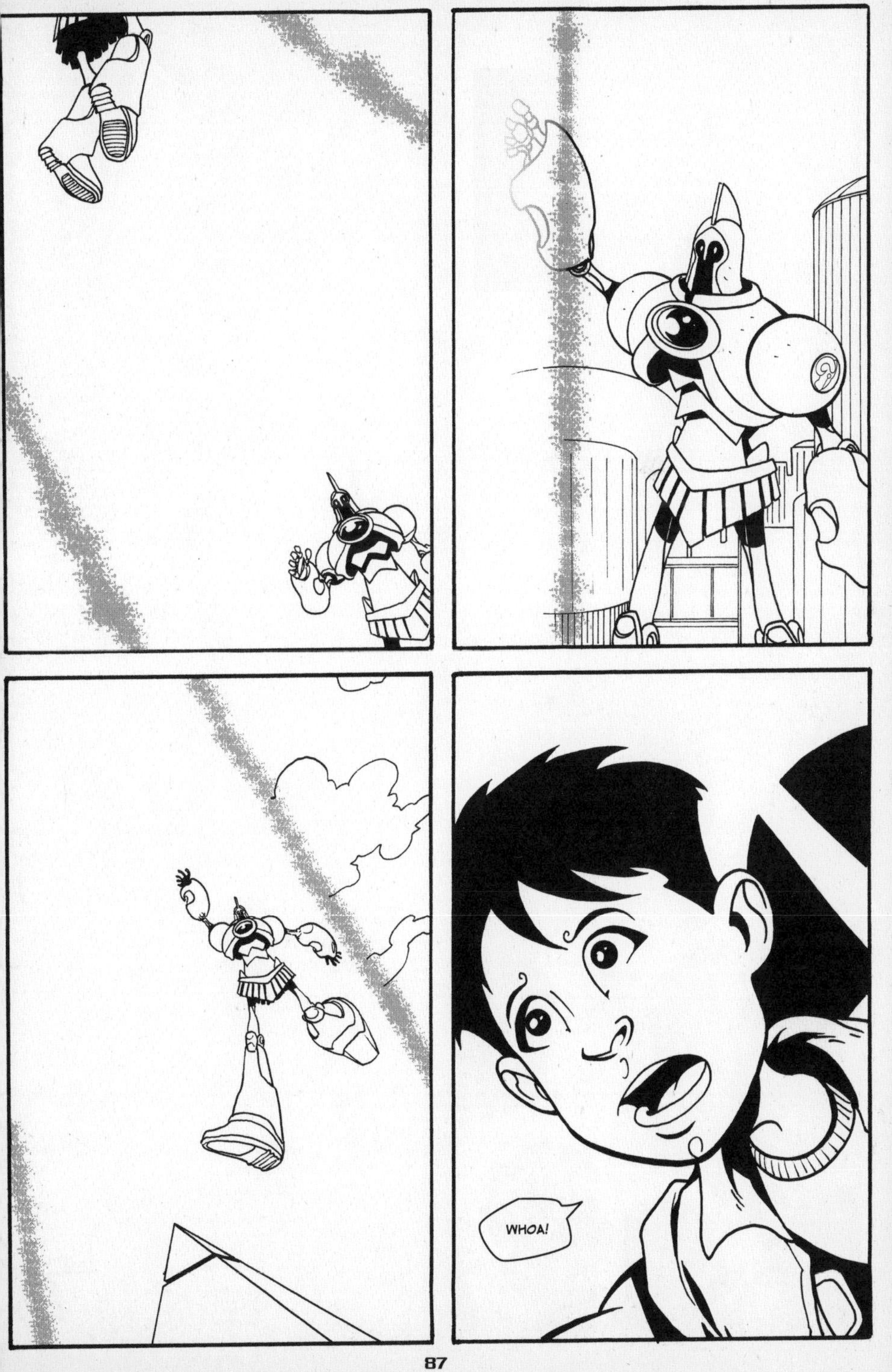
WHOA!

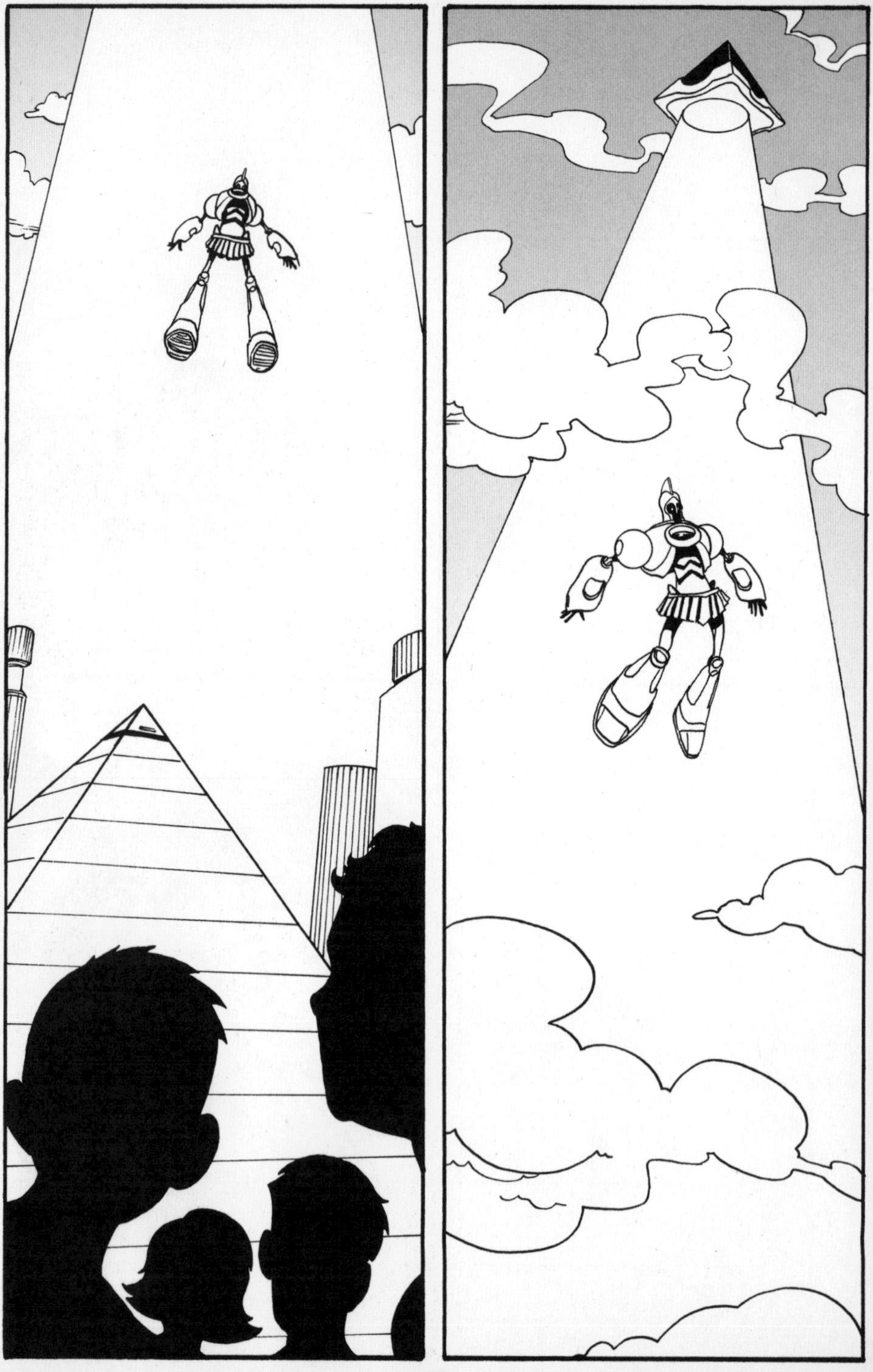

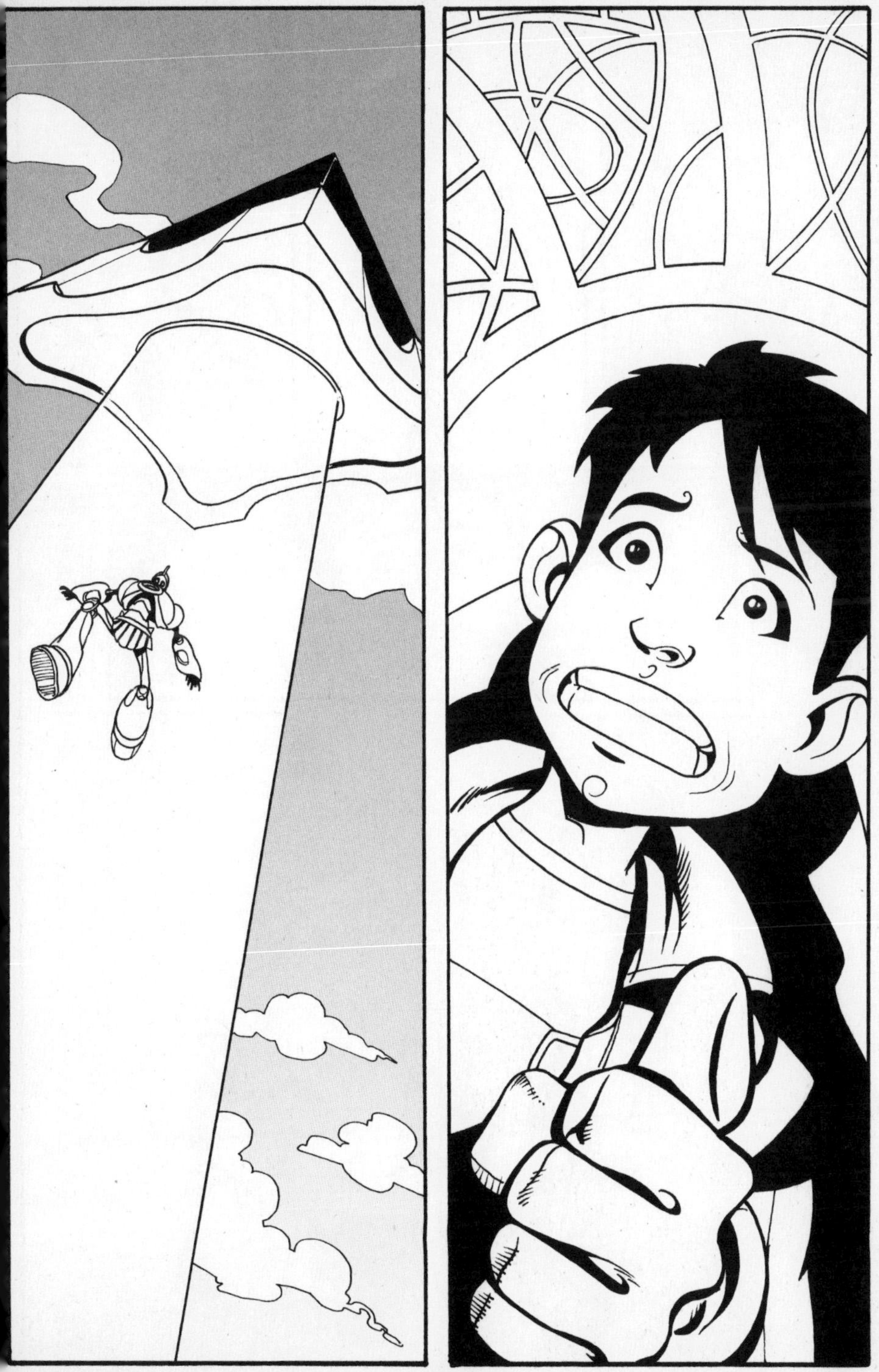

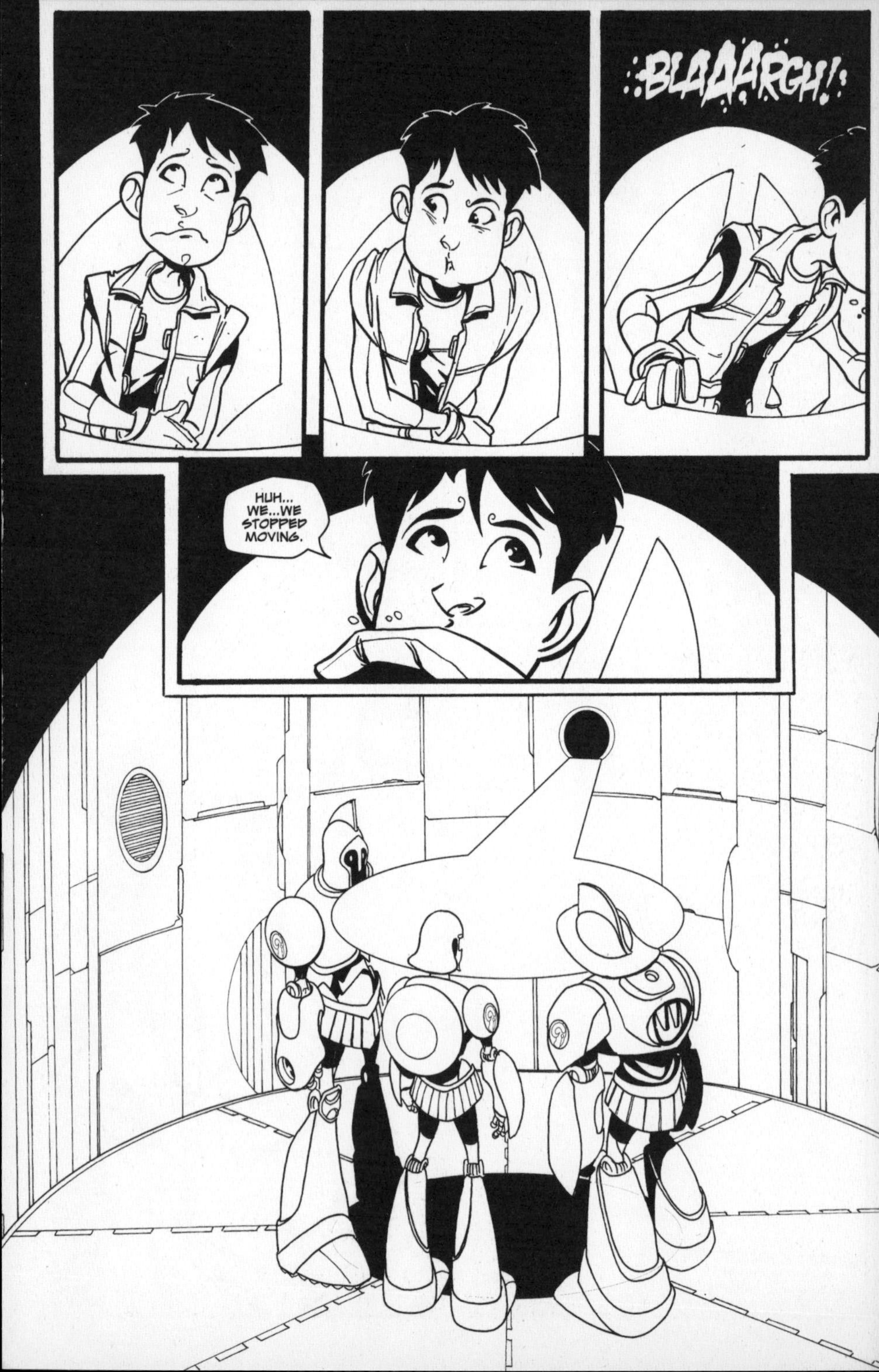
BLAAARGH!
HUH... WE...WE STOPPED MOVING.

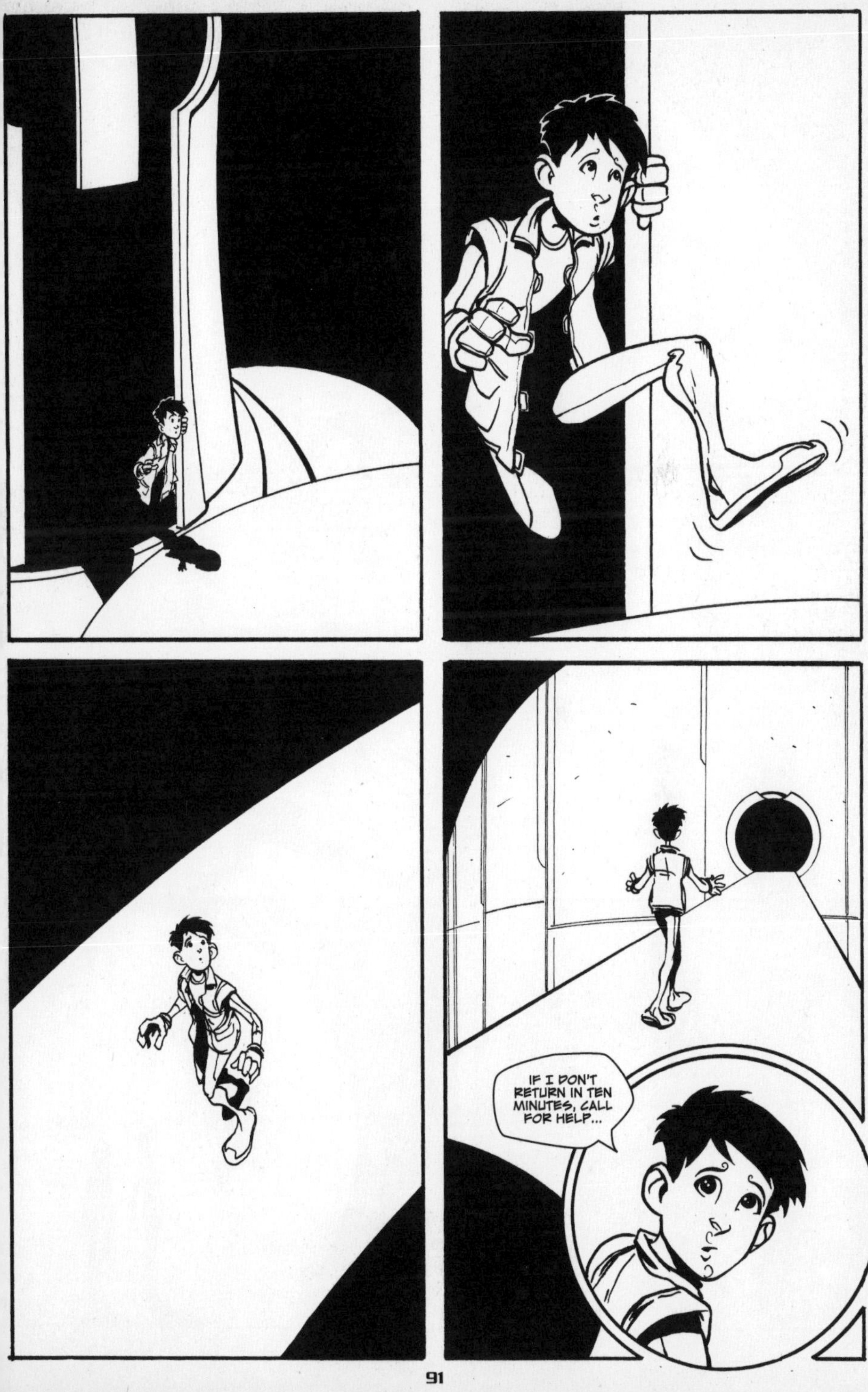
IF I DON'T RETURN IN TEN MINUTES, CALL FOR HELP...

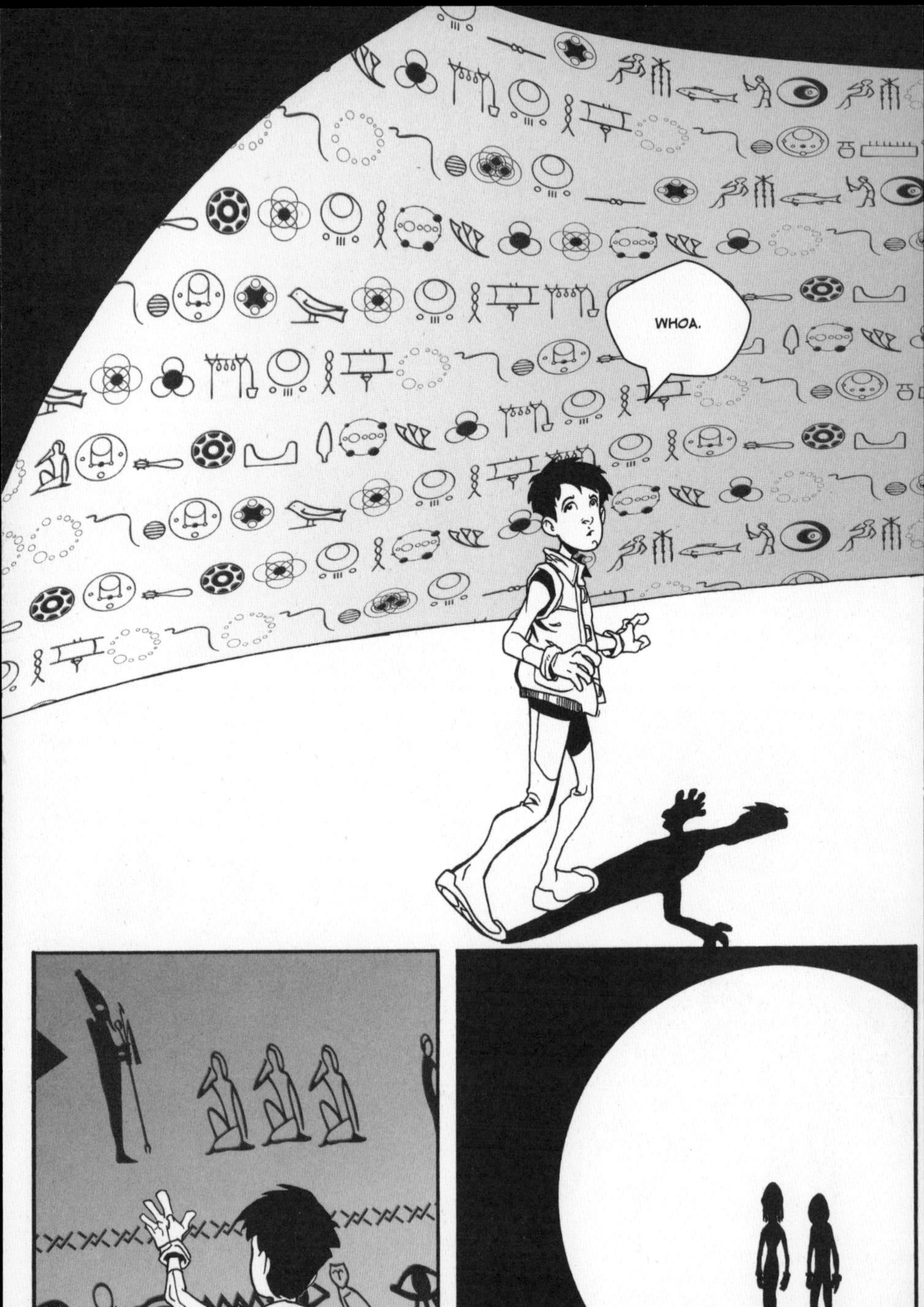
WHOA.

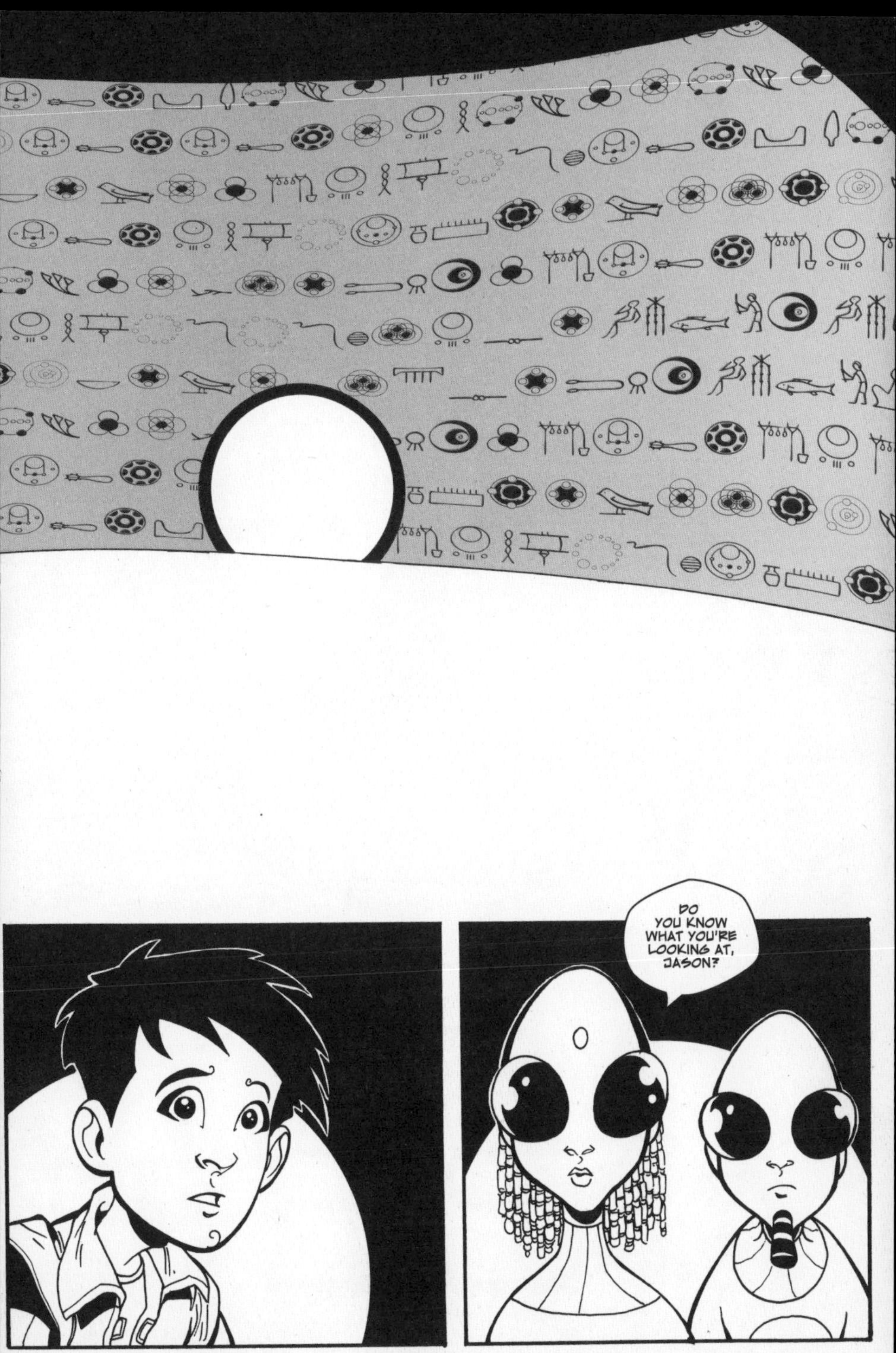
DO YOU KNOW WHAT YOU'RE LOOKING AT, JASON?

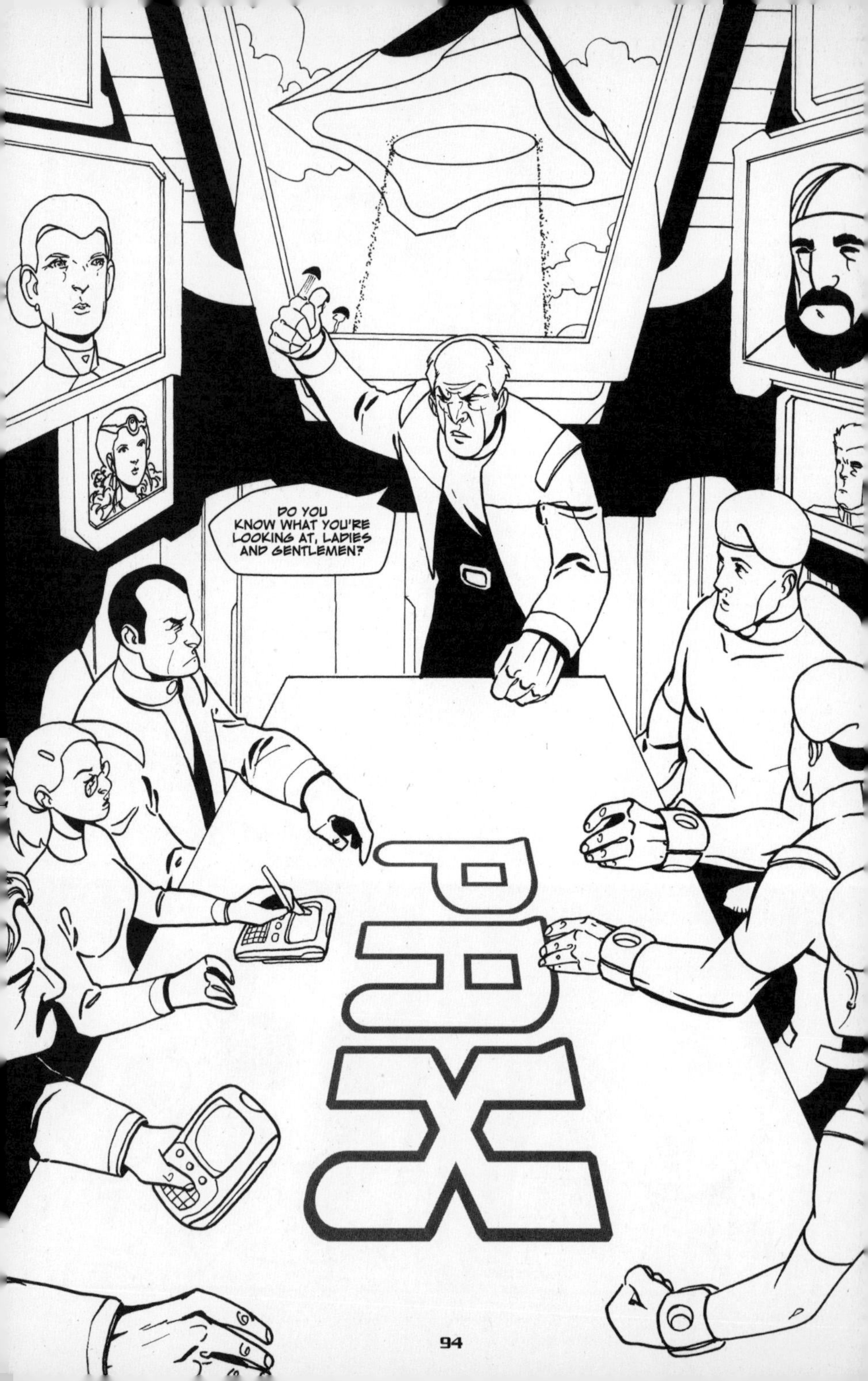
DO YOU KNOW WHAT YOU'RE LOOKING AT, LADIES AND GENTLEMEN?
PRX

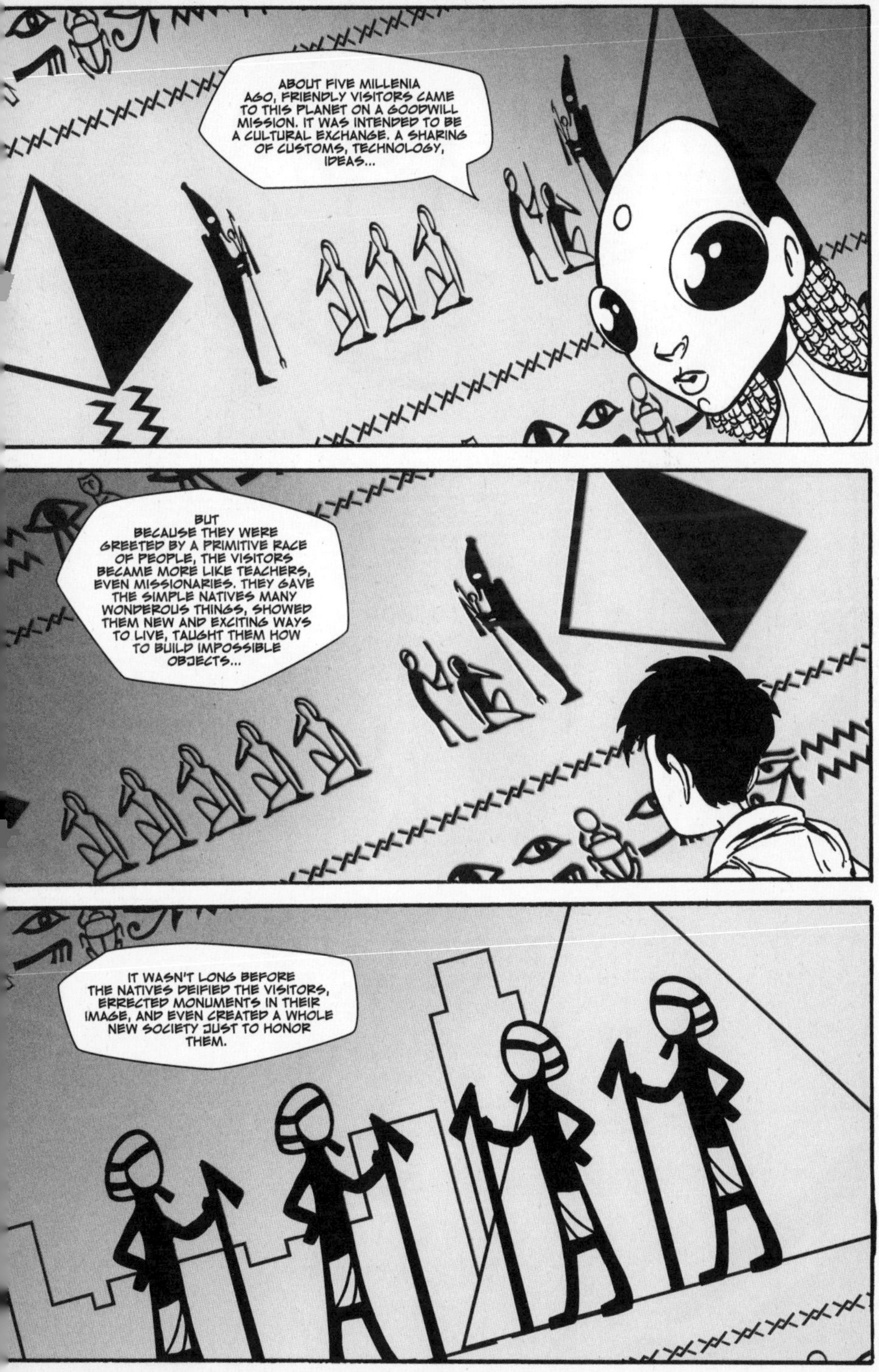
ABOUT FIVE MILLENIA AGO, FRIENDLY VISITORS CAME TO THIS PLANET ON A GOODWILL MISSION. IT WAS INTENDED TO BE A CULTURAL EXCHANGE. A SHARING OF CUSTOMS, TECHNOLOGY, IDEAS...
BUT BECAUSE THEY WERE GREETED BY A PRIMITIVE RACE OF PEOPLE, THE VISITORS BECAME MORE LIKE TEACHERS, EVEN MISSIONARIES. THEY GAVE THE SIMPLE NATIVES MANY WONDEROUS THINGS, SHOWED THEM NEW AND EXCITING WAYS TO LIVE, TAUGHT THEM HOW TO BUILD IMPOSSIBLE OBJECTS...
IT WASN'T LONG BEFORE THE NATIVES DEIFIED THE VISITORS, ERRECTED MONUMENTS IN THEIR IMAGE, AND EVEN CREATED A WHOLE NEW SOCIETY JUST TO HONOR THEM.

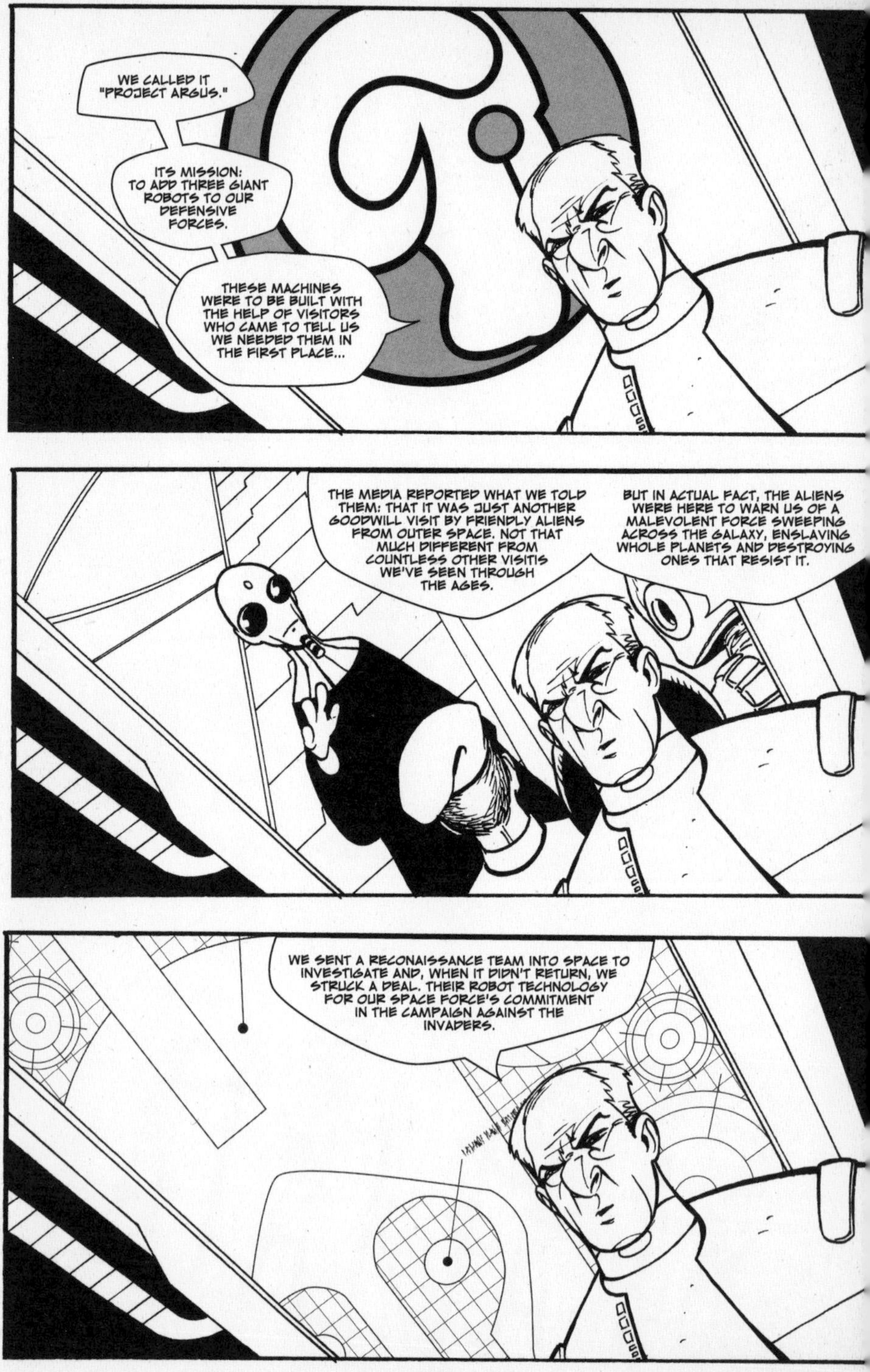
WE CALLED IT "PROJECT ARGUS."
ITS MISSION: TO ADD THREE GIANT ROBOTS TO OUR DEFENSIVE FORCES.
THESE MACHINES WERE TO BE BUILT WITH THE HELP OF VISITORS WHO CAME TO TELL US WE NEEDED THEM IN THE FIRST PLACE...
THE MEDIA REPORTED WHAT WE TOLD THEM: THAT IT WAS JUST ANOTHER GOODWILL VISIT BY FRIENDLY ALIENS FROM OUTER SPACE. NOT THAT MUCH DIFFERENT FROM COUNTLESS OTHER VISITIS WE'VE SEEN THROUGH THE AGES.
BUT IN ACTUAL FACT, THE ALIENS WERE HERE TO WARN US OF A MALEVOLENT FORCE SWEEPING ACROSS THE GALAXY, ENSLAVING WHOLE PLANETS AND DESTROYING ONES THAT RESIST IT.
WE SENT A RECONAISSANCE TEAM INTO SPACE TO INVESTIGATE AND, WHEN IT DIDN'T RETURN, WE STRUCK A DEAL. THEIR ROBOT TECHNOLOGY FOR OUR SPACE FORCE'S COMMITMENT IN THE CAMPAIGN AGAINST THE INVADERS.

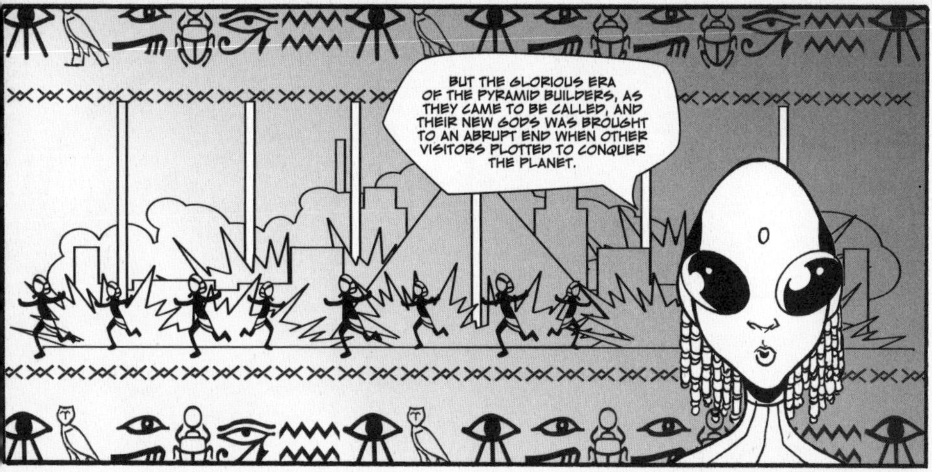
BUT THE GLORIOUS ERA OF THE PYRAMID BUILDERS, AS THEY CAME TO BE CALLED, AND THEIR NEW GODS WAS BROUGHT TO AN ABRUPT END WHEN OTHER VISITORS PLOTTED TO CONQUER THE PLANET.

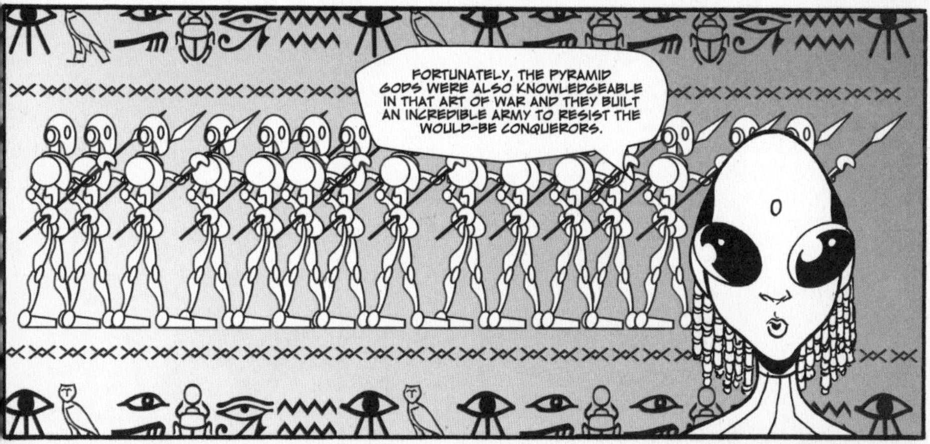
FORTUNATELY, THE PYRAMID GODS WERE ALSO KNOWLEDGEABLE IN THAT ART OF WAR AND THEY BUILT AN INCREDIBLE ARMY TO RESIST THE WOULD-BE CONQUERORS.

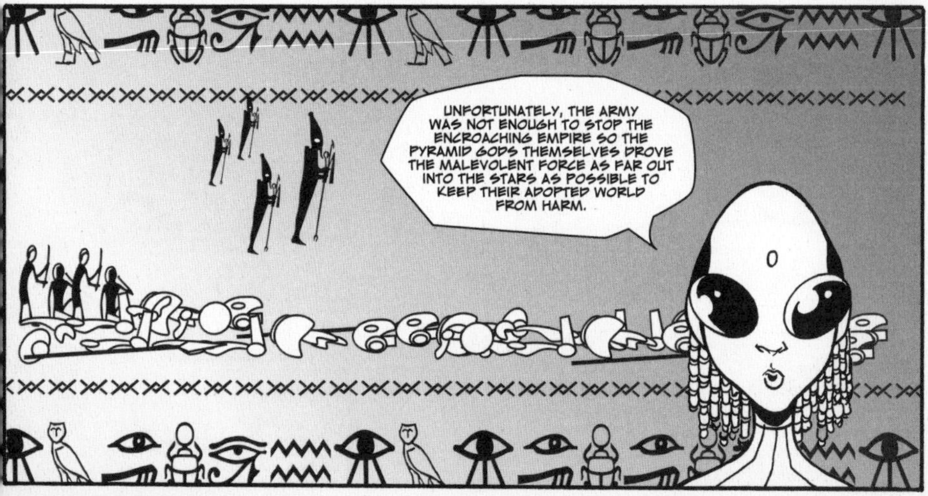
UNFORTUNATELY, THE ARMY WAS NOT ENOUGH TO STOP THE ENCROACHING EMPIRE SO THE PYRAMID GODS THEMSELVES DROVE THE MALEVOLENT FORCE AS FAR OUT INTO THE STARS AS POSSIBLE TO KEEP THEIR ADOPTED WORLD FROM HARM.

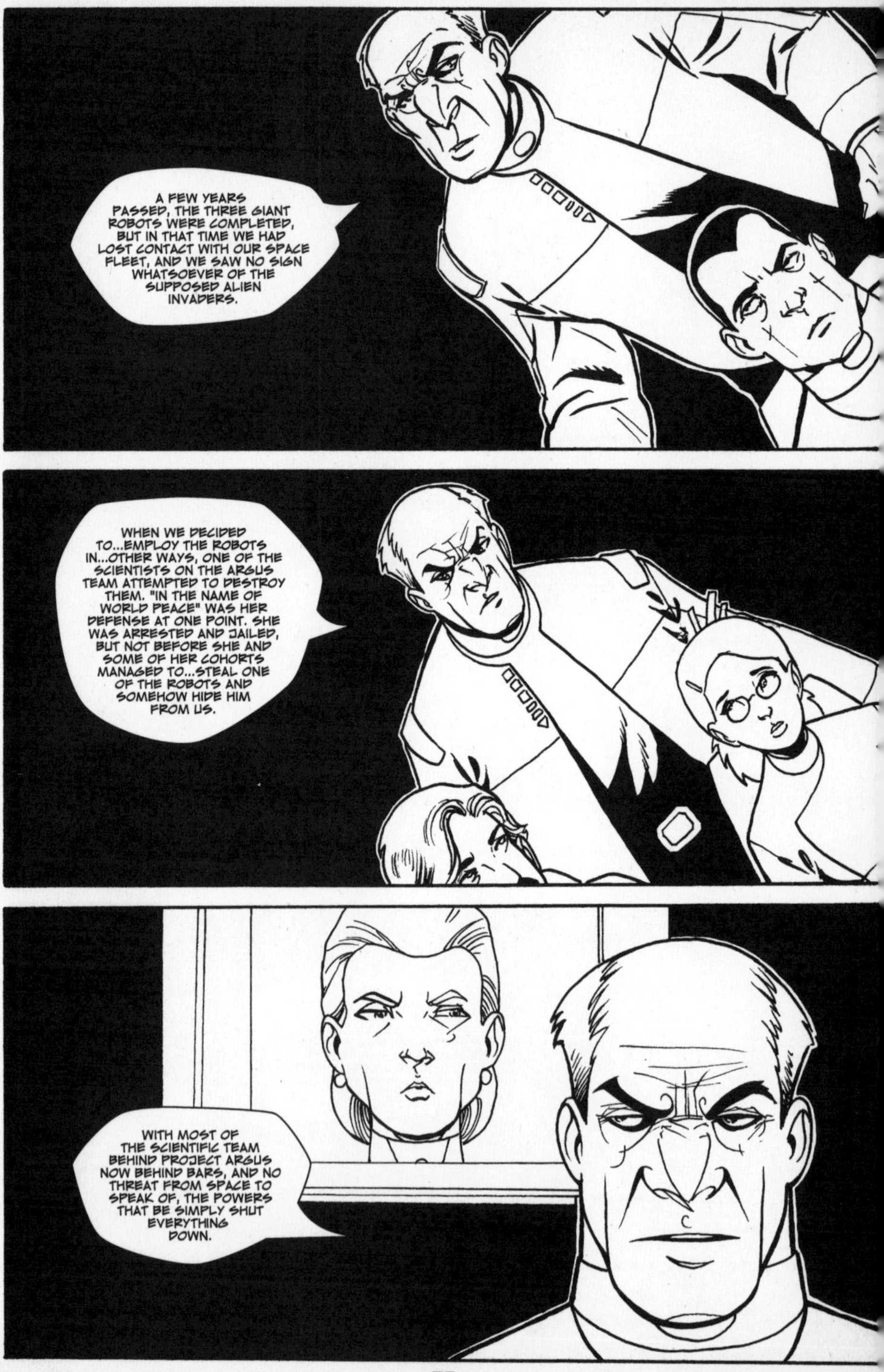
A FEW YEARS PASSED, THE THREE GIANT ROBOTS WERE COMPLETED, BUT IN THAT TIME WE HAD LOST CONTACT WITH OUR SPACE FLEET, AND WE SAW NO SIGN WHATSOEVER OF THE SUPPOSED ALIEN INVADERS.
WHEN WE DECIDED TO...EMPLOY THE ROBOTS IN...OTHER WAYS, ONE OF THE SCIENTISTS ON THE ARGUS TEAM ATTEMPTED TO DESTROY THEM. "IN THE NAME OF WORLD PEACE" WAS HER DEFENSE AT ONE POINT. SHE WAS ARRESTED AND JAILED, BUT NOT BEFORE SHE AND SOME OF HER COHORTS MANAGED TO...STEAL ONE OF THE ROBOTS AND SOMEHOW HIDE HIM FROM US.
WITH MOST OF THE SCIENTIFIC TEAM BEHIND PROJECT ARGUS NOW BEHIND BARS, AND NO THREAT FROM SPACE TO SPEAK OF, THE POWERS THAT BE SIMPLY SHUT EVERYTHING DOWN.

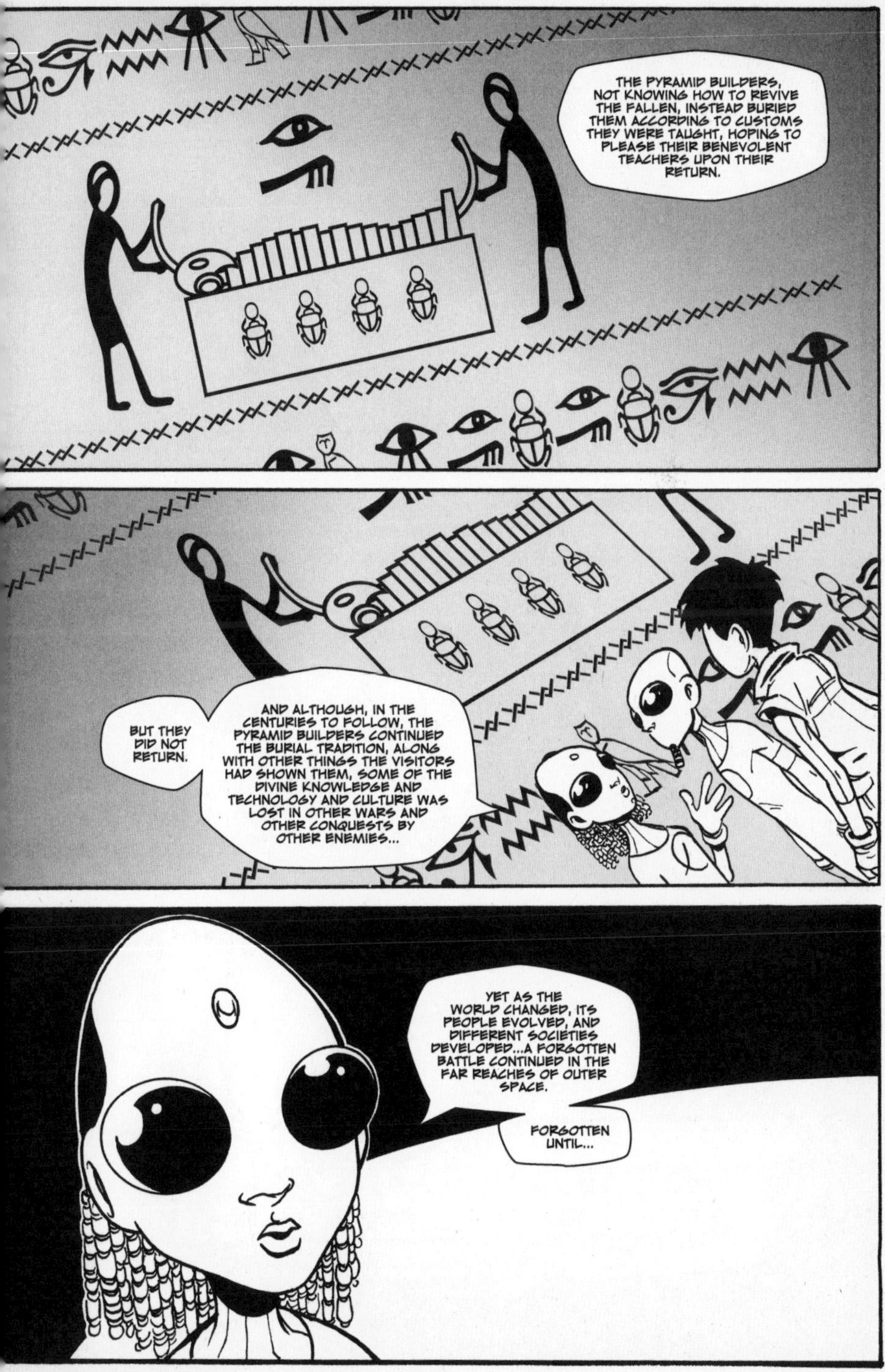
THE PYRAMID BUILDERS, NOT KNOWING HOW TO REVIVE THE FALLEN, INSTEAD BURIED THEM ACCORDING TO CUSTOMS THEY WERE TAUGHT, HOPING TO PLEASE THEIR BENEVOLENT TEACHERS UPON THEIR RETURN.
BUT THEY DID NOT RETURN.
AND ALTHOUGH, IN THE CENTURIES TO FOLLOW, THE PYRAMID BUILDERS CONTINUED THE BURIAL TRADITION, ALONG WITH OTHER THINGS THE VISITORS HAD SHOWN THEM, SOME OF THE DIVINE KNOWLEDGE AND TECHNOLOGY AND CULTURE WAS LOST IN OTHER WARS AND OTHER CONQUESTS BY OTHER ENEMIES...
YET AS THE WORLD CHANGED, ITS PEOPLE EVOLVED, AND DIFFERENT SOCIETIES DEVELOPED...A FORGOTTEN BATTLE CONTINUED IN THE FAR REACHES OF OUTER SPACE.
FORGOTTEN UNTIL...

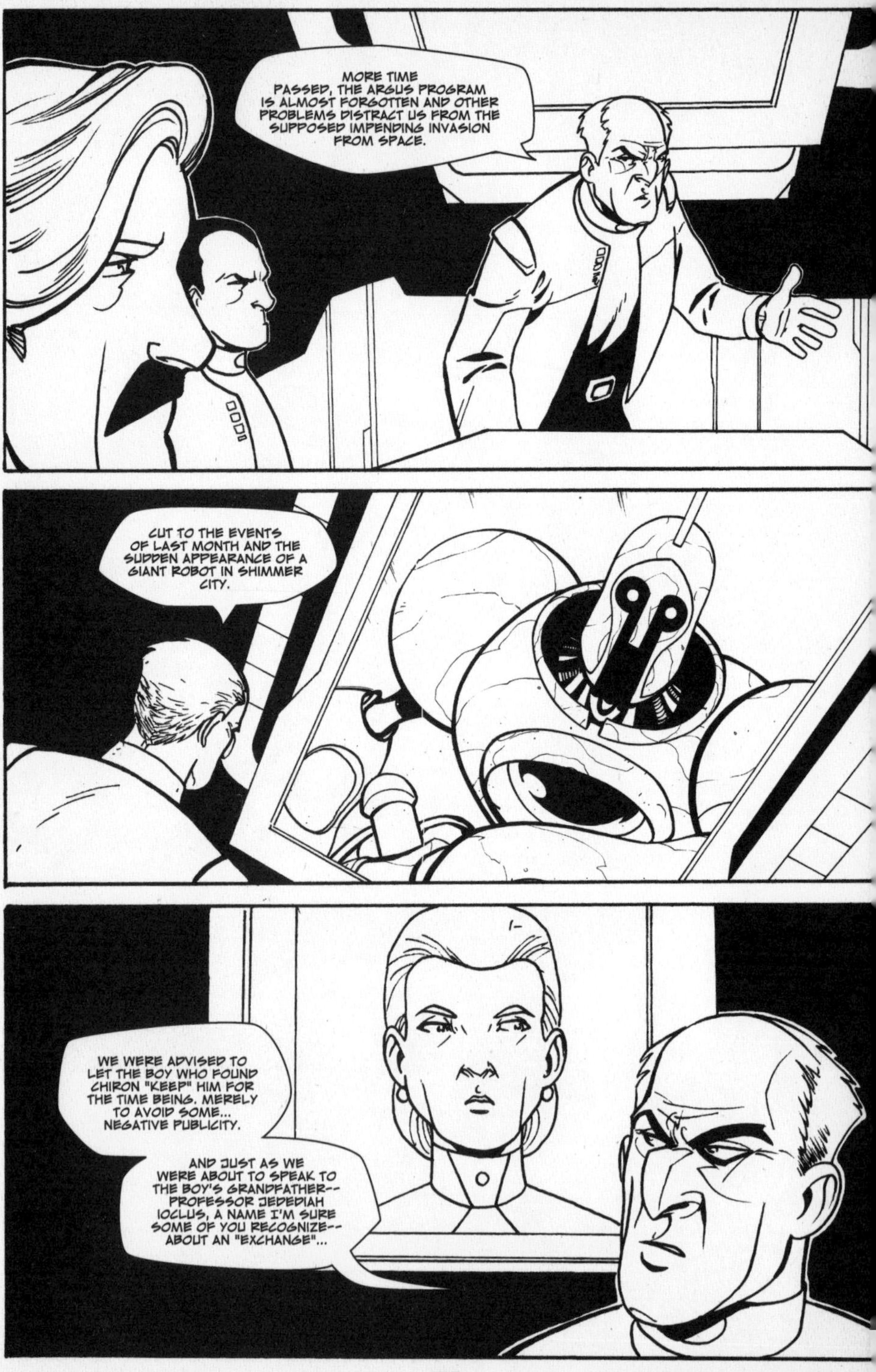
MORE TIME PASSED, THE ARGUS PROGRAM IS ALMOST FORGOTTEN AND OTHER PROBLEMS DISTRACT US FROM THE SUPPOSED IMPENDING INVASION FROM SPACE.
CUT TO THE EVENTS OF LAST MONTH AND THE SUDDEN APPEARANCE OF A GIANT ROBOT IN SHIMMER CITY.
WE WERE ADVISED TO LET THE BOY WHO FOUND CHIRON "KEEP" HIM FOR THE TIME BEING. MERELY TO AVOID SOME... NEGATIVE PUBLICITY.
AND JUST AS WE WERE ABOUT TO SPEAK TO THE BOY'S GRANDFATHER--PROFESSOR JEDEDIAH IOCLUS, A NAME I'M SURE SOME OF YOU RECOGNIZE--ABOUT AN "EXCHANGE"...

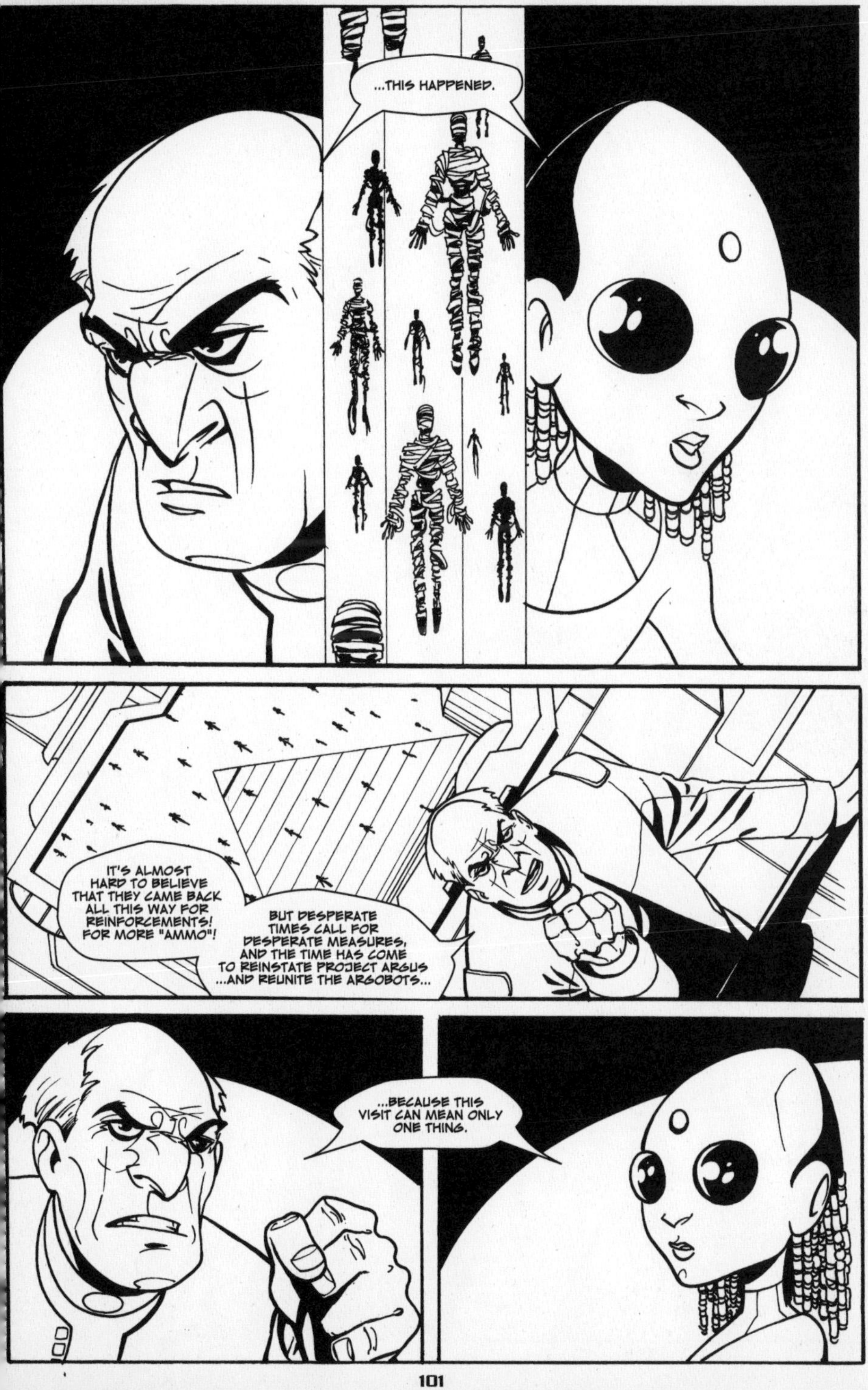
...THIS HAPPENED.
IT'S ALMOST HARD TO BELIEVE THAT THEY CAME BACK ALL THIS WAY FOR REINFORCEMENTS! FOR MORE "AMMO"!
BUT DESPERATE TIMES CALL FOR DESPERATE MEASURES, AND THE TIME HAS COME TO REINSTATE PROJECT ARGUS ...AND REUNITE THE ARGOBOTS...
...BECAUSE THIS VISIT CAN MEAN ONLY ONE THING.

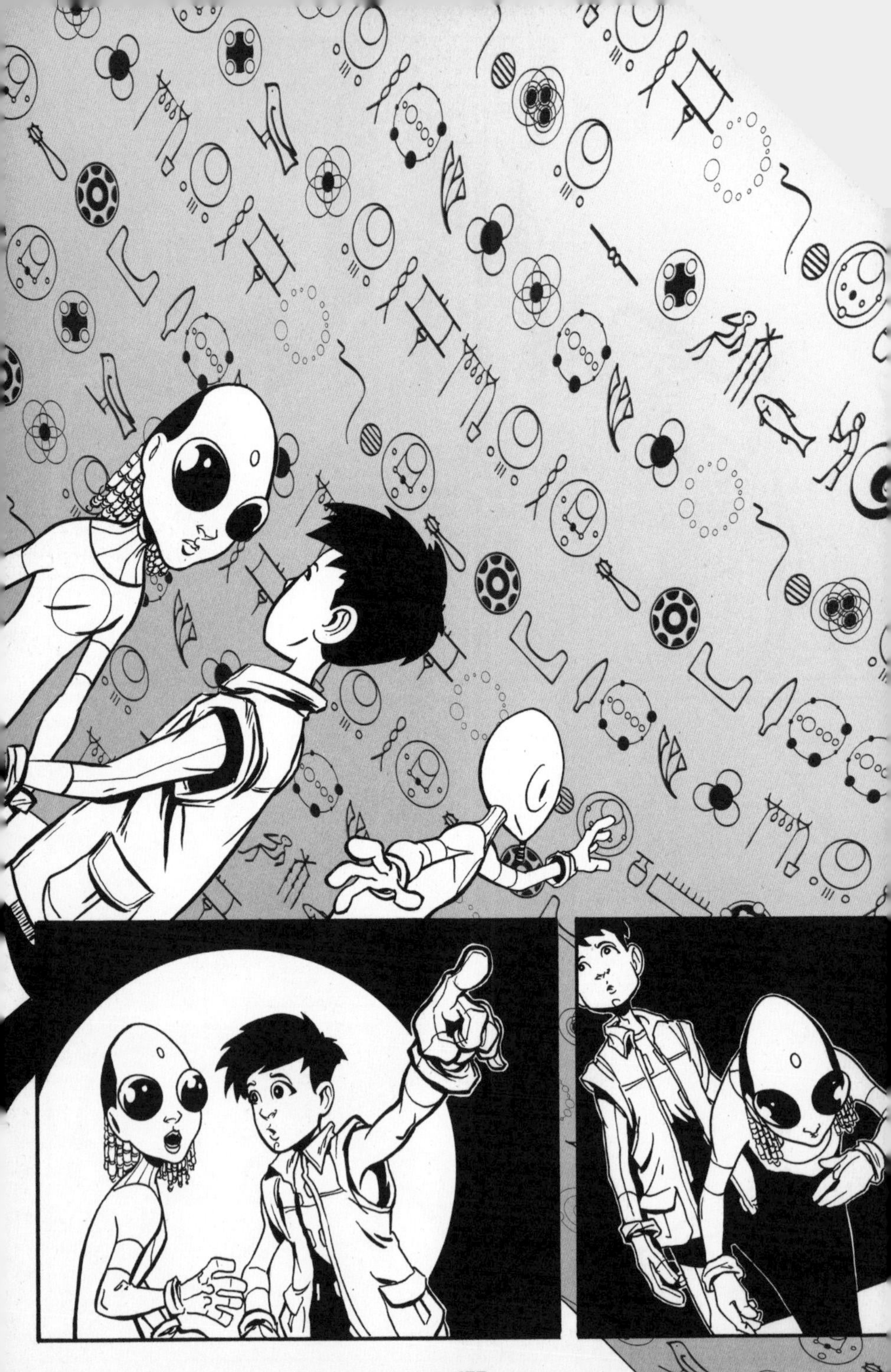

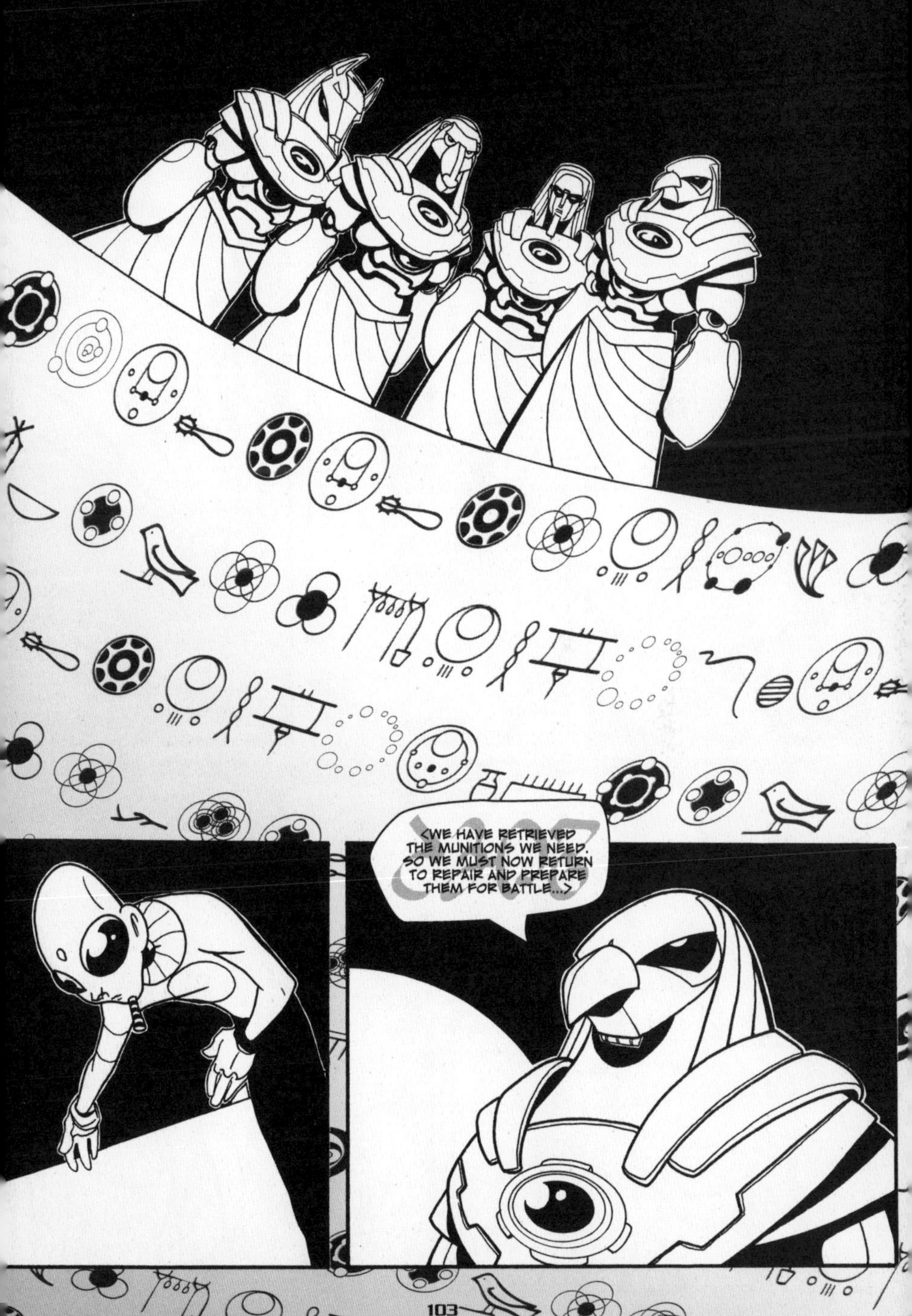
<WE HAVE RETRIEVED THE MUNITIONS WE NEED. SO WE MUST NOW RETURN TO REPAIR AND PREPARE THEM FOR BATTLE...>

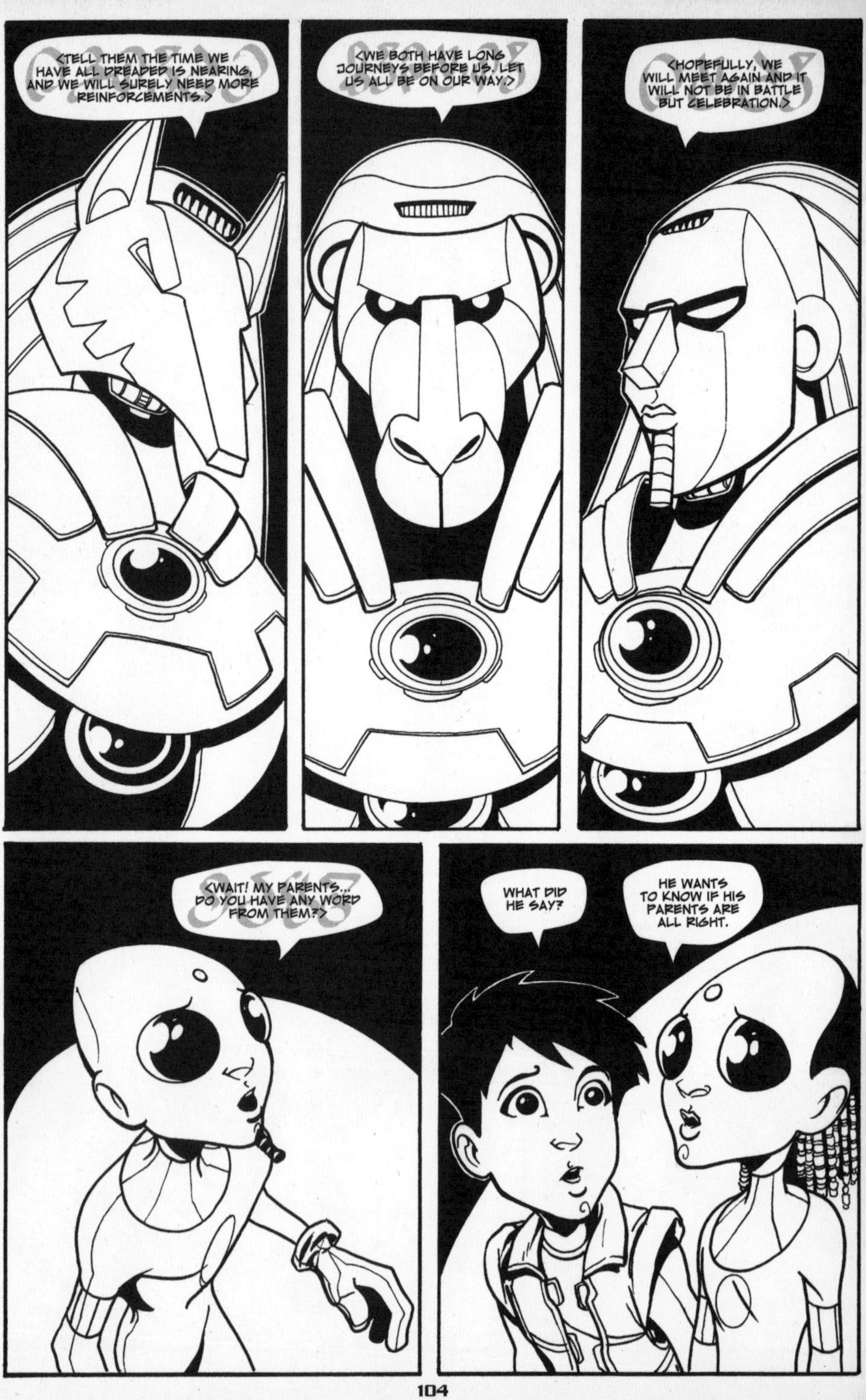
<TELL THEM THE TIME WE HAVE ALL DREADED IS NEARING, AND WE WILL SURELY NEED MORE REINFORCEMENTS.>
<WE BOTH HAVE LONG JOURNEYS BEFORE US. LET US ALL BE ON OUR WAY.>
<HOPEFULLY, WE WILL MEET AGAIN AND IT WILL NOT BE IN BATTLE BUT CELEBRATION.>
<WAIT! MY PARENTS... DO YOU HAVE ANY WORD FROM THEM?>
WHAT DID HE SAY?
HE WANTS TO KNOW IF HIS PARENTS ARE ALL RIGHT.

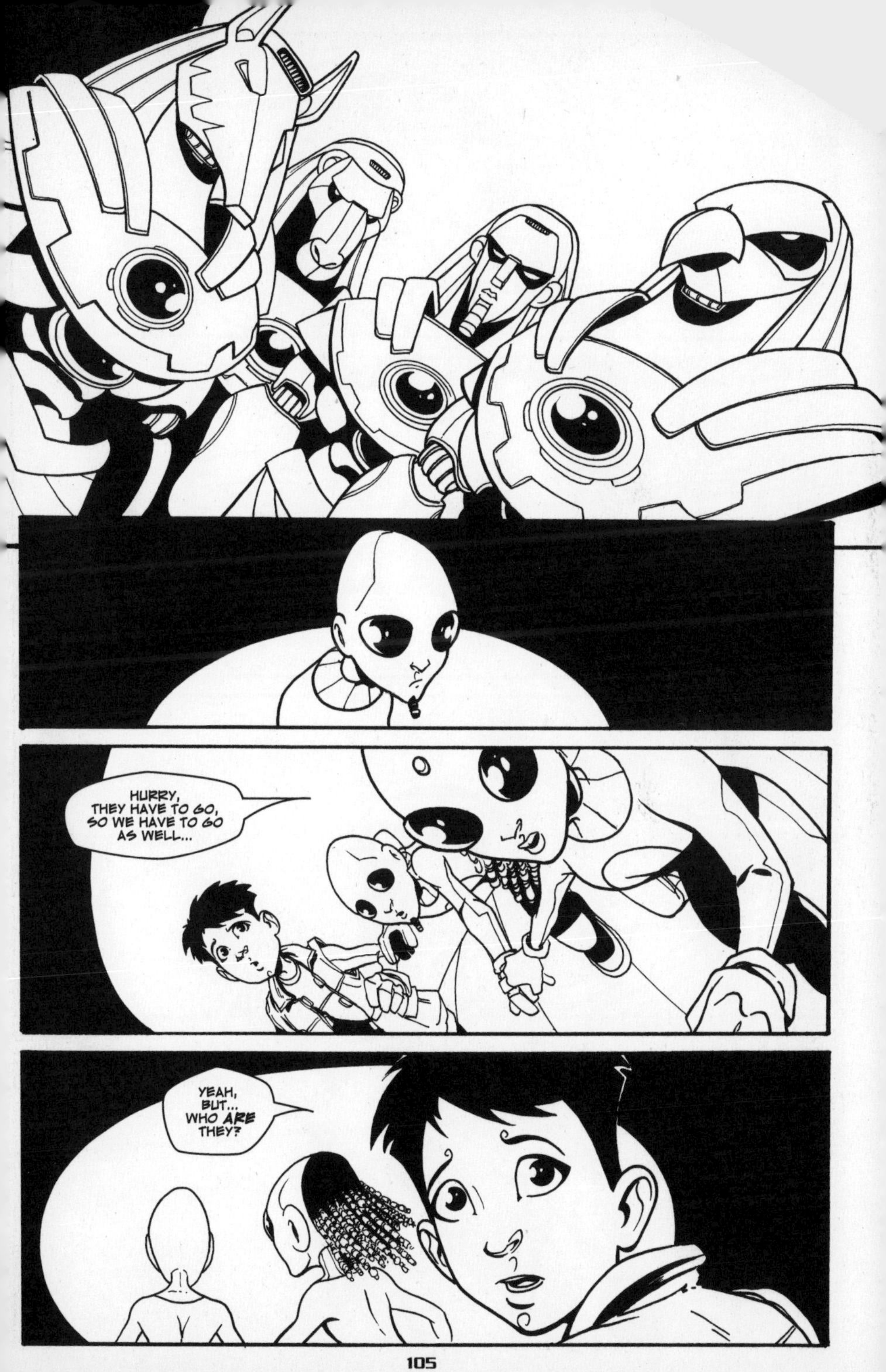
HURRY, THEY HAVE TO GO, SO WE HAVE TO GO AS WELL...
YEAH, BUT... WHO ARE THEY?

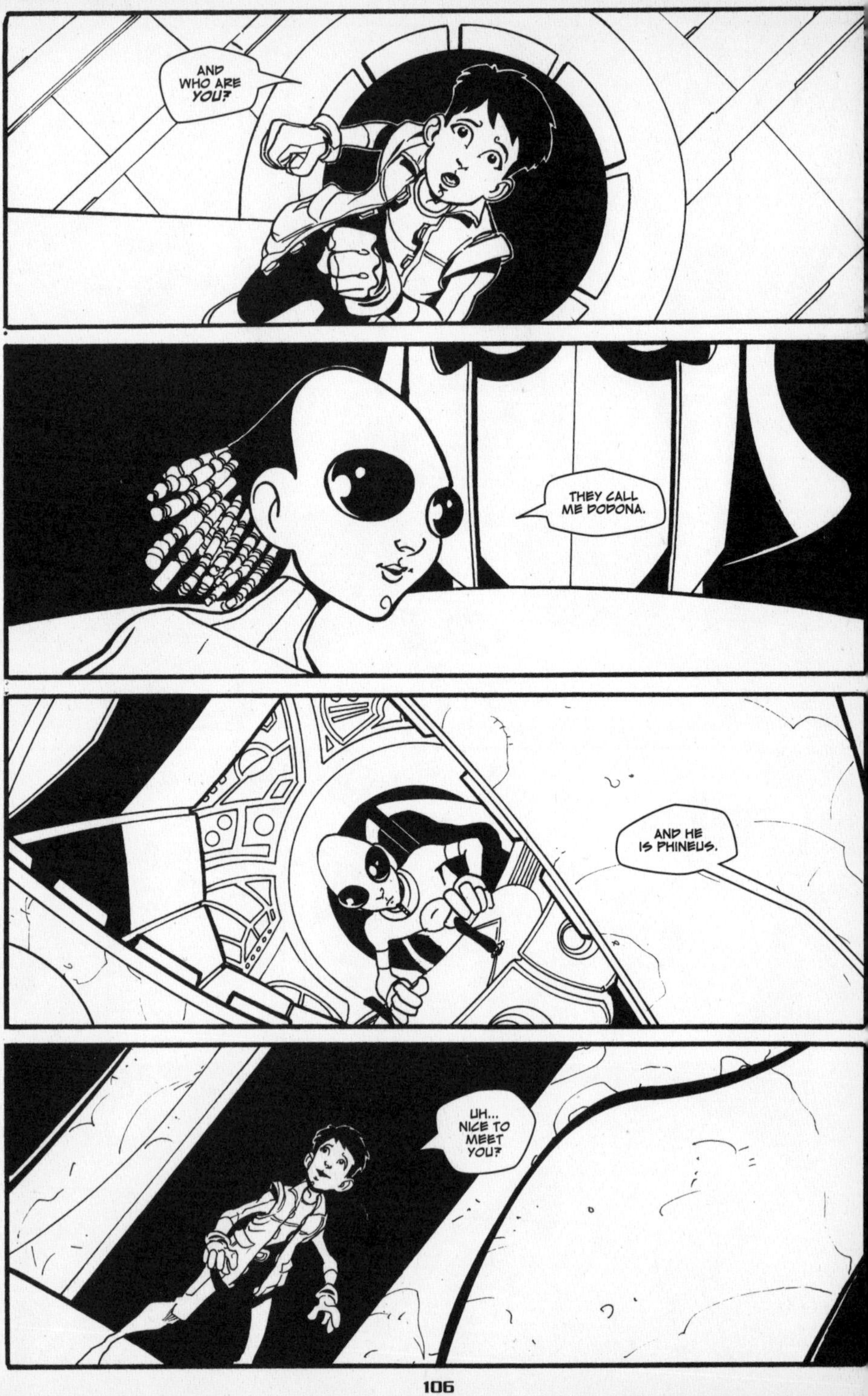
AND WHO ARE YOU?
THEY CALL ME DODONA.
AND HE IS PHINEUS.
UH... NICE TO MEET YOU?

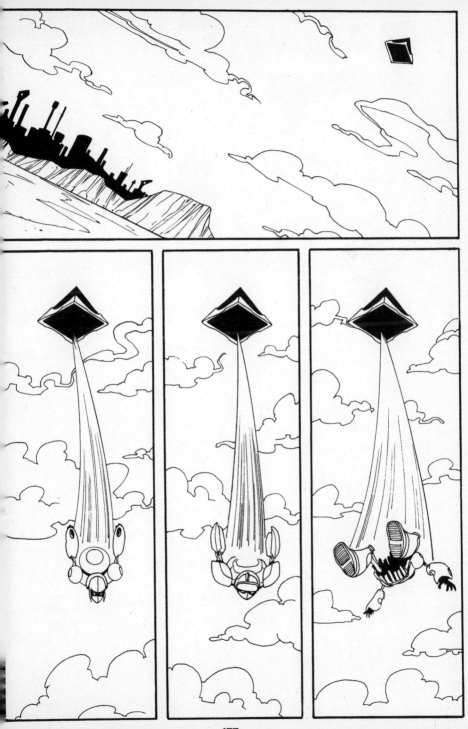

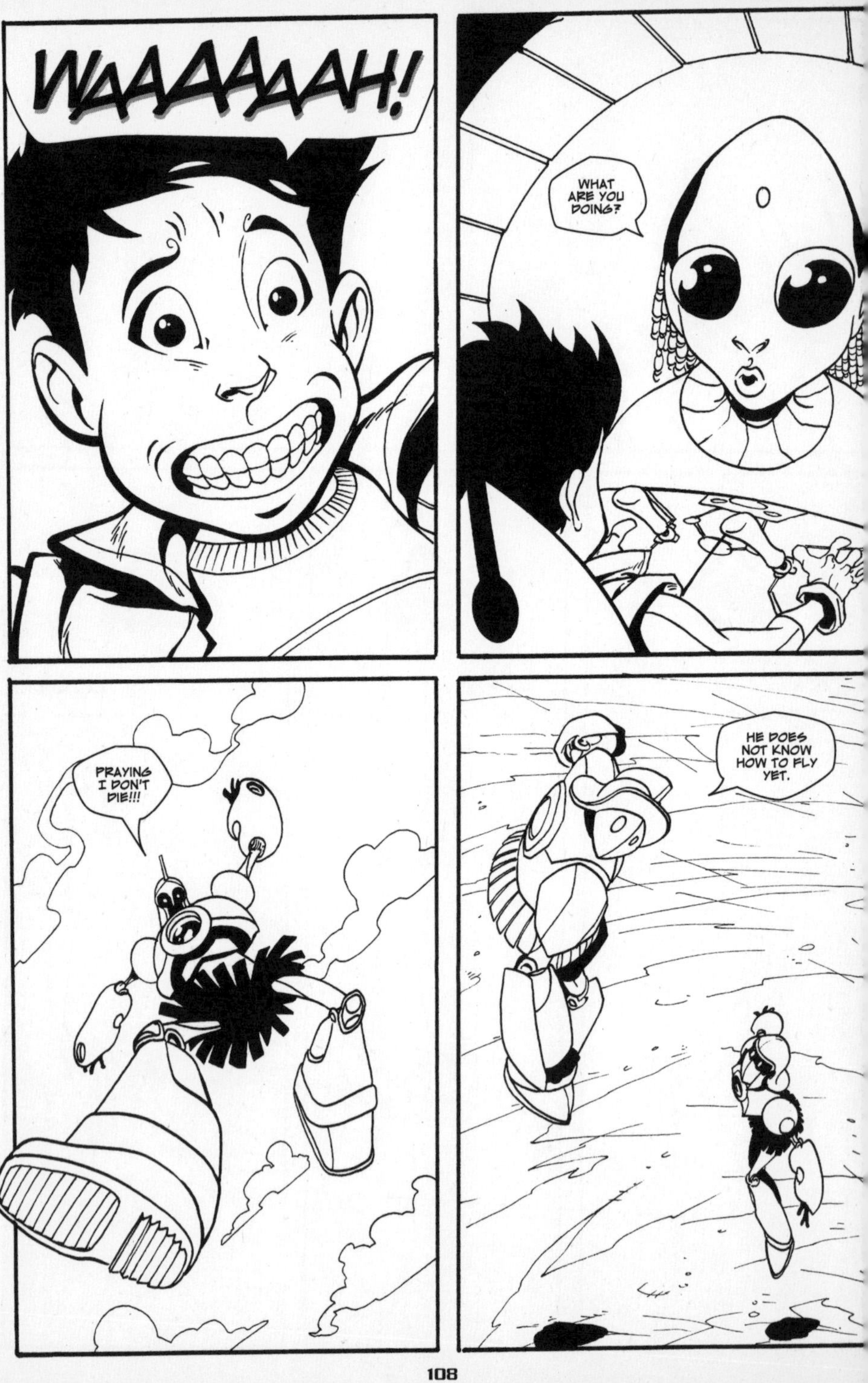
WAAAAAAH!
WHAT ARE YOU DOING?
PRAYING I DON'T DIE!!!
HE DOES NOT KNOW HOW TO FLY YET.

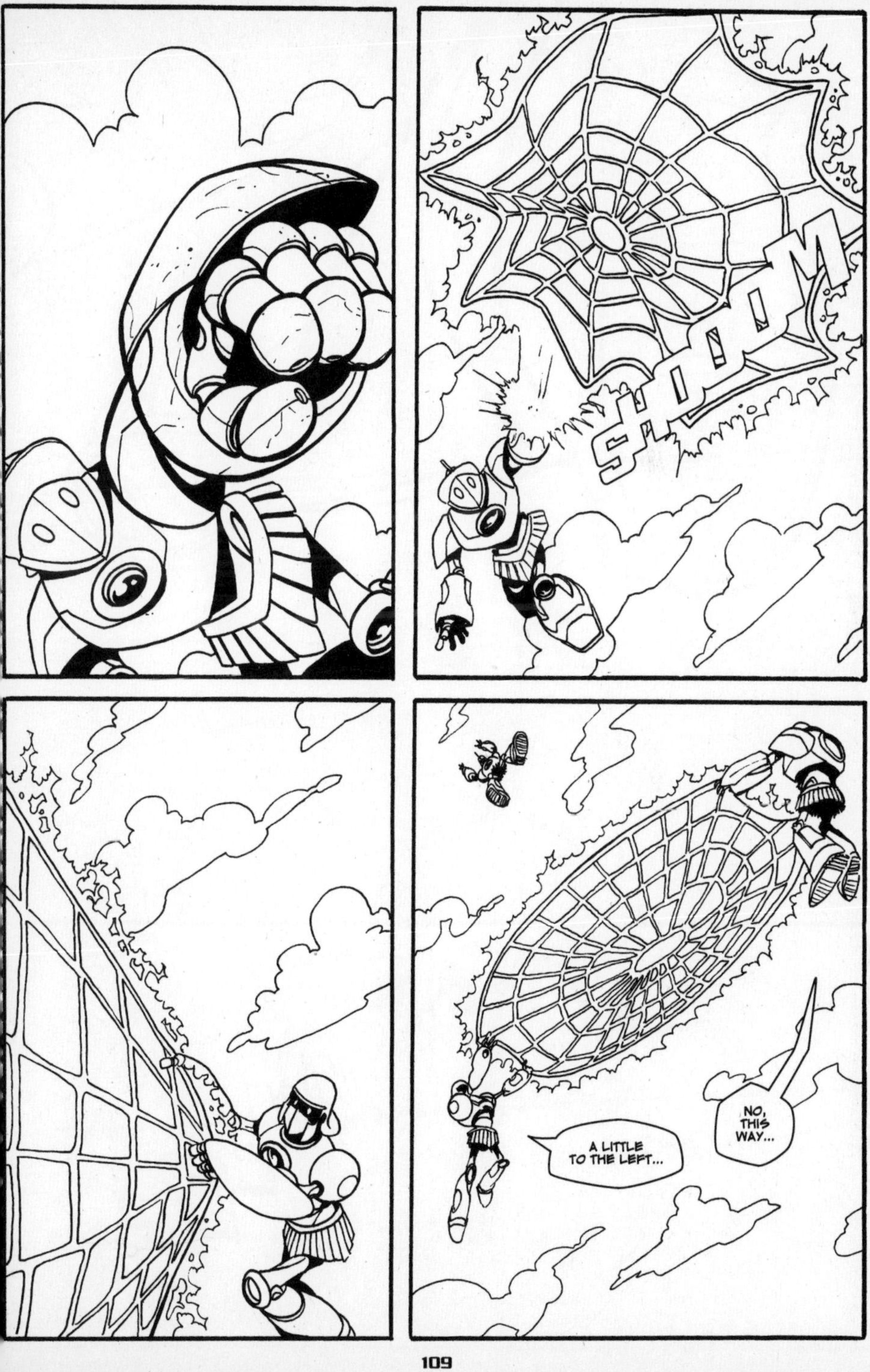
SHOOM
A LITTLE TO THE LEFT...
NO, THIS WAY...

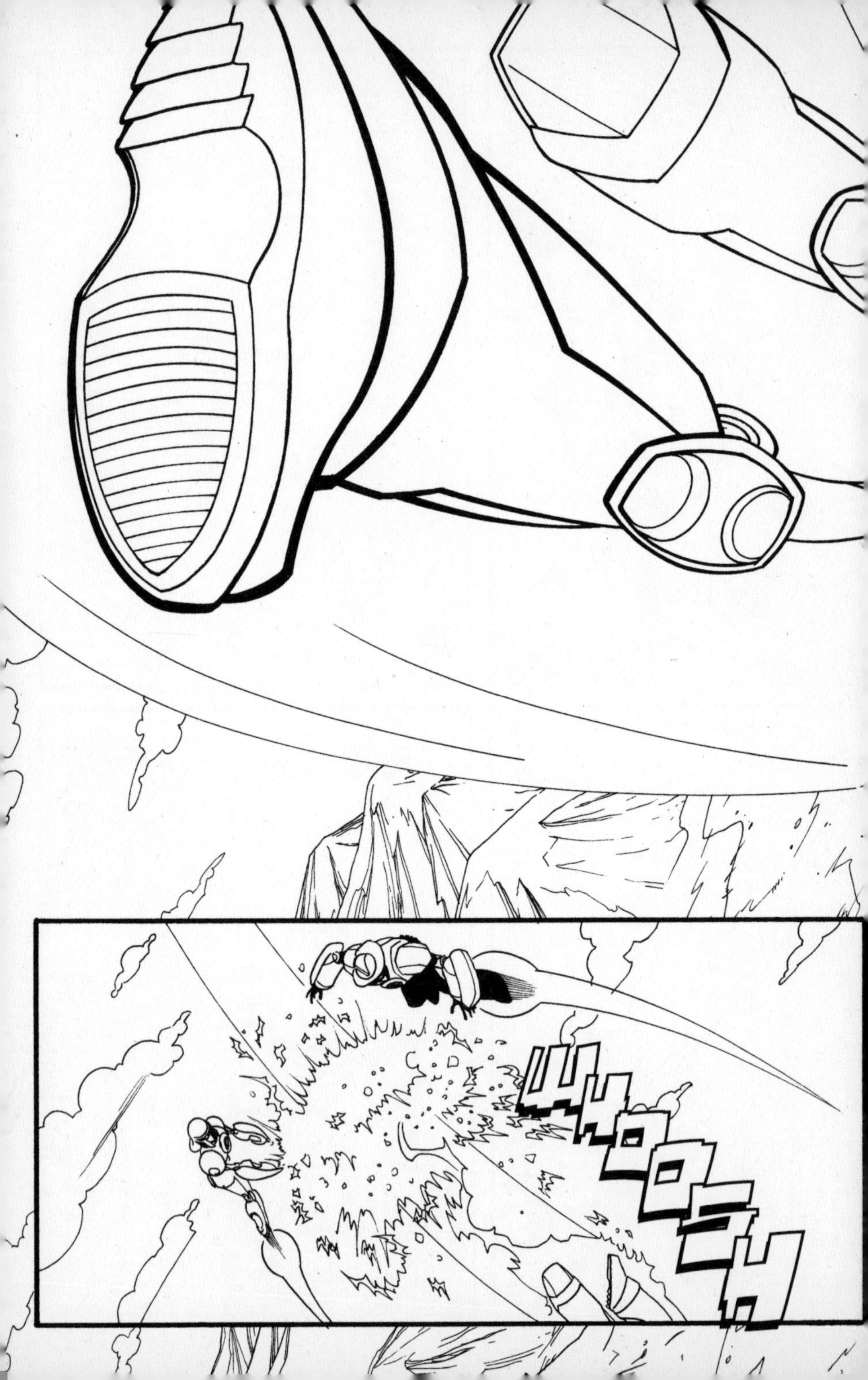
WHOOOSH

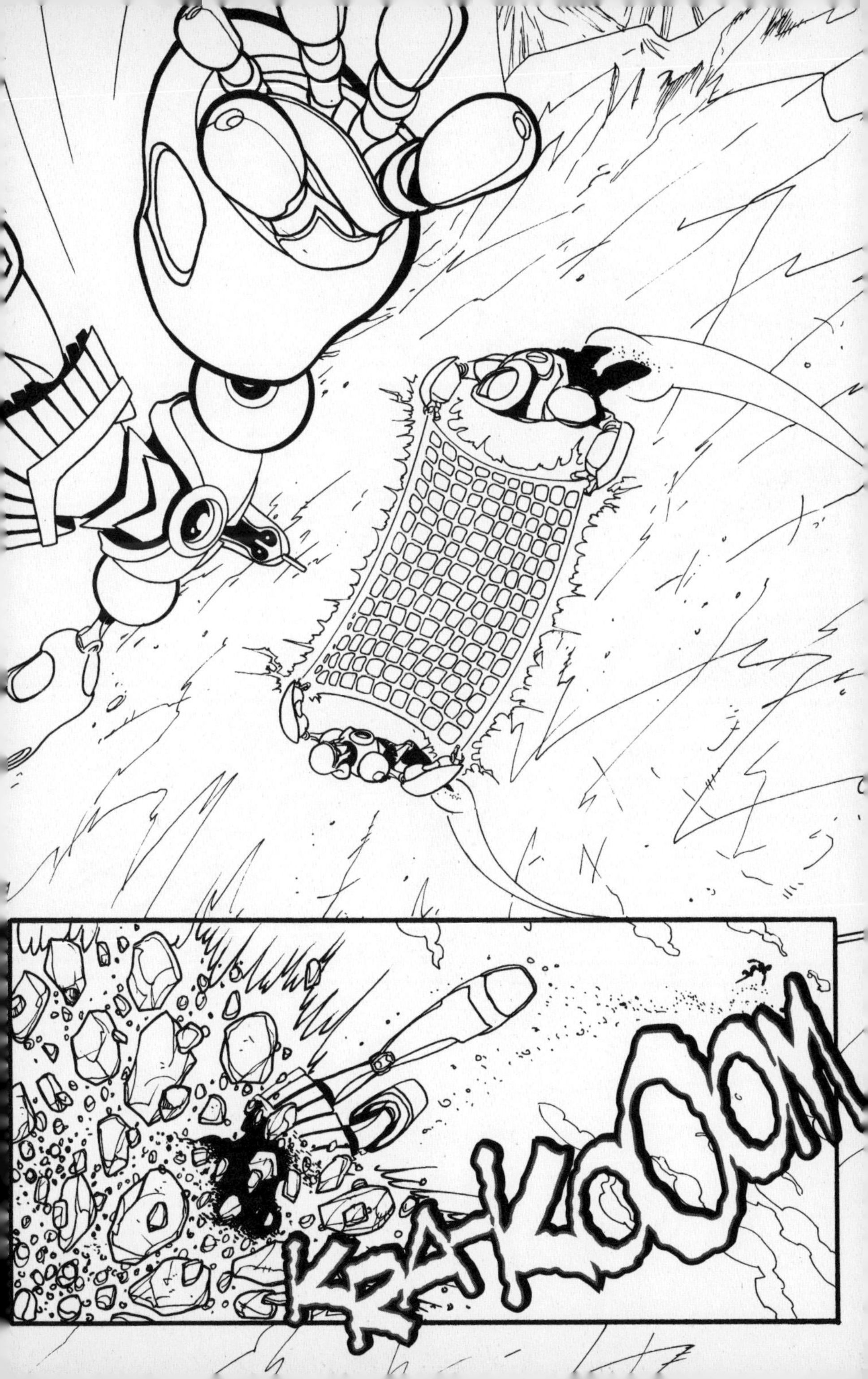
KRAKOOOM

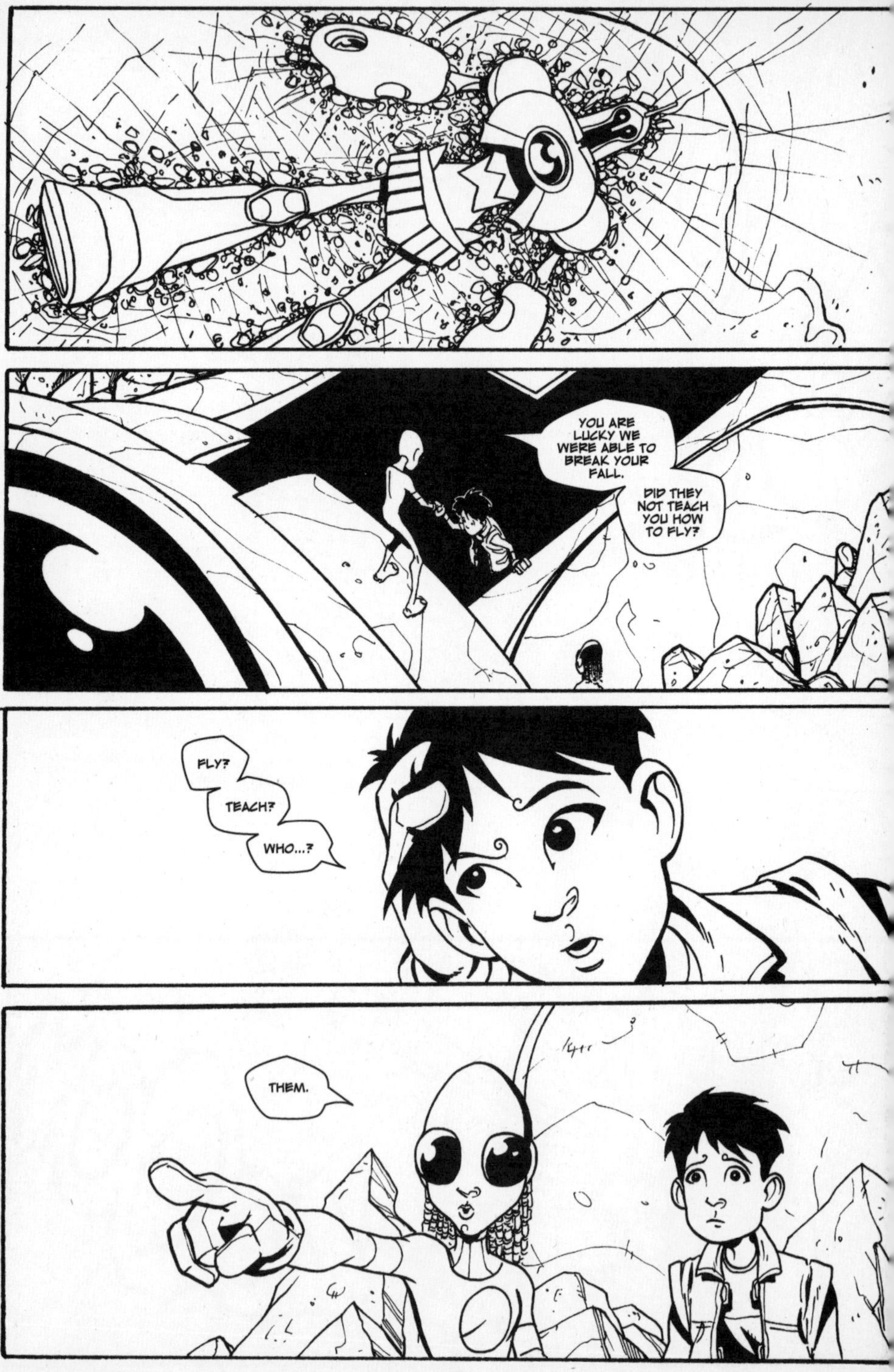
YOU ARE LUCKY WE WERE ABLE TO BREAK YOUR FALL.
DID THEY NOT TEACH YOU HOW TO FLY?
FLY?
TEACH?
WHO...?
THEM.

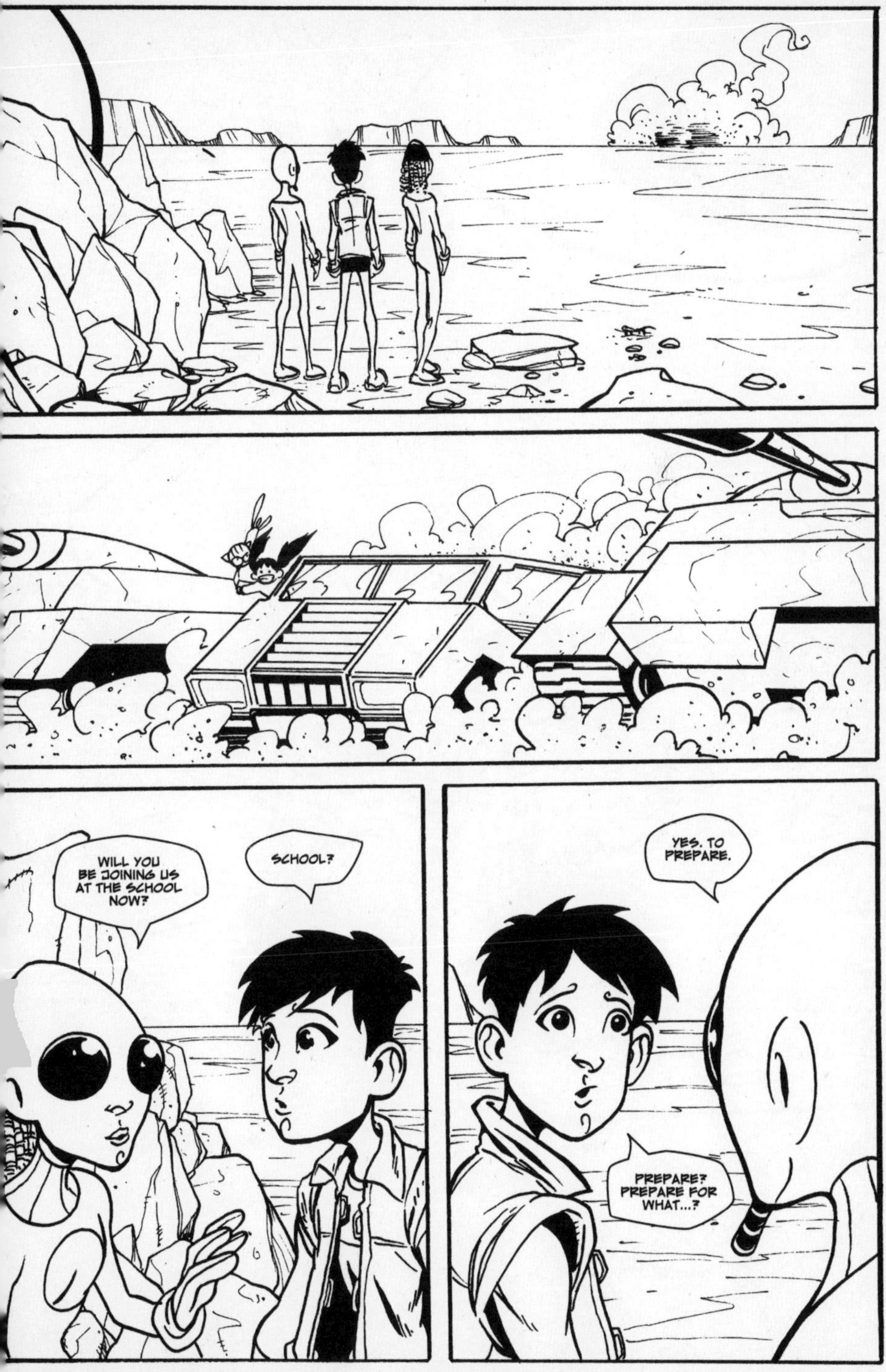
WILL YOU BE JOINING US AT THE SCHOOL NOW?
SCHOOL?
YES. TO PREPARE.
PREPARE? PREPARE FOR WHAT...?

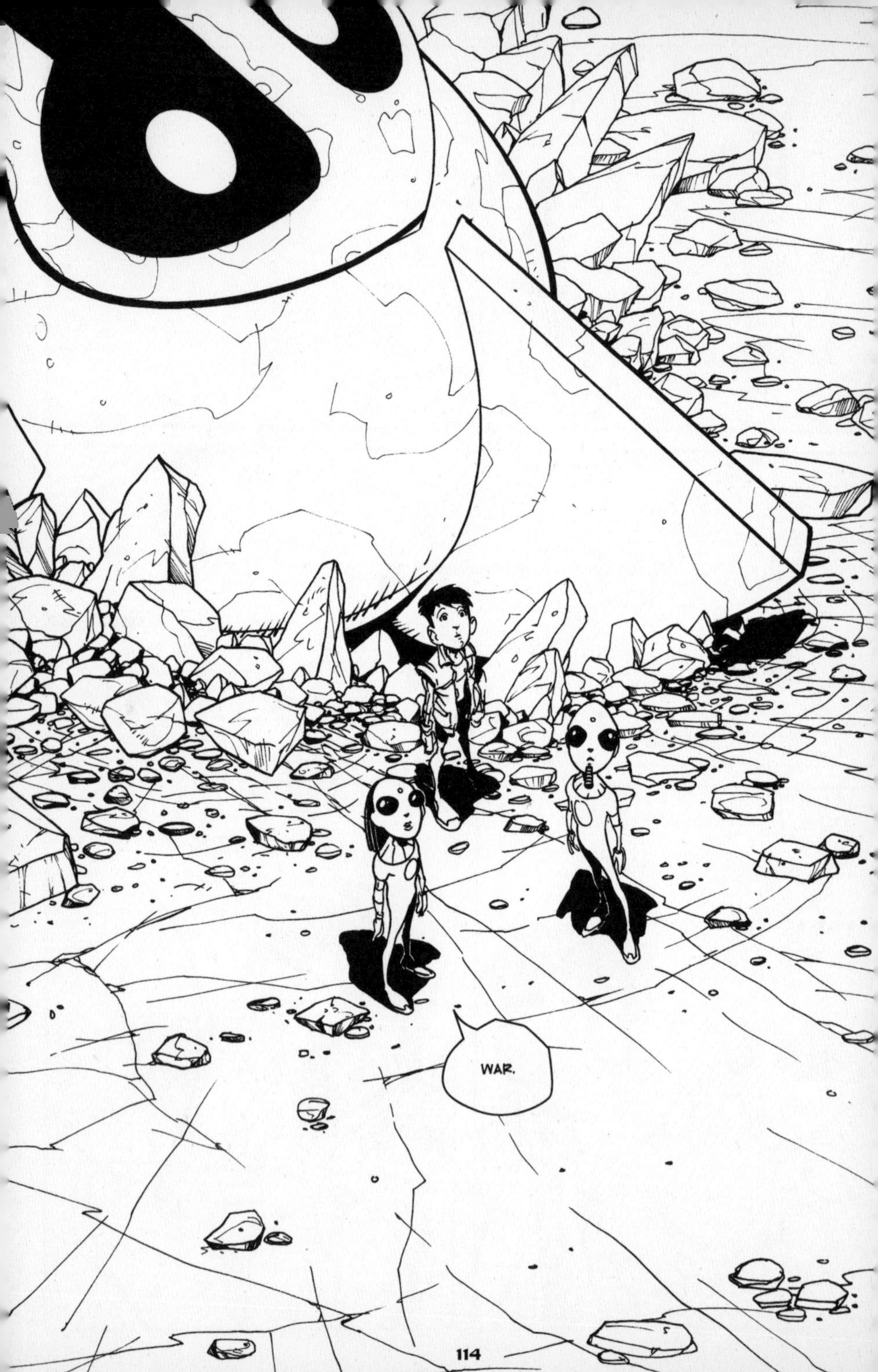
WAR.

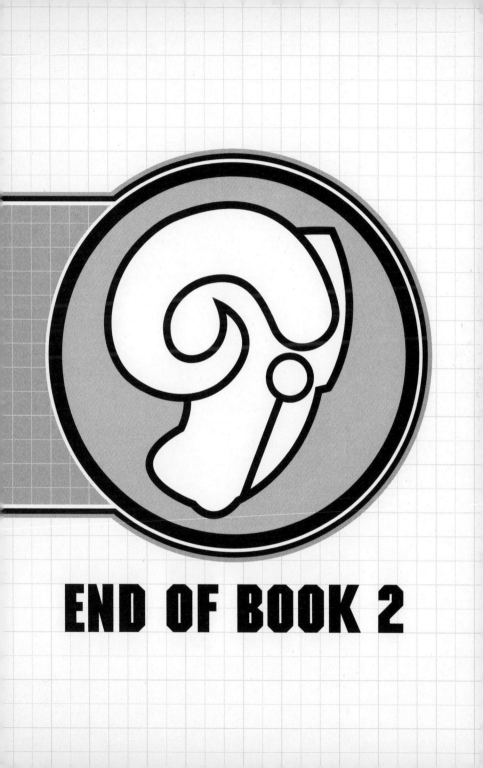

END OF BOOK 2

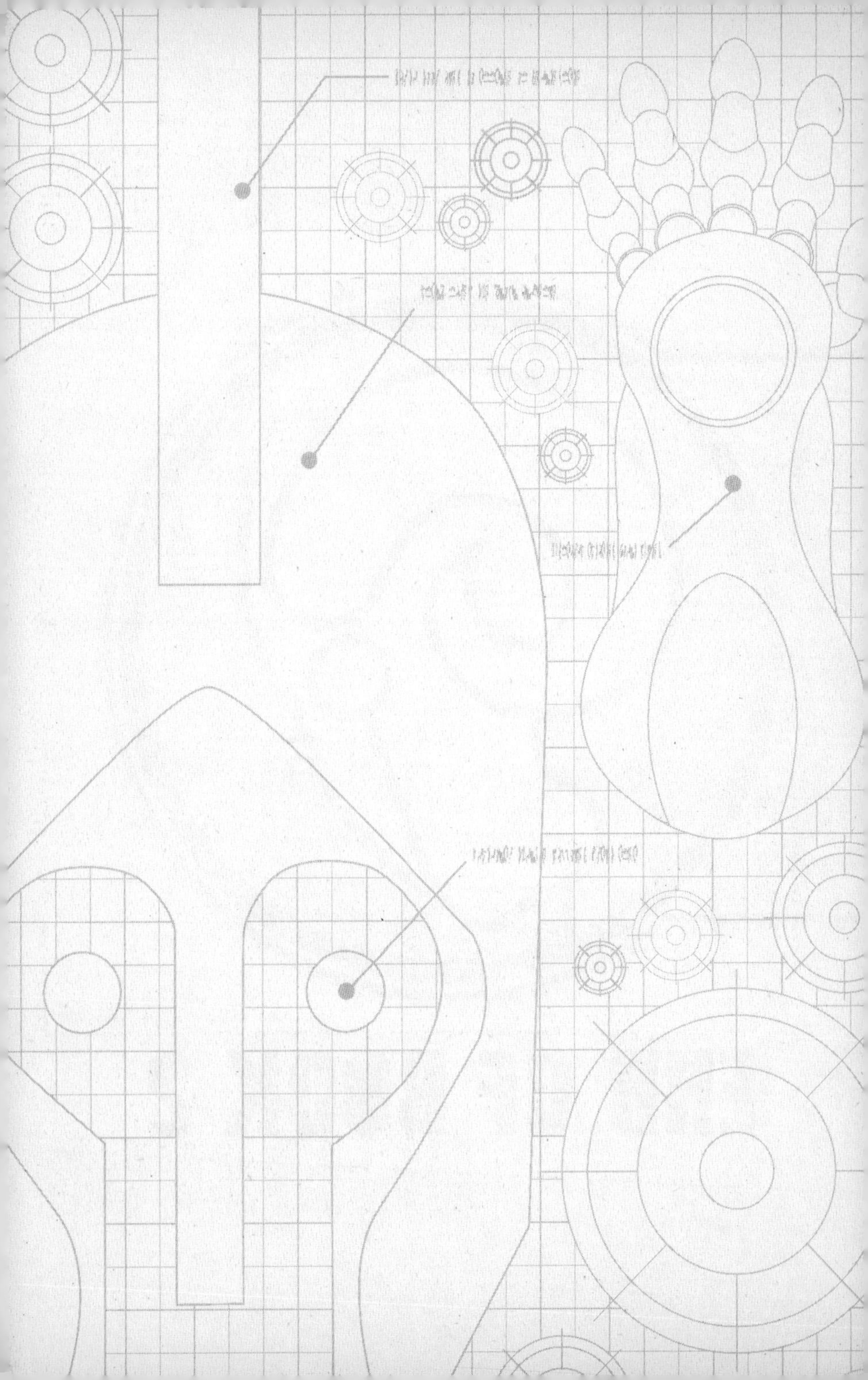

ARGOBOTS

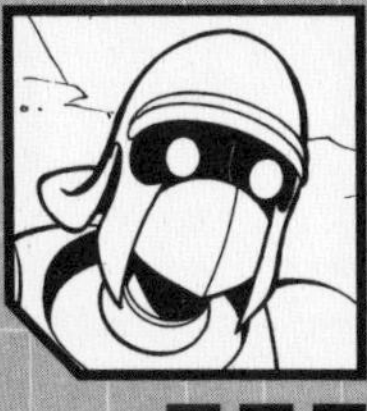

ATALANTA

POWERS: Diana's Shield, Cloud of Circe, Medusa Stare, and other classified moves.
QUOTE: "..."
LIKES: Dodona.
HATES: Standing around idle in the silo.
Theme Song: "Turn the Beat Around" (Vicki Sue Robinson)

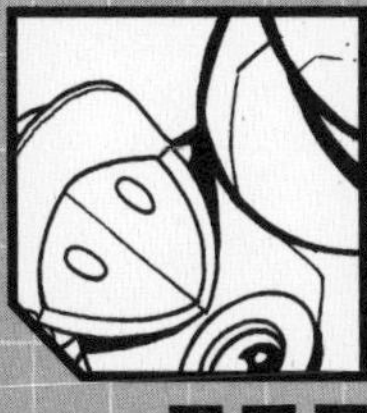

PHRIXUS

Powers: Poseidon's Trident, Retiarius Net, Cyclops Stare, and other classified moves.
Quote: "..."
Likes: Phineus.
Hates: Leaving the peace and quiet of the silo.
Theme Song: "The Warrior" (Patti Smyth)

HANDBOOK

MR. NEKKO NEKKO

Powers: Classified.
Quote: "Civilization is defined by the presence of cats."
Likes: Juni.
Hates: Being dragged around by one arm.
Theme Song: "Memory" (Sarah Brightman)

DODONA

Powers: Responsible, diplomatic, and brave, a born leader. Scores off the charts on scholastic aptitude tests; vocational placement tests indicate she would excel in a career in the military or government. Likely candidate for Pax Forces Academy.
Quote: "Follow me!"
Likes: Braiding her hair, macaroni art projects, history, storytelling.
Hates: People who don't pay attention, people who don't follow directions, people who don't know what they're doing.
Theme Song: "Powerpuff Girls (Main Theme)" (Jim Venable)

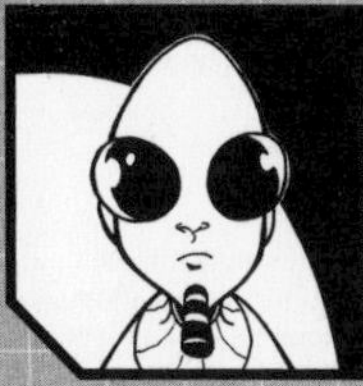

PHINEUS

Powers: Caring and loyal, but requires direction, a born follower. Holds high score on Robo Rumble Arcade in all of Shimmer City. Likely candidate for Pax Forces Academy.
Quote: "I *am* sitting up straight!"
Likes: Playing Robo Rumble Arcade, hanging from monkey bars, recess, Miss Elder.
Hates: Macaroni art projects, people telling him to sit up straight, not knowing how his parents are doing.
Theme Song: "Robo Rumble Arcade (Title Theme)" (DJ X-Machina)

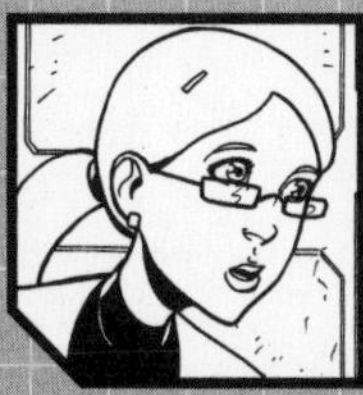

EMILY ELDER

Powers: Gifted teacher, nurturing maternal figure, can find 101 artistic uses for macaroni.
Quote: "I know you can do it."
Likes: Teaching, kids, Captain Marcus Moyen.
Hates: The insult "Those who can, do. Those who can't, teach." because it undermines that "those who can" were obviously taught by someone.
Theme Song: "ABC" (Jackson 5)

OTHER BOOKS BY J. TORRES...

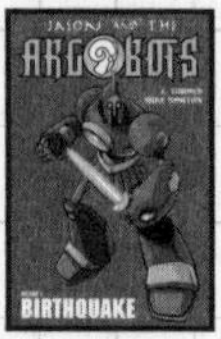
JASON AND THE ARGOBOTS
BIRTHQUAKE

JASON & THE ARGOBOTS, VOLUME 1: BIRTHQUAKE™
Illustrated by Mike Norton
120 pages, black-and-white interiors
$11.95 US
ISBN 1-929998-55-4

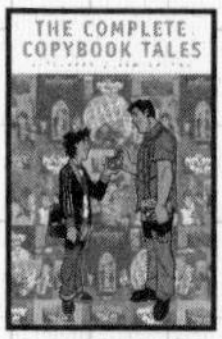
THE COMPLETE
COPYBOOK TALES

THE COMPLETE COPYBOOK TALES™
Illustrated by Tim Levins
with Jeff Wasson
240 pages, black-and-white interiors
$19.95 US
ISBN 1-929998-39-2

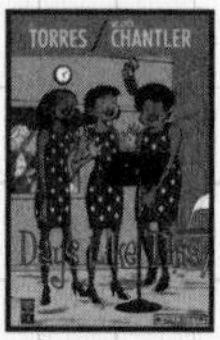
TORRES / CHANTLER

DAYS LIKE THIS™
Illustrated by Scott Chantler
88 pages, black-and-white interiors
$8.95 US
ISBN 1-929998-48-1

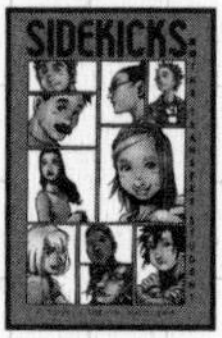
SIDEKICKS:

SIDEKICKS: THE TRANSFER STUDENT™
Illustrated by Takeshi Miyazawa
104 pages, black-and-white interiors
$8.95 US
ISBN 1-929998-40-6

OTHER ALL-AGES BOOKS FROM ONI PRESS...

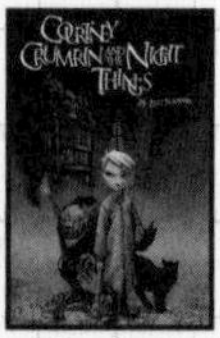
COURTNEY CRUMRIN AND THE NIGHT THINGS

COURTNEY CRUMRIN & THE NIGHT THINGS™
by Ted Naifeh
128 pages, black-and-white interiors
$11.95 US
ISBN 1-929998-42-2

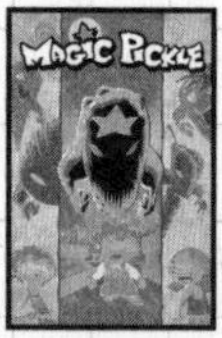
MAGIC PICKLE

MAGIC PICKLE™
by Scott Morse
128 pages, black-and-white interiors
$11.95 US
ISBN 1-929998-33-3

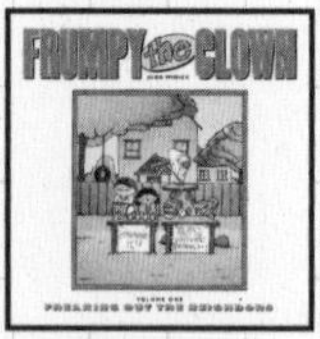
FRUMPY the CLOWN

FRUMPY THE CLOWN, VOLUME 1: FREAKING OUT THE NEIGHBORS™
by Judd Winick
144 pages, b&w interiors
$15.95 US
ISBN 1-929998-11-2

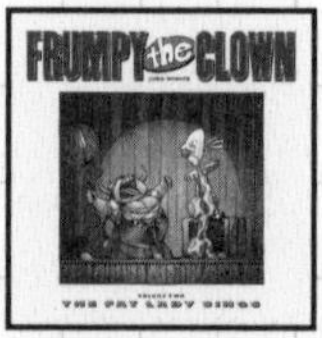
FRUMPY the CLOWN

FRUMPY THE CLOWN, VOLUME 2: THE FAT LADY SINGS™
by Judd Winick
136 pages, b&w interiors
$15.95 US
ISBN 1-929998-12-0

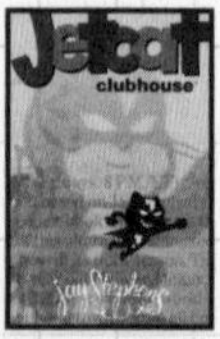
Jetcat
clubhouse

JETCAT CLUBHOUSE™
By Jay Stephens
80 pages, 24 color pages
$10.95 US
ISBN 1-929998-30-9

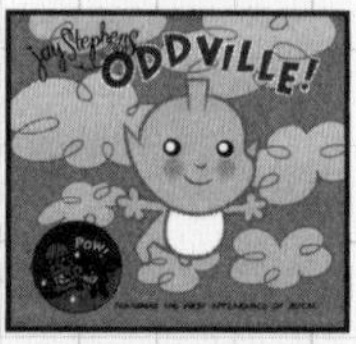
Jay Stephens
ODDVILLE!

ODDVILLE!™
by Jay Stephens
88 pages, balck-and-white
$10.95 US
ISBN 1-929998-25-2

Available at finer comics shops everywhere. For a comics store near you, call 1-888-COMIC-BOOK or visit www.the-master-list.com. For more Oni Press titles and information visit www.onipress.com.